Kamala's Way

Kamala's Way

An American Life

Dan Morain

THORNDIKE PRESS
A part of Gale, a Cengage Company

Thorndike Press, a part of Gale, a Cengage Company.

Thorndike Press® Large Print Basic.
The text of this Large Print edition is unabridged.
Other aspects of the book may vary from the original edition.
Set in 16 pt. Plantin.

LIBRARY OF CONGRESS CIP DATA ON FILE.
CATALOGUING IN PUBLICATION FOR THIS BOOK
IS AVAILABLE FROM THE LIBRARY OF CONGRESS.

ISBN-13: 978-1-4328-8693-6 (hardcover alk. paper)

Published in 2021 by arrangement with Simon & Schuster, Inc.

Printed in Mexico
Print Number: 01 Print Year: 2021

To Claudia, my everything

CONTENTS

1
Shyamala's Daughter

If Kamala Harris owes her place in history to anyone, it is to the twenty-six-year-old Indian immigrant who gave birth to her at Kaiser Hospital in Oakland, California, in the fall of 1964. Perhaps it was no coincidence that her birth came just two weeks before Election Day, and that it came in California. It was a year and a state that proved to be the perfect incubator for a girl who grew up proving that social progress and bare-knuckle politics go hand in hand.

That little girl grew up to be a tough, sharp-witted, exacting, hardworking, smart, multilayered, and multicultural woman. Kamala Harris misses little and forgets even less. She has loyal supporters who have been part of her political organization from the start, and she has alienated people who were once as close as family. When the cameras aren't on, she has exhibited empathy and acts of kindness for people who could not help her, and some people who have known her well see her as cold and calculating. Though she lives on a national stage, Harris shares few personal details. She is a foodie who finds joy in cooking and dining at fine restaurants and out-of-the-way joints. The one time we had lunch she picked a small family-owned Caribbean place across from the capitol in Sacramento; she talked about the varied spices and ate slowly, unlike me, she noted. Mostly, she is her mother's daughter. People who work closely with her say hardly a week goes by that she doesn't recall some nugget of wisdom passed along by Shyamala Gopalan Harris, who died in 2009. The one she most often repeats publicly: "You may be the first to do many things, but make sure you are not the last." Sometimes, at big moments in her life, she wells up when she remembers her mom, clearly wishing she were by her side.

"My mother, Shyamala Gopalan Harris, was a force of nature and the greatest source of inspiration in my life," Harris wrote on Instagram in a post honoring her mother during Women's History Month in 2020. "She taught my sister Maya and me the importance of hard work and to believe in our power to right what is wrong."

Shyamala Gopalan stood a little taller than

this father, 'a neegroe from da eyelans' " — a "Yankee stereotype" that suggested such a father "might just end up eating his children for breakfast!"). He wrote, "Nevertheless, I persisted, never giving up on my love for my children."

The final divorce judgment, dated July 23, 1973, shows Shyamala gained physical custody, but that Donald was entitled to take the girls on alternating weekends and for sixty days in the summer. He writes about bringing his daughters to Jamaica to meet relatives and show them the world he knew as a child: "I tried to convey this message in very concrete terms, through frequent visits to Jamaica and engaging life there in all its richness and complexity."

"Of course," Donald Harris wrote, "in later years, when they were more mature to understand, I would also try to explain to them the contradictions of economic and social life in a 'poor' country, like the striking juxtaposition of extreme poverty and extreme wealth, while working hard myself with the government of Jamaica to design a plan and appropriate policies to do something about those conditions."

Try as he did, lessons taught by Harris's mother seems to have stuck more. Harris weaves references to her mother throughout her autobiography. She mentions her father on fewer than a dozen pages. "My father is a good guy, but we are not close," she told an interviewer in 2003.

In her official biography on the California attorney general's website, Harris describes herself as "the daughter of Dr. Shyamala Gopalan, a Tamilian breast cancer specialist who traveled to the United States from Chennai, India to pursue her graduate studies at UC Berkeley." That biography makes no mention of her father.

In an essay about his Jamaican ancestors, Donald Harris writes about a Hamilton in his family's past, although the Harris family's Hamilton, Hamilton Brown, shared little in common with Alexander Hamilton, one of this nation's Founding Fathers and an abolitionist. "My roots go back, within my lifetime, to my paternal grandmother, Miss Chrishy (née Christiana Brown, descendant of Hamilton Brown who is on record as plantation and slave owner and founder of Brown's Town)." Hamilton Brown was born in about 1775 in County Antrim, Ireland, and sailed as a young man to the Caribbean island of Jamaica. His first recorded act in his new homeland took place in 1803, when he sold Black people to another man. In the next three decades, Brown became a willing participant in and perpetrator of the brutal system of Jamaican slavery and was one of its outspoken defenders against the abolitionist movement led by Baptists and Methodists.

The work was a common route to prosperity for White men of his era and provenance. "Managing slaves was a means of employment, and for white men, owning slaves was a path to material betterment, to independence, and to greater freedom," Christer Petley, a history professor at the University of Southampton, writes in his book *Slaveholders in Jamaica.*

Indeed, Hamilton Brown ascended in Jamaican society, attaining a seat in the House of Assembly, the island's lawmaking body. An attorney, he was listed as the agent, assignee, executor, guardian, manager, receiver, or trustee for more than fifty estates. Petley writes that estates in Jamaica had as many as two hundred enslaved people.

Whites owned vast sugar, pimento, and coffee plantations, while enslaved Black people provided the labor. Jamaican slave-produced sugar was central to transatlantic trade, and "more than a third of all slave vessels trading to British America docked there," Petley writes. At the height of Jamaica's slave economy, 354,000 Black people were held in bondage by 8,000 to 10,000 White people.

"In Jamaica, sexual relations between white men and enslaved women were common, and since legal status passed from one generation to the next via the female line, the children of enslaved mothers were born into slavery, regardless of their father's status," Petley writes.

Whatever specific acts of violence Hamilton Brown perpetrated against the people he enslaved almost 220 years ago is lost to history. What of his DNA lives on cannot be known without genetic testing. But Petley writes that "the sexual opportunism of white men was an important vestige of their coercive power and high social status."

Among his many roles, Brown became a ranking member of the militia. In the early 1830s, when enslaved people rebelled, he and his militia were deployed to help put the uprising down. At one stop, he and his soldiers located insurgents. Ten were hanged and thirteen received three hundred lashes.

"Brown worked hard to repress the uprising and was proud of what he did," Petley writes.

In 1833, after the slave rebellion, the British government bowed to the abolitionist movement and passed legislation freeing Jamaican slaves. In later years, Brown tried to supplement the shortage of plantation workers by importing laborers from Ireland. In 1842, he offered an apology for not having greater wealth to bequeath to the next generation and lamented the financial hit he took because of "the great deterioration of Jamaican property." He died in 1843.

Shyamala and Donald Harris lived in Berkeley and Oakland when the East Bay Cities were at the center of the free speech movement and of many kinds of transformative politics for the nation. The anti–Vietnam War movement, the rise of environmentalism, demands for racial justice, the nascent prisoners' rights movement, and more were part of the swirl of their times.

"They fell in love in that most American way, while marching for justice in the civil rights movement of the 1960s. In the streets of Oakland and Berkeley, I got a stroller's-eye view of people getting into what the great John Lewis called 'good trouble,' " Harris said at the 2020 Democratic National Convention when she accepted her party's nomination to be Joe Biden's running mate.

They were heady days, and deadly serious. The National Guard was called to the UC Berkeley campus regularly. Tear-gas canisters were launched from the ground and from helicopters. Police shot to death an unarmed protester at a 1969 demonstration over a plot of vacant land that came to be known as People's Park. The Black Panther Party for Self-Defense was born in 1966, cofounded by Huey Newton and Bobby Seale. Panthers openly carried guns as they observed police stops of people of color in Oakland. The notion that young Black men could legally display guns alarmed authorities. In May 1967, shortly after Ronald Reagan became governor, Newton and Seale led two dozen Panthers, wearing berets, dark glasses, and leather jackets and carrying unloaded guns, into the California capitol in Sacramento. The *Sacramento Bee*'s headline read: "Armed Black Panthers Invade Capitol." The Panthers were there to protest legislation that sought to forbid the open carrying of loaded firearms. Authored by a Republican assemblyman from the affluent Oakland Hills, the legislation included a provision that banned carrying firearms into the capitol. It passed overwhelmingly with Republican and Democratic support.

five feet. She was the eldest of four children of a senior civil servant in a family of high achievers, in a nation that gained its independence from Britain in 1947, nine years after she was born. She was nineteen in 1958 when she graduated with a degree in home science from Lady Irwin College in New Delhi, India, and with her father's blessing, traveled to Berkeley in search of a higher and more meaningful education. Studying nutrition and endocrinology, she received her Ph.D. and, in the decades ahead, gained recognition for her research in breast cancer. Her work was cited more than one hundred times in other research papers, and she raised no less than $4.76 million in grants for her work.

"My mother had been raised in a household where political activism and civic leadership came naturally," Kamala Harris wrote in her 2019 autobiography, *The Truths We Hold.* She went on to explain, "From both of my grandparents, my mother developed a keen political consciousness. She was conscious of history, conscious of struggle, conscious of inequities. She was born with a sense of justice imprinted on her soul."

In the fall of 1962, Shyamala Gopalan attended a gathering of Black students where the speaker was a young graduate student from Jamaica, Donald Jasper Harris, who was studying to become an economist. He emigrated from Jamaica in 1961, arriving in Berkeley also in search of an education. He was a bit of a radical, or, as economists might say, a "heterodox." He did not adhere to the traditional economic theories then favored by U.S. universities. Donald Harris told the *New York Times* that Gopalan, wearing a traditional sari, came up to him after his lecture and was "a standout in appearance relative to everybody else in the group of both men and women." She charmed him, they met and spoke a few more times, and, as he said, "the rest is now history."

Gopalan and Harris married in 1963, the year after Jamaica gained its own independence from the United Kingdom. Their wedding announcement in the *Kingston Gleaner* on November 1, 1963, reported that they were both pursuing their Ph.D.s. Kamala Devi was born in 1964, and her sister, Maya Lakshmi, two years after that. Devi is the Hindu mother goddess. Lakshmi is the lotus goddess of wealth, beauty, and good fortune. Shyamala told a *Los Angeles Times* reporter in 2004 that she gave her daughters names derived from Indian mythology to help preserve their cultural identity and said, "A culture that worships goddesses produces strong women."

In the mid- to late 1960s, both parents were active in the civil rights movement. Harris tells of being wheeled to demonstrations in a stroller. She tells the family tale that on one occasion, as she was fussing in the stroller, her mother asked what she wanted.

"Fee-dom!" she is said to have answered.

Like many academics, Donald Harris was an itinerant in his early years, moving from Berkeley to the University of Illinois at Urbana-Champaign, Northwestern University, the University of Wisconsin, and back to the Bay Area and Stanford in 1972. The student newspaper, the *Stanford Daily,* characterized his economic philosophy as Marxist. Whether it was or not, it was not classical. That made his continued employment fraught with risk. In 1974, as his visiting professorship was ending, some of Stanford's economics professors were reluctant to recommend him for a full-time position. The Union for Radical Political Economics got involved on Harris's behalf, and the issue became a subject for the *Stanford Daily.* Students started a petition signed by more than 250 people demanding that the economics department make a "formal commitment" to Marxian economics and maintain a staff of three faculty members working in the field, and that the faculty recommend Harris for a full-time, tenure-track position. Donald Harris has written that he had "no great anxiety or desire to remain" at Stanford. But he was ultimately hired and became the first Black economist to achieve tenure in the Stanford Economics Department. He remained at the university until 1998, when he retired from teaching. Harris still holds professor emeritus status.

Shyamala and Donald separated in 1969, when Donald was teaching at the University of Wisconsin and when Kamala was five and Maya was three. They filed for divorce in January 1972. Harris wrote in her autobiography that "had they been a little older, a little more emotionally mature, maybe the marriage could have survived. But they were so young. My father was my mother's first boyfriend."

In a 2018 essay, Donald Harris lamented that close contact with Kamala and Maya "came to an abrupt halt" after a contentious custody battle. He blamed the custody arrangement on "the false assumption by the State of California that fathers cannot handle parenting (especially in the case of rights leader Nina Simone; and poet Maya Angelou.

"This #BlackHistoryMonth, I want to lift up my mother and the community at Rainbow Sign who taught us anything was possible, unburdened by what has been," Harris posted on social media in 2020.

But that lesson was not always true for Shyamala. She had been working at UC Berkeley with a friend, Dr. Mina Bissell, who recalled that Shyamala had been promised a promotion that ultimately went to a man. The single mom of Kamala, twelve, and Maya, ten, reacted by getting a job teaching at McGill University in Montreal in 1976 and researching breast cancer at Jewish General Hospital in that city.

Shyamala had traveled extensively as a child. Her father was a high-ranking civil servant in India who, over the course of Shyamala's childhood, took posts in Chennai, New Delhi, Mumbai, and Kolkata. It likely would have felt natural for her to move from California to Quebec in pursuit of a new opportunity. For her eldest daughter, however, the move was intimidating. Kamala recalls in her memoir that "the thought of moving away from sunny California in February, in the middle of the school year, to a French-speaking foreign city covered in twelve feet of snow was distressing." Shyamala enrolled her in Notre-Dame-des-Neiges, a French-speaking primary school, and later Westmount High School, one of the oldest English-speaking schools in Quebec.

At Westmount, Kamala Harris took part in pep rallies and started a dance troupe called "Midnight Magic," and with five friends by her side, she danced to early 1980s pop in glittery, homemade costumes. She also learned a hard reality.

Wanda Kagan and Kamala Harris were the best of friends in high school in Montreal, but as happens with teenage friendships, they lost touch after graduation. They reconnected in 2005. Kagan was watching when her friend appeared on *The Oprah Winfrey Show* talking about her experience as California's first Black woman to be elected as a district attorney.

Kagan called Harris and the two had a long conversation, catching up and reminiscing about their shared memories, including the time Kagan lived with Kamala, Maya, and Shyamala Harris. She was escaping abuse that was occurring at home.

In that conversation, Kagan said, Harris told her that she was inspired to become a prosecutor largely because of "what she

went through with me." She told H
living with the Harris family was
few good memories she had fr
years. Kagan, who first told her s
licly to the *New York Times,* rec
the Harris family cooked and a
together. Usually, they were India
She had never had good food lik
was a special time for her. In th
home, Kagan wasn't simply "a per
ing in our house now." She was w
as a member of the family. Shyamal
that she get counseling. Kagan's ex
was so profound that she named he
ter Maya. The story of that bond
teenage girls decades ago in Montre
become a part of the 2020 presiden
paign.

Harris's high school yearbook ent
that she yearned to return to the
States. She described happiness as
long distance phone calls," and h
ished memory entry reads, "Cal
Angelo; summer '80." She's smilin
yearbook photo, and she soon w
entering her freshman year at H
University, a historically Black co
Washington, D.C. In that yearboo
Harris encourages her sister: "Be C
YA!" Maya would become Kamala

sest confidante as she rose in politics. yamala's daughter pays homage to the ce of nature that was her greatest source inspiration: "Sp Thks to: My mother."

2
That Little Girl

It is impossible to understand Harris without understanding the unique contradictions of California's politics. There are many Californias. Some parts of the state are as conservative as the reddest parts of the nation. Others are among the nation's most liberal. To leave a mark on its history, as Harris has, a politician must know how to navigate among all of them. Her ascent, as you will see, is largely due to her talent at doing just that.

But most of all, you have to understand California's particularly contradictory record on race — a record that Harris would come to know intimately from the day she was born.

Election Day 1964 fell on November 3, two weeks after October 20, the day Shyamala Gopalan Harris gave birth to her first daughter. To the extent the new parents were paying attention to election results, and not their infant, Shyamala and Donald Harris would have seen a momentous turn of events that night. President Lyndon Johnson won in a landslide over Senator Barry Goldwater, an Arizona Republican, and gained a mandate that for a time would help him expand his domestic policy of the Great Society and civil rights. He captured nearly 60 percent of California's vote, the first time in sixteen years that a Democrat carried California.

Across San Francisco Bay, Willie Lewis Brown Jr., a thirty-year-old Black man, campaigning as a "responsible liberal," won a state assembly race against an Irish American politician who had held the seat since 1940. Phillip Burton had won a congressional seat in a special election earlier that year. With Burton's younger brother, John Burton, also winning an assembly seat, Brown became a charter member of the Burton political machine, later called the "Burton-Brown machine" and then, simply, "Willie Brown's machine." Whatever its name, the organization dominated San Francisco politics for decades to come.

Brown, the son of a maid and a waiter, grew up in Mineola, Texas, a separate and unequal town of 3,600 people eighty-four miles east of Dallas. He was seventeen in 1951 when he escaped the Jim Crow South and arrived in San Francisco wearing worn-out shoes and holding his possessions in a cardboard suitcase. His sole San Francisco contact was his uncle, Rembert "Itsie" Collins, a high-living gambler who wore silk suits and diamond rings and who taught Brown his first lessons about the city he would come to dominate.

Like Shyamala Gopalan and Donald Harris and so many others, Brown had come west in search of opportunity. That meant getting an education. Brown worked his way through San Francisco State College as a janitor and got his law degree at the University of California Hastings College of the Law, located in the city's Tenderloin district. Then, as now, the Tenderloin was home to new Americans and broken souls who were down, out, and addicted. Unable to get a job in the downtown law firms, Brown represented clients who were accused of vice crimes. That would change in the ensuing decades, when he would become one of California's most powerful politicians of the later decades of the twentieth century. Kamala Harris would see that up close in the years ahead. And she herself would learn how to manage the treacherous political dichotomies of the state her parents had adopted.

On that Election Day, California voters decided the fate of a ballot measure, Proposition 14, which gave property owners "absolute discretion" to sell or not sell to whomever they chose and sought to prohibit the state government from in any way dictating who property owners could sell to. Funded by real estate interests and apartment owners, the measure was a mere 270 words long. Its goal was simple, although not explicitly stated: White property owners should have the right to keep Black people out of suburban neighborhoods, a siren sounded many decades later by President Trump in the 2020 presidential campaign.

In the official voter guide that went to all California registered voters, Proposition 14's backers made the argument: If the government could require owners to rent or sell to anyone who could pay the price, "what is to prevent the Legislature from passing laws prohibiting property owners from declining to rent or sell for reasons of sex, age, marital status or lack of financial responsibility?"

California attorney general Stanley Mosk, a liberal, took the opposite view: "It would legalize and incite bigotry. At a time when our nation is moving ahead on civil rights, it proposes to convert California into another Mississippi or Alabama and to create an atmosphere for violence and hate."

Like many cities, Berkeley long had been carved in two, a legacy of redlining. People of color generally could not rent or buy houses to the east of Grove Street, now Martin Luther King Jr. Way. The hills to the east, with their eucalyptus and oak trees, were where White people lived. The Harris family rented in the flats.

Proposition 14 was a reaction to the Rumford Fair Housing Act. Signed by Governor Edmund G. "Pat" Brown in 1963, the Rumford Fair Housing Act guaranteed people the right to rent where they wanted and banned discrimination in public housing. The legislation passed on the last night of the legislative session, after conservative senators watered it down by exempting single-family homes.

Its author, Assemblyman William Byron Rumford, represented the district that encompassed the Berkeley flats and West Oakland where the Harris family lived. Rumford, a pharmacist educated at the University of California, San Francisco, another public university, won his seat in

1948, the first Black legislator elected from the Bay Area.

Realtors saw California as the battleground for a national showdown over open housing, and they "felt that if in so-called 'liberal' California they could defeat this legislation, their chance of defeating it in other areas was very good," Rumford said in an oral history.

The outcome wasn't close.

On the day they voted overwhelmingly for LBJ and sent Willie Brown to Sacramento, Californians approved Proposition 14, 65 percent to 35 percent. Voters in fifty-seven of the state's fifty-eight counties, including liberal San Francisco, voted for it. In Alameda County, where the Harris family lived, 60 percent of the voters approved it.

Proposition 14 would not stand. The California Supreme Court struck it down in 1966, finding it violated the U.S. constitutional requirement that all citizens receive equal protection. On May 29, 1967, the U.S. Supreme Court agreed that the ballot measure violated the Fourteenth Amendment by the narrowest of margins, 5–4.

Supreme Court justice William O. Douglas wrote separately: "This is not a case as simple as the one where a man with a bicycle or a car or a stock certificate or even a log cabin asserts the right to sell it to whomsoever he pleases, excluding all others whether they be Negro, Chinese, Japanese, Russians, Catholics, Baptists, or those with blue eyes." Rather, the issue involved "a form of sophisticated discrimination," intended to keep neighborhoods White.

Quoting James Madison, Douglas wrote, "And to those who say that Proposition 14 represents the will of the people of California, one can only reply: 'Wherever the real power in a Government lies, there is the danger of oppression.' "

Translation: The Constitution protects minorities against unbridled majority rule for good reason.

Dissenters cited the will of the people, contending courts should not second-guess legislators or, by extension, the people through the ballot on such matters.

Decades later, California attorney general Kamala Harris would use a variation of that argument when she advocated for marriage equality. But first and more directly, she would experience the outcome of a major showdown over race.

Berkeley school superintendent Neil V. Sullivan was the Harvard-educated son of a mother who knew that education was the ticket out of their Irish ghetto in Manchester, New Hampshire. He also was a leading proponent of school desegregation.

On behalf of the Kennedy administration, Sullivan spent 1963 working to reopen schools in Prince Edward County, Virginia, after segregationists sought to evade integration orders by shutting down all public schools. Parents of White kids placed their children in special private schools. Black kids had no school. Sullivan's job was tough. Townsfolk regularly dumped garbage on the steps and veranda of Sullivan's rented house. There were bomb threats. Someone fired a shotgun through his window. But he managed to reopen the schools, and U.S. attorney general Robert F. Kennedy visited Sullivan in Prince Edward County in 1964, after his brother, President John F. Kennedy, was assassinated.

"The children fell in love with him, and it was obvious that they gave him the psychological lift he so badly needed," Sullivan later wrote.

Sullivan arrived in Berkeley in September 1964, having been recruited by the school board. It was dicey, initially. School board members were facing a recall over their efforts to integrate the schools, but they survived. That ensured Sullivan could carry out his mandate. In May 1967, Sullivan told the Berkeley School Board: "These schools shall be totally desegregated in September, 1968, and we might make history on that day."

Sullivan chronicled his Berkeley experiences in a book, *Now Is the Time,* a reference to Martin Luther King Jr.'s exhortation at the March on Washington in 1963, "Now is the time to make real the promise of democracy."

Dr. King, who had become a friend, wrote in the foreward to Sullivan's book, dated September 1, 1967, "I believe that our schools must and can take the lead in this mighty effort." Dr. King, however, did not live to see the result.

In 1968, that year of the assassinations and civil uprising, Sullivan made good on his promise. Buses transported Black kids from the Berkeley flats to schools in the hills, and White kids rode buses to schools in the flats. Berkeley became the largest city in America to integrate its schools.

"Is it possible for one middle-sized city with the familiar array of white bigots capable of flooding the mails with hate literature, one city surrounded by cities full of racism — both white and black — to succeed?

"The answer in this city of Berkeley is a resounding 'YES,'" Sullivan wrote.

Kamala Harris was not on those buses in 1968. She was too young. Nor did she ride on those buses in 1969, the year she entered kindergarten. That year, her parents enrolled her in a Montessori school in Berkeley.

But in the fall of 1970, that little girl did board a bus bound for first grade at Thousand Oaks Elementary, a 2.3-mile ride from her apartment. Before desegregation, 11 percent of Thousand Oaks's students were Black. By 1970, more than 40 percent of the kids were Black.

"Whether or not we can change adults, we can change children. Our children will grow up in a community where justice is a way of life, and, we hope, they will spread justice," Sullivan wrote. Sullivan's sentiment was noble and aspirational, though clearly not simple.

A half century later, in the heat of a race for the presidency, Harris was determined to take Americans back to that moment in history. On the big stage at the Adrienne Arsht Center for the Performing Arts in Miami, Florida, U.S. senator Kamala Harris, the prosecutor turned politician and the daughter of a mother from India and a father from

Jamaica, was not about to be silenced.

"I would like to speak on the issue of race," the first-term senator from California said, breaking up the back-and-forth an hour into the first Democratic presidential primary debate in the race to unseat President Donald J. Trump.

One of the moderators, Rachel Maddow of MSNBC, asked that she take no more than thirty seconds. Harris smiled and composed herself. What she had in mind on June 27, 2019, would take a little longer than a half minute.

She turned to Joe Biden, the former vice president and front-runner, a man twenty-two years her senior, from another generation. Harris started gently. She didn't believe he was a racist, she said, with the implication hanging over the moment that perhaps he could be. Then she pivoted. In the past, Biden had sounded almost romantic about his days in the Senate, when politics were civil and he, a Delaware liberal, worked with Senators James O. Eastland of Mississippi and Herman E. Talmadge of Georgia, old Democrats, who were segregationists. The legislation they worked on sought to block busing to desegregate public schools. Harris called that "hurtful."

"You know, there was a little girl in Cali-

fornia who was part of the second class to integrate her public schools and she was bused to school every day, and that little girl was me," Harris said in what became the debate's signature line.

In the days ahead, Harris's supporters and detractors would argue over whether the orchestrated attack was politically wise or below the belt, crass or a much-needed breakout moment for a candidate seeking to rise into the top tier of Democrats seeking the nomination for president of the United States. At a minimum, Kamala Harris had staked her claim as being the embodiment of a multicultural America and a direct beneficiary of hard-won policies that segregationists fought to prevent. Hand-wringing aside, the drama of the immediate political episode obscured the context of the era in which she was born.

The moment was intended to catapult Harris to front-runner status, cement her place with the Democratic base, particularly Black voters, and hobble Biden, the front-runner. It worked for a minute. Harris's campaign seized on the moment, tweeting a photo of Harris as a young girl, her hair in pigtails tied with bows and an unsmiling look of determination on her face. Biden's team was on the defensive. Harris's cam-

paign team sought to monetize the moment by selling T-shirts with the image of the girl in pigtails and the words THAT LITTLE GIRL WAS ME. Sales price: $29.99 to $32.99.

Harris entered the presidential race fully intending to win. To do that, she had to defeat the front-runner. That she fell short can be attributed to missteps by her and by factors beyond her control. But though her campaign sputtered and halted before the first votes were cast, Harris left a big impression. Something about her always cuts through.

That is Kamala Harris's way.

3
An Education, Apartheid, and a Slaughter

On May 13, 2017, 150 years after Howard University's founding and thirty-one years after she graduated, Senator Harris returned to her alma mater to deliver the commencement address. Harris, like many Howard alumni, is loyal to her alma mater and speaks of it with great affection. She talks of the great Howard graduates who came before her — author Toni Morrison, Supreme Court justice Thurgood Marshall, and many more. In her commencement speech, she dwelled on Howard University's motto, *Veritas et utilitas* — truth and service. Without mentioning Donald Trump by name, she left no doubt who she was referring to.

"At a time when there are Americans, disproportionately black and brown men, trapped in a broken system of mass incarceration, speak truth and serve. At a time when men, women, and children have been detained at airports in our country simply because of the god they worship, speak truth and serve. At a time when immigrants have been taken from their families in front of schools and outside courthouses, speak truth and serve."

Howard University occupies a unique place in American history, even more so now with Harris's ascent. It was named after Oliver O. Howard, the Civil War major general who headed the Bureau of Refugees, Freedmen, and Abandoned Lands, and fought to ensure that the four million people who were freed by the Emancipation Proclamation and the Civil War would have the right to marry, own land, earn a living, vote, and get an education. Howard was to play an important role in educating teachers and others who would help formerly enslaved people gain their place in society.

President Andrew Johnson — who was anti-Black, drank heavily, and was given to conspiracy theories — signed the legislation creating Howard University on March 2, 1867. That was the same day that Congress overrode Johnson's veto of the first Reconstruction Act, and a year before the House of Representatives impeached him. In a history of Howard University, Rayford W. Logan, a history professor for nearly thirty years at Howard, writes that given Johnson's racist views, the decision to sign the act was "probably not altruistic." Perhaps, he wrote, Johnson did not realize the significance of the bill he was signing.

On November 7, 2020, the day Joe Biden declared victory in his long run for the presidency, Vice President–elect Kamala Harris stepped to the dais wearing white, in honor of the one hundredth year of women's suffrage, and wearing pearl earrings in honor of Alpha Kappa Alpha, the nation's first sorority created by and for Black women. Harris paid tribute to the women who came before her — Shirley Chisholm, Hillary Clinton, and many others — and became the living embodiment of the promise that any girl can become whatever she aspires to be so long as she has the talent and drive, and a measure of good fortune. Her rise is especially significant for her sorority, Alpha Kappa Alpha, which was founded in 1908: members of that sorority and others that make up the "Divine Nine" sororities, founded by Black women, undoubtedly helped propel the Biden-Harris ticket.

"Tonight, I reflect on their struggle, their determination, and the strength of their vision to see what can be unburdened by what has been," Harris told the crowd gathered in Wilmington, Delaware, and watching from around the nation and world. Many who watched are part of the Howard family.

Karen Gibbs was watching from her home in suburban Washington, D.C. She and Harris lived next door to each other at Howard and became best of friends.

"Pure exuberance, an abundance of pride and thankfulness," Gibbs said, summing up what was going through her mind as she watched the godmother of her children. "I've been overwhelmed with emotion."

The university is a little less than a two-and-a-half-mile walk from the White House. It has produced mayors, senators, a Supreme Court justice, Nobel laureates, and now someone who will take her place in the White House. Harris, like others who chose to attend Howard, could have gone to some other top university. But she sought out a historically Black college because she would be respected for who and what she was, to be with people who looked like her, and as one not to the manor born, would not have to struggle for a place at the table.

"It is finally Kamala who gets us there. You can't help but feel so, so, so much joy and hope," said Ron Wood, an attorney and prominent graduate of Howard, who watched her speech from his Los Angeles home.

Having grown up in Berkeley and Oakland and attended protests since she was a toddler, Kamala Harris fit right in at Howard University in the mid-1980s.

"We would dance on Friday nights and we would protest on Saturday mornings," Harris said of her days at Howard, in a presidential campaign video addressed to alumnae of Historically Black Colleges and Universities, specifically her Alpha Kappa Alpha sorority sisters, a network of accomplished college-educated women. Harris writes in *The Truths We Hold:*

> On any given day, you could stand in the middle of the Yard and see, on your right, young dancers practicing their steps or musicians playing instruments. Look to your left and there were briefcase-toting students strolling out of the business school, and medical students in their white coats, heading back to the lab. Groups of students might be in a circle of laughter, or locked in deep discussion. . . . That was the beauty of Howard. Every signal told students that we could be anything — that

we were young, gifted, and black, and we shouldn't let anything get in the way of our success.

Harris graduated with a degree in political science and economics in 1986. That year's Howard University yearbook shows that Shirley Chisholm was honored for her career. Wynton Marsalis and Run-DMC performed. Younger students were upset that the national age for alcohol consumption had increased to twenty-one from eighteen in 1984, and Howard students were starting to use personal computers, which cost upward of $3,000. Students organized a boycott of Coca-Cola for doing business in White-ruled South Africa. On January 20, 1986, the nation for the first time celebrated Martin Luther King Jr. Day. The Reverend Jesse Jackson spoke about King on that day at Howard.

Harris and Karen Gibbs shopped together, shared whatever bounty that came in care packages from home, regularly went with each other to worship at different churches in Washington on Sundays, and cooked together.

"She used to laugh at my cooking. I ate bland," Gibbs said.

Harris visited Gibbs's home in Delaware and Gibbs visited Harris's in Oakland. Gibbs gave Harris the high compliment of inviting her to be godmother to her children. Harris was honored. To this day, Gibbs thinks of Shyamala Harris when she cooks a recipe that Shyamala taught her: green apples fried in butter and cinnamon. At Howard, Harris and Gibbs were focused on achieving their goals of becoming lawyers and prosecutors. Both did. "That is where we came of age, where we found out who we were. It was a flurry of excitement. There were so many people who were young, gifted, and Black," Gibbs said. Senator Harris invited Gibbs to attend the Senate Judiciary Committee's confirmation hearing for Supreme Court nominee Brett Kavanaugh. Her opinion of Harris's performance was important to her old friend, as someone who often had questioned hostile witnesses herself. Gibbs thought the Kavanaugh questioning by Harris was masterful.

While at Howard, Harris got an internship in U.S. senator Alan Cranston's office; she would go on to hold the seat Cranston once held. She also marched against apartheid. In a speech at Howard shortly after President Reagan's reelection in 1984, the South

African leader Bishop Desmond M. Tutu accused the Reagan administration of collaborating with South Africa to perpetuate racism in his homeland, the Associated Press reported on November 7, 1984. Tutu said U.S. policy under Reagan proved to be "an unmitigated disaster for blacks" in his homeland and that Reagan's policy encouraged the regime to "increase its repressiveness" and "be more intransigent."

Back in Harris's home state of California, people in positions of power were taking actions intended to topple the South African regime. An influential Republican played an outsized role in that effort.

For years, Congresswoman Maxine Waters, then an assemblywoman from Los Angeles, had been pushing legislation without success to force managers of California's massive public employee pension fund to divest holdings in companies doing business in South Africa. California Assembly Speaker Willie Brown was helping in any way he could. In June 1985, Brown called on the University of California Board of Regents to divest the university's pension fund holdings in South Africa. Although Brown was at the height of his power and could exert control over the university's funding, the board rejected his request. Governor George Deukmejian, a Republican, agreed with that decision, at first.

As students continued to protest apartheid, Brown went to work on the governor, making a point of bumping into Deukmejian where the governor ate lunch, the cafeteria in the basement of the capitol. Brown never would have eaten in the basement on his own. He preferred finer dining. Deukmejian was happy with tuna sandwiches on white bread. Tuna was one of Brown's least favorite foods. The Speaker sacrificed his good taste for an important cause, writing in his autobiography, *Basic Brown:* "We talked of many things during those lunches, including the genocide of the Armenian people at the hands of the Turks in 1915 — a horror that was present in Deukmejian's life, since members of his own family had suffered terribly then. I pointed out the parallels between the condition of the Armenian people then and the black citizens of South Africa now."

Deukmejian's position evolved. In mid-1986, Deukmejian's chief of staff, Steven Merksamer, phoned the University of California chancellor to say that the governor was rethinking his opposition to divestment.

Deukmejian then appealed to his friend

President Reagan. No legislator had been closer to Reagan during his time as governor than Deukmejian. In a letter to President Reagan, Deukmejian urged that he "turn up the pressure against apartheid South Africa." He signed the letter "Duke."

On July 16, 1986, Deukmejian wrote to the regents: "We must not turn our backs on black South Africans at this moment of great crisis. As the world's seventh largest economy, California can make a difference. We must stand up for freedom and stand up against violations of human rights wherever they occur."

Two days later, with Deukmejian in attendance, the regents reversed their position and voted to divest billions in pension fund holdings in companies doing business in South Africa.

In Sacramento, Assemblywoman Waters reintroduced legislation in 1986 to force state pension funds to sell their holdings in companies operating in South Africa. Major businesses, Deukmejian's main source of political support, lobbied hard against the legislation. But the legislature passed it, with Republican votes. On the day he signed Waters's bill, Deukmejian raised the question he'd been asking himself: "How would we feel if our rights and if our individual

freedoms were denied and the rest of the world turned its back on us?"

If Harris was paying attention to the events back home, she would have seen that actions taken in Sacramento matter. California was again proving that it could lead a movement, if not a nation. Nelson Mandela, for one, noticed.

In 1990, the year Harris started working as an Alameda County prosecutor, South African authorities freed Mandela after twenty-seven years in prison. In June, Mandela made a triumphal appearance before sixty thousand people chanting "freedom, freedom" at the Oakland Coliseum. On that stop in Oakland, Mandela praised the California political leaders who had pressured South Africa by fighting for divestment.

"I don't think there was anything we did that had more of a worldwide impact," Brown said years later. "We brought the key to the jail for Nelson Mandela."

Shyamala had returned to Oakland with Maya, having gotten a research position in Berkeley, across the bay from Oakland. Kamala decided to come home, too. Her next stop was the UC Hastings College of the Law, in downtown San Francisco.

She entered law school in 1987. That was the year after California voters ousted three liberal California Supreme Court justices in a campaign led by Deukmejian. Deukmejian replaced the three Democratic appointees with conservatives, giving Republican appointees a majority on the court that would stand for the next three decades.

Harris's law class produced numerous lawyers who went on to much success. One, McGregor Scott, became U.S. attorney in Sacramento under Presidents George W. Bush and Donald Trump. Another, J. Christopher Stevens, joined the U.S. Foreign Service and was appointed U.S. ambassador to Libya by President Obama in 2012. Stevens died when terrorists attacked the consulate in Benghazi on September 11, 2012. Harris became president of Hastings's Black Law Students Association. But people who knew her there say she was not a standout. She did not graduate summa cum laude, magna cum laude, or cum laude.

"There was nothing about her that would suggest that she would one day become district attorney, or attorney general, or senator, or vice president," said San Francisco attorney Matthew D. Davis, a classmate, friend, and campaign supporter.

■ ■ ■ ■

Kamala Harris was finishing her time at Hastings when on January 17, 1989, California and the nation learned of a new kind of hell.

Patrick Purdy, a hate-filled young man wearing combat fatigues and wielding an AK-47 assault weapon of war, took aim at children on the playground at Cleveland Elementary School in Stockton. By the time he was finished firing 106 rounds, five children were dead and twenty-nine others were wounded, as was a teacher. Parents of nearly all the victims had left the strife of Southeast Asia for the freedom promised in America. Purdy, who shot himself in the head, wasn't the first gunman to carry out a mass killing in the United States. But his special evil targeting children would be repeated at many more schools in the decades ahead.

In Sacramento, about fifty miles to the north, Democratic legislators responded by reviving long-stalled legislation to ban assault weapons. Then attorney general John Van de Kamp, a proponent of gun control, already had established a task force to help shape the legislation. One of the advocates was Richard Iglehart, the chief assistant for the Alameda County district attorney. Iglehart provided expertise in shaping the legislation and, with others from law enforcement, garnering support for politicians worried about a backlash for supporting the bill. "We were able to hit the ground running," Iglehart said at the time.

Governor Deukmejian was elected in 1982 in no small part because his Democratic opponent, former Los Angeles mayor Tom Bradley, supported an initiative on the ballot that year that would have imposed strict gun control. So Deukmejian was not the sort to readily sign gun control legislation. But as he neared the end of his time in elective office, the Stockton slaughter shook him.

"You do not grieve alone," Deukmejian said, addressing two thousand people at the children's funeral, which was conducted in four languages. Willie Brown was there and saw the governor tear up. "Your sorrow is our sorrow. Your pain is our pain. This terrible tragedy has shocked and greatly saddened the people of this state."

Deukmejian decided that assault weapons had to be restricted. Despite intense lobbying by the NRA and Gun Owners of California, the legislature answered with what would be the first measure in the nation to ban assault weapons. Four months after the slaughter at Cleveland Elementary School, Deukmejian signed the bill:

"These bills are not going to bring back the lives of the five beautiful young children who died so tragically on the school grounds in Stockton, but we hope and pray that these measures, along with the others that we are seeking, will help our brave and courageous law enforcement community."

The new law was far from perfect. Because it banned specific models, gunmakers made small modifications and continued selling their deadly wares. But in California, the 1989 assault weapons ban marked the beginning of the gun advocates' decline. In 2000, the NRA's political action fund spent $373,000 on California campaigns. By 2010, the year Harris was elected California attorney general, the NRA reported spending zero on California campaigns. It would have been a waste of money. The vast majority of California voters had come to support strong gun control.

In the years ahead, the legislature tightened the law so that rapid-fire assault weapons that hold more than ten rounds are illegal in California. Other laws require background checks for all gun purchases, restrict the sale of cheap handguns, deny guns to people who have a history of alcohol abuse or domestic violence, prohibit guns on university campuses, limit the number of guns people can buy in a given month, and allow ammunition sales only to people who are legally entitled to own guns. There are many more restrictions.

Kamala Harris was learning early in her career about the brutal reality of guns in the wrong hands. As a prosecutor, she would be an aggressive enforcer of the California laws that seek to keep guns away from people who should not have them.

4
A Taste of Politics

Prosecutors know they are not meant to see the finer side of life. Even so, the criminal world of Alameda County stood out. In 1990, when Kamala Harris, rookie prosecutor, walked through the door of the Alameda County District Attorney's Office, the number of murders in the county seat of Oakland reached a record 146, exceeding the record set the year before. And it reached a new height in 1992 when there were 165. A few years earlier, a horse-drawn funeral procession for a drug kingpin, who was murdered in prison, wended its way through the length of Oakland and drew one thousand mourners.

On some mornings, people waiting to handle their traffic infractions would stand in a line that snaked around the Wiley W. Manuel Courthouse, a utilitarian building named for a son of Oakland who became the first Black California Supreme Court justice. A bridge connects the courthouse to the Oakland Police Department headquarters and Alameda County jail. The criminal justice complex is hard by the freeway that skirts the east shore of San Francisco Bay, not far from where the double-deck Cypress Structure freeway pancaked onto itself in the Loma Prieta earthquake on October 17, 1989, killing forty-two of the sixty-three people who died in that temblor.

This was where Deputy District Attorney Kamala Harris, twenty-five-year-old daughter of high-minded Berkeley intellectuals, began her career, after passing the notoriously tough California State Bar exam on her second try.

In her presidential campaign kickoff speech thirty years later, Harris explained her decision to become a prosecutor: "I knew that the people in our society who are most often targeted by predators are also most often the voiceless and vulnerable."

Harris would walk through the courthouse doors and climb the stairs to the second floor where the district attorney's warren of offices was located, or, if she was so inclined, ride an elevator with jurors, defendants, witnesses, and defense lawyers. Cops would catch a few minutes of sleep before having to testify. As many as five trials would be in progress. Alpha Kappa Alpha was a world away.

As a law student in 1988, Harris worked as an Alameda County District Attorney's Office law clerk, a coveted job because clerks would gain courtroom experience and get paid. The office's storied history is a draw for ambitious young lawyers. Earl Warren, a California governor and chief justice of the U.S. Supreme Court, was an Alameda County district attorney. President Reagan's attorney general, Edwin Meese III, came from the Alameda County District Attorney's Office. So did California Supreme Court justices Ming Chin and Carol A. Corrigan. At noon, Harris and other young lawyers would bring brown bags to the law library, where senior prosecutors would describe cases and offer pointers on trial strategies.

"She did stand out a bit from the crowd. She had a different confidence," Alameda County district attorney Nancy O'Malley, then one of Harris's supervisors, said. Harris was energetic, willing to take tough cases, laser focused, driven to be successful. She knew early where to get the education she needed. "She paid very close attention when old-timers were talking."

Like other rookies, Harris handled misdemeanors, many of them driving under the influence cases, and the very early procedural stages of felony cases. She went on six-month rotations to branch courthouses in Fremont, Hayward, and, in December 1991, back to the Wiley Manuel Courthouse, all the while learning the questioning skills that would serve her when she became a U.S. senator.

No young lawyer could have ignored what was going on in Washington in October 1991. U.S. senator Joseph Biden was chairing the Judiciary Committee during the confirmation hearing for Supreme Court nominee Clarence Thomas. Law professor Anita Hill appeared before the all-White, all-male committee and testified that Thomas had pressured her for dates and talked about pornographic films when she was his underling at the Department of Education and the Equal Employment Opportunity Commission. Men on the committee insulted and minimized Hill. Thomas denounced the hearings as a "high-tech lynching."

The Judiciary Committee sent Thomas's nomination to the Senate floor without a recommendation, and senators confirmed him 52–48. Biden voted no, but his performance angered the many women who believed Anita Hill.

A year later, in October 1992, Harris took on an assignment to work in juvenile court. It was tough duty. Oakland schools were so troubled that half the district's fifty-three thousand students scored below the 50th percentile on standardized tests. Truancy was rampant. The California State Legislature had installed a trustee to oversee Oakland school finances in 1990, as the district teetered on the brink of insolvency. Everything that happens in juvenile court is confidential. The cases she handled are sealed. But Harris talks often of hearing the stories of children being abused and exploited sexually. She would use that experience in later years when she got into positions to affect policy and shape law — and as she was thinking about elective office.

On election night, November 7, 1992, Harris drove her Corolla across the San Francisco Bay Bridge to the Fairmont Hotel on Nob Hill, where Democrats were celebrating. It was a good night to be a Democrat. Bill Clinton had been elected president, and Barbara Boxer and Dianne Feinstein were basking in their respective victories in their U.S. Senate races. Boxer, the more liberal of the two senators, had

been one of seven Democratic co
women who marched to the Senate i
demanding to discuss the Thomas con
tion with Senate Democrats, only
denied admittance to their regular Tu
caucus, a closed event. Boxer used A
Hill's mistreatment and Thomas's confir
tion to energize voters and win electio
1992, the "Year of the Woman."

No one could have imagined that Kam
Harris would go from being a twenty-seve
year-old face in the crowded Fairmon
ballroom to replacing Boxer as U.S. senato
in 2016 and then gaining a seat on the Senate Judiciary Committee. But there she was, twenty-seven years later, when Christine Blasey Ford, a psychologist from the San Francisco suburb of Menlo Park, took the brave step of coming forward to testify that Trump's second Supreme Court nominee, Brett Kavanaugh, sexually assaulted her when they were teenagers. The parallel to the Thomas confirmation hearing was unmistakable, and the outcome was the same.

Democrats had tried without success to elicit Kavanaugh's view of *Roe v. Wade,* the landmark 1973 abortion rights case. Harris used her time and the skills she learned in the Alameda County District Attorney's Office to cut through the clutter:

"Can you think of any laws that give the overnment power to make decisions about ne male body?"

Kavanaugh tripped over his words: "I'm not aware — I'm not — thinking of any right now, Senator."

Harris's path to that hearing went through Sacramento.

Harris's life took a turn in 1994. She had become involved with one of the nation's most talented politicians, California State Assembly Speaker Willie Brown. The relationship was imbalanced; he was thirty years her senior. But they shared the common traits of drive and intelligence, and they both rose from little to attain a great deal, though Brown's path was especially daunting, coming, as he did, from Texas during the days of Jim Crow.

In order to rise to a position of dominance, Brown had to make himself known, and so he forged a crucial friendship with *San Francisco Chronicle* columnist Herb Caen. Caen told me one of the secrets of his success: San Francisco was not a town with celebrities, so he had to create them. It's one way his three-dot column became a must-read for San Franciscans for fifty years. He defined the city, was its champion,

its scold, its arbiter of class, and the classless. And no one played a bigger part in the world he chronicled than his good friend Willie Brown. They had Friday lunch dates at Le Central bistro and traveled to Paris. Ever clever with a quip, stylish in his Wilkes Bashford suits and fedoras or riding in his new Ferrari, Brown was a regular ingredient in the snappy, irreverent, melancholy, funny, never-dull columns that appeared next to the Macy's ads.

On March 22, 1994, Brown provided Caen with especially rich material. Brown celebrated his sixtieth birthday at billionaire Ron Burkle's estate, known as Greenacres, a thirty-six-thousand-square-foot villa originally built by silent film star Harold Lloyd on fifteen verdant acres in Benedict Canyon. Burkle and Brown were friends, and for a time, Burkle retained Brown as one of his lawyers. Throughout the 1990s, Burkle hosted political fund-raisers for President Clinton and other prominent Democrats at Greenacres. The *Los Angeles Times* called it the Versailles of fund-raising venues. Caen reported that Barbra Streisand was at Brown's sixtieth and that Clint Eastwood "spilled champagne on the Speaker's new steady, Kamala Harris." It was quite a public introduction of Brown and

Harris's relationship.

Over the course of the relationship, Brown gave Harris a BMW, and she traveled with him to Paris, attended the Academy Awards with him, and was part of the entourage that flew to Boston with him in 1994. While he was in Boston, Brown got a call from New York billionaire Donald Trump. Trump wanted to discuss a hotel project he had in mind for Los Angeles and sent his jet to Boston to fly Brown and his friends, Harris included, to New York City. The jet was gilded, had valuable paintings on its cabin walls, and had notes left for Trump by his then wife, Marla Maples. Brown and Trump had lunch at the Plaza Hotel. The Los Angeles deal never materialized. Trump and Harris likely did not meet then, but she was a long way from the Wiley Manuel Courthouse.

In 1994, Willie Brown was facing the term-limited conclusion of his time in the assembly. The beginning of that end dates to 1986, when businessmen from Georgia persuaded a legislator to introduce a bill to allow for the construction of a shrimp processing plant and greased the legislation's path by handing out money. The bill passed both houses of the legislature. But there was no shrimp processing plant or businessmen. It was all a mirage, part of an FBI sting. The scandal became public in 1988 when the FBI agents searched the capitol offices of several lawmakers. Like other reporters who covered the scandal, I assumed Brown was the target, as did he. A dozen legislators, lobbyists, and others were convicted or pleaded guilty. But Brown knew the rules and the law and hadn't stepped over any lines. There was, however, another more lasting price to pay. Capitalizing on the scandal, conservatives promoted an initiative in 1990 to impose term limits on legislators. Dislodging Brown, who had famously called himself the "Ayatollah of the Assembly," was the immediate goal. Campaign mailers using unflattering images of Brown were sent to voters in more conservative parts of the state. Voters in San Francisco overwhelmingly opposed the term limits measure, but it passed statewide, 52 percent to 48 percent. The 1994 election would be Brown's final assembly election. His end would be more abrupt than he had hoped.

In 1994, Governor Pete Wilson won reelection over California treasurer Kathleen Brown, Pat Brown's daughter and Jerry Brown's sister, on a platform that included support for capital punishment, the anti–illegal immigration initiative known as Proposition 187, and a singularly harsh version of three strikes, Proposition 184. Funded by the California Correctional Peace Officers Association and the NRA, California's three-strikes law led to life sentences for many people convicted of shoplifting. Analysts predicted California would need twenty-five new prisons to house the coming deluge of as many as one hundred thousand prisoners.

Nationally, Republicans led by Newt Gingrich took control of the U.S. House of Representatives. In California, Republicans flipped the assembly for the first time in twenty-five years, gaining a 41–39 edge. That meant Willie Brown would lose his speakership when the legislature convened in December, or so it was thought. First, though, Brown had plums to pass out.

In 1994, Harris took a leave from her job as Alameda County deputy district attorney when Brown placed her on the state board responsible for hearing appeals from people who were denied jobless benefits. The term for that position would end on January 1, 1995, beyond the point where he would still have power. So in late November, he placed her on a separate part-time board that oversees California's Medi-Cal contracts, then a $72,000-a-year job, the salary paid to legislators. She would hold that post through 1998, three years after their relationship ended. The first time I wrote about Harris was when she got that appointment. She declined to be interviewed at the time, and Brown's office ducked my calls. Republicans protested but were powerless to stop it.

"It's safe to say that these are not appointments we would necessarily make," Phil Perry, the spokesman for Assembly Republican Leader Jim Brulte, the man in line to succeed Brown as Speaker, said at the time.

Brown didn't leave the speakership quietly. I was in the assembly chamber on December 5, 1994, the day of the speakership vote, taken by roll call. When the clerk got to Assemblyman Paul Horcher, a back-bench Republican from a town east of Los Angeles, Horcher banged his fist on his desk and roared, "Brown," creating a 40–40 split and sending the house into chaos. For a year, Brown managed to maintain control by installing Republican allies as Speakers. The inevitable occurred in 1996 when Republicans managed to install their own Speaker, though the GOP lost the house in the 1996 election and haven't come close to regaining it since.

By then, Brown was gone.

In 1995, after representing San Francisco in the assembly for thirty-one years, Brown decided to challenge the incumbent mayor Frank Jordan, an affable former San Francisco police chief who was seeking a second term. Harris often was by Brown's side as he campaigned for the mayor's job, going to fund-raisers, engaging in strategy sessions, learning the details of how to wage a campaign. Jordan might have eked out a victory, except that inexplicably, he agreed to a stunt pulled by two Los Angeles disc jockeys by disrobing with them and stepping naked into a shower. The embarrassing photo of the mayor with the disc jockeys, all of them naked, was front-page news in the *San Francisco Examiner* for no fewer than five days in the week leading up to the election. Jordan tried to laugh it off by saying he was squeaky clean and by calling on Brown to prove he had nothing to hide. It didn't work.

Brown held his election-night victory party at a union hall near Fisherman's Wharf. As the happy results came in, Harris stepped up to Brown and presented him with a baseball cap with the words DA MAYOR emblazoned in gold lettering on it.

He beamed, as did she. That was December 12, 1995. On December 14, Caen ran an item describing Harris as the "new first-lady-in-waiting." It wasn't to be.

Years before, Brown had begun living a separate life from his wife, Blanche, the mother of his children. He made no secret that he dated other women. But Brown and Blanche have never divorced, and never will. When that became apparent, Harris and Brown split.

The end, like the beginning, played out in Herb Caen's column, on the day after Christmas, 1995, with one final three-dot item.

" 'It's all over,' " Caen wrote in the *San Francisco Chronicle.* "With those words, mayor-elect Brown let word get around over the weekend that his long affair with Kamala Harris, an Alameda County asst. district attorney, has ended."

For Harris, who is intensely private, the idea that her personal life played out in Caen's column must have pained her. But the relationship was unbalanced from the start. Brown had all the power. He used that clout to open doors for Harris early in her career, part of a long tradition in politics of mentorship and patronage. No one rises on his or her own: Phil Burton had helped young Willie Brown. But once those early doors were opened, Harris had to make her own way. She moved on, got married in 2014, and long ago stopped discussing Brown publicly, making no mention of him in her autobiography. In 2019, Brown, the octogenarian, still spoke of her, telling a radio interviewer that he was not as committed to the relationship as she was. He also made clear that it was all about him: "It was a real love affair. I loved me and she loved me."

On January 8, 1996, 7,500 people crowded into a downtown square in front of San Francisco's main memorial to Martin Luther King Jr. for Brown's inauguration. A telephone, specially installed at the podium for the event, rang. An operator put the mayor-to-be on hold. Brown feigned being offended and returned to his seat, and the Reverend Cecil Williams, the iconic San Francisco pastor and civil rights leader, proceeded with the ceremony, briefly.

Then the caller in chief came on the line.

"Willie?"

"No, this is Cecil Williams, Mr. President."

Brown hustled from his seat to the dais and took the phone.

"You should be here with us. It is just

incredible. There is no snow and no Republicans," Brown told his old friend President Clinton, then in the midst of an epic battle with Speaker Gingrich over the Republican-led government shutdown.

"Can the people hear me there?" Clinton asked.

Loud and clear.

Clinton got to his point, praising Brown for his "tenacity, determination, and the never-surrender attitude, and the worldview you have that I think is the biggest issue we're facing today: that our future has to include everybody in our community.

"You know, the City of San Francisco has a commitment to community, to the idea that diversity is our strength, that I want America to embrace. . ..

"This great battle we're fighting here in Washington today is not a battle over balancing the budget. It's over whether we're going to be a winner-take-all country or a country in which everybody has a chance to win."

The call from the president was a reflection of the position Brown held in American politics at the time. Clinton was warm and gracious. His words reflected the self-image of many San Franciscans. That was years before Twitter, Google, Uber, Facebook,

Juul, and a hundred other new economy companies vastly increased San Francisco's wealth and deepened the gap between the haves and have-nots. Housing prices, for decades high in San Francisco, would reach into the stratosphere in the 2000s. The city that Herb Caen knew would become prohibitively expensive for cops, teachers, waitstaffers who served fine food at fancy restaurants, and the Uber and Lyft drivers who chauffeured San Francisco's tech titans to their destinations. Mayor Brown and his successors would preside over a high-rise building boom, while the city's homeless population would reach crisis proportions.

All that was to come. On this day, Brown gathered a select group on the stage: his three grown children and a grandchild. He raised one hand to take the oath of office and placed the other hand on a Bible owned by his mother so many years before in Mineola, Texas. Holding the Bible was his wife, Blanche.

In 1995, Harris decided to return to the Alameda County District Attorney's Office. Tom Orloff, who had prosecuted Huey Newton twenty years earlier, had become the Alameda County district attorney and welcomed Harris back.

"She was very bright and personable. Juries liked her," Orloff said. "We had 150 attorneys then. She was one of the ones who was very good."

Harris busied herself by prosecuting people accused of felonies. In one of her trials, she won a conviction of a man who used a shotgun to kill another man. He's doing life behind bars. In another, she prosecuted three people who committed a dozen armed robberies. She sometimes used California's new three-strikes law to seek lengthy sentences against repeat offenders. Her cases rarely attracted press attention, though there was an exception. A man high on meth and rum used a Ginsu knife to slice a four-inch square out of his girlfriend's scalp. He had tried this once before, only to be foiled because the blade was dull. She survived. He's serving life in prison.

"It's appropriate for what he did," Harris said after the sentencing, as quoted in the *San Francisco Chronicle* in 1996. "The manner in which this crime was committed was incredibly sadistic."

Nancy O'Malley, the current district attorney, could see that Harris was especially good in dealing with young victims of sexual assault. She could calm them and reassure them. Some would contact her long after

their cases were over, believing that Harris understood what they were going through.

Harris and O'Malley also began talking about the young prosecutor's career options. She had ambition. Richard Iglehart, an old boss in Alameda County and the one who had lobbied for California's assault weapons ban, was working for the San Francisco district attorney, Terence Hallinan, and he had a job for Harris. That was 1998. The move made sense.

Having gotten a taste of politics, she wanted more.

5
Setting Her Sights

Kamala Harris left the storied district attorney's office in Alameda County at the start of 1998, drove 12.7 miles west across the Bay Bridge, and arrived for work in the hothouse of San Francisco criminal justice politics. The district attorney's office, the police department, the courts, the coroner, the sheriff, and other agencies all shared the same building they called the "Hall." Right out back, on the other side of the parking lot, was the jail.

If police inspectors and prosecutors and defense lawyers all played the angles for and against one another, they also shared the common misery of working in a building that was falling apart. Famous as a set in the Dirty Harry movies and other major and minor cinematic efforts, the Hall of Justice was infamous for toilets that backed up and electrical outages. Lights flickered and elevators stalled, and criminals and cops alike feared the next Big One.

From downtown to South Beach, massive residential towers, new condos, high-rises occupied by lawyers and financiers, and maybe the most scenic baseball park in America occupied block after formerly gritty block. But not Bryant Street and the streetscape around the Hall. To this day, it is a collection of auto body shops, bail bond offices, and graffiti-covered walls, though a shared work space and strategically located cannabis dispensary have slipped into the layout.

Richard Iglehart recruited Harris to be a supervisor and to help right the whole judicial operation. It was a tall order. The man at the helm, District Attorney Terence Hallinan, was having a tough time, even if he had spent a lifetime proving that he could win a fight.

In 1995, the year Willie Brown was elected San Francisco mayor, Hallinan, a termed-out San Francisco supervisor, unseated three-term incumbent district attorney Arlo Smith and beat a former prosecutor, Bill Fazio, who had spent twenty years in the DA's office. To win, Hallinan had to overcome opposition from the *San Francisco Chronicle* editorial board, which suggested he was a "political hack," and a late revelation that a paternity suit had been filed against him a decade earlier by a flight attendant who had been a law client. Once the child was proven to be his, he took responsibility.

Hallinan was the radical son of Vincent Hallinan, an iconic figure of the Left in the Bay Area who ran for U.S. president on the Progressive Party ticket in 1952. A Black woman, newspaper publisher Charlotta Bass, was his running mate. The old man took the view that if his kids were going to hold radical opinions, they'd need to be able to fight. Terence Hallinan learned at his father's knee, or maybe his clenched fist, and gained the nickname "Kayo," a tribute to his ability and willingness to fight. Hallinan also inherited his father's sense of justice. In 1963, the year before Harris was born, Hallinan was arrested for loitering and littering while registering Black voters in Mississippi. The charges didn't stick. He would be arrested many more times protesting against racial injustice.

Hallinan graduated from the UC Hastings College of the Law and passed the bar exam. But the California State Bar, citing his criminal history and pugilistic tendencies, refused to grant him a license to practice law in 1966, even though two young assemblymen, Willie Brown and John Burton, testified to his good character. The California Supreme Court overruled the bar, and Hallinan built a practice representing people busted for drugs (business was very good in San Francisco in the late '60s and '70s), leftists, and serial murderer Juan Corona.

The *Washington Post,* detailing Hallinan's rocky transition from defense attorney to DA, reported that Hallinan "vehemently denies almost dying from a heroin overdose administered by rock singer Janis Joplin, as claimed in her biography, 'Pearl.' " A deft non-denial denial.

Although he was the city's top prosecutor, Hallinan stayed true to his past. He refused to seek the death penalty in murder cases, tried to block the execution of a man prosecuted by his predecessor, supported the use of medical marijuana before it was legal, and refused to seek life sentences under California's three-strikes sentencing law. None of that was a problem in San Francisco. Voters knew what they were getting when they elected him. But the turmoil he caused in his own office did become an issue.

First, there was the story about two prosecutors caught in flagrante delicto in the office. He fired the man, not the woman, and later was sued for wrongful termination.

Shortly after taking office, Hallinan gave tersely worded notes to fourteen prosecutors thanking them for their service and firing them. One of them was a twenty-six-year-old rookie lawyer named Kimberly Guilfoyle. Several others who received pink slips had donated to Fazio, his opponent, though Hallinan claimed that had nothing to do with his decision. He merely wanted to install his own team.

A fight broke out between Hallinan and a friend of one of the dismissed lawyers at a birthday bash for Willie Brown's political adviser Jack Davis. *San Francisco Chronicle* political affairs columnists Phil Matier and Andy Ross quoted Hallinan's explanation for why he had no choice but to deploy his fists: "I didn't choose it, but I can't back down. I'm the DA." Matier and Ross added a tongue-in-cheek "Tale of the Tape" to their account, listing the men's ages, weight, height, and reach. Of Hallinan, they wrote, "Leads with his left, but can go with a right if it means a few extra votes."

Realizing he needed help, Hallinan turned to the Alameda County DA's Office and hired Richard Iglehart to be his third chief of staff. Iglehart was a top-flight prosecutor who provided expert testimony that helped pass California's assault weapons ban and was a widely respected expert on the three-strikes sentencing law. Iglehart, in turn, hired Harris.

"She's a terrific prosecutor and has a great reputation," Hallinan told the *Chronicle*.

From Day One in San Francisco, Harris laid down a marker that nobody would outwork her. Fazio, who quit the district attorney's office after losing to Hallinan in 1995 and was working as a defense attorney, knew Harris from her days in Oakland, having shared dinner on occasion with her and other friends in the criminal justice business. A buddy on the San Francisco murder-prosecution team told him in the earliest days of the new assistant who had just come over from the other side of the bay:

"This friend of mine, he was working a big murder case, and he went into the office one weekend to work on it, before it went to trial," Fazio said. "He goes into the office, and he sees that she's there, too, working on some kind of felony case. He'd never met her, and he introduced himself, and she told him she'd just gotten hired and came in to work on some pretrial motions."

Not long into her San Francisco tenure,

Hallinan promoted Harris to the chief assistant position in charge of the career criminal division. Fazio was representing a client facing a long stretch in prison for robbery and thought his client, a drug user, was a candidate for diversion to Delancey Street, San Francisco's well-regarded therapeutic community for ex-offenders.

"So I set up a meeting with the two of them, Kamala and Hallinan. Kamala, she was a DA. She wasn't a probation officer. She wasn't a social worker. She was a prosecutor who prosecuted people and put them in jail."

Hallinan turned to Harris and asked what she thought, "and she said, 'I don't think this guy should go to Delancey Street. He did a violent robbery, and he belongs in state prison." Fazio's client accepted the offer of six years in prison.

Harris supported Hallinan's 1999 reelection. But in January 2000, Governor Gray Davis appointed Harris's boss, Iglehart, to a superior court judgeship. Rather than promote Harris to be his second in command, Hallinan turned to a lawyer with no prosecutorial experience, Darrell Salomon. Harris led an office protest against the selection, without success.

In one of his first acts, Salomon rehired

Kimberly Guilfoyle. A San Francisco native and the daughter of an influential figure in the city's Democratic politics, Guilfoyle had become San Francisco supervisor Gavin Newsom's girlfriend. She later became Mayor Newsom's wife, then a Fox News commentator, and then Newsom's ex-wife. In a weird twist of political fate years later, Guilfoyle became Donald Trump Jr.'s girlfriend and one of President Trump's chief surrogates and fund-raisers. With Salomon entrenched, Harris decided it was time to move on.

In San Francisco, the city attorney's office oversees family issues, including child abuse and foster care. Deputies in the office derisively called it the "kiddie law section." City Attorney Louise Renne wanted to elevate the Family and Children's Services section and hired Harris to run it.

No part of the law is more personal or emotional. It takes a special sort of lawyer to handle family law cases, one who is part therapist, part social worker, and one who understands the law. Renne said she saw in Harris "an intelligent lawyer who had a heart and had compassion." One day, Harris burst into Renne's office with teddy bears and asked Renne to come with her to the courtroom where children were about to be adopted. There, the two women passed out teddy bears as mementos of the children's momentous day.

Matthew D. Davis, a friend from Hastings, had stayed in touch with Harris off and on. They reconnected when Harris went to work for the San Francisco City Attorney's Office in 2000. Harris's demeanor surprised Davis.

"Suddenly, she had become this glamorous person," Davis, who is among her political supporters, said. "She continued to grow at a remarkable pace after law school. She had become more cosmopolitan and very focused."

Harris would not stay long in the city attorney's office. She had set her sights on running for elective office.

6
Becoming a Boldface

In the late 1990s and early 2000s, Kamala Harris's name was far more common in the society pages than it was in stories about her day job prosecuting criminals.

Alameda County Deputy District Attorney Harris had become a trustee of the prestigious San Francisco Museum of Modern Art in 1996, part of a larger plan. In his autobiography, *Basic Brown,* Willie Brown dispenses counsel for aspiring politicians: "Being able to cross over into the white community is essential for any black, female or male, to succeed as a political figure." He had specific advice for Black women: they should "lay the groundwork by looking to become active on the boards of social, cultural, and charitable institutions like symphonies, museums, and hospitals."

Harris undoubtedly used her position as trustee to make contacts with influential people. But she also used the opportunity to do good. She visited Libby Schaaf, now mayor of Oakland, who was then running the Marcus Foster Education Institute from a small office in a Victorian house in West Oakland. The institute is named for the Oakland school superintendent who was mindlessly assassinated by members of the radical Symbionese Liberation Army on November 6, 1973. Its mission is to improve the education of Oakland public school kids. Harris asked Schaaf to help her create a mentoring program for Oakland high school students at the Museum of Modern Art.

"She was very determined that this elite institution not just host a field trip, but that it become a deeper part of Oakland," Schaaf said.

Toward that end, Harris also visited Jackie Phillips, who was principal of Cole School, a performing and visual arts magnet program in Oakland. Phillips had known Harris as a bright-eyed high school kid who traveled between Montreal and Oakland and would pull up at Phillips's house in a white Chrysler convertible to pick up Phillips's daughter, Terry. The two were always ready to have fun. But Phillips also could see that Harris had a strong will to excel. As a museum trustee, Harris asked Phillips to help her recruit kids. Phillips did. On one occasion, they met actor Danny Glover. On another, they met director and actor Robert Redford.

"And they were treated like little kings and queens," Phillips said. Several Cole School students went on to pursue the arts in college. The mentoring program continues, introducing the arts to kids who might not otherwise have access.

Harris arrived in San Francisco in 1998 without money or pedigree, but she was becoming a boldface name. She was photographed in an elegant gown, drink in hand, at the 1999 wedding of Vanessa Jarman and oil heir Billy Getty in Napa Valley. The bride rode up on a horse, sidesaddle, and William Newsom, the retired state court of appeal justice and father of California's current governor, Gavin Newsom, officiated.

A piece in *Harper's Bazaar* about the style of San Francisco featured Harris in 2001, along with other women, such as Kimberly Guilfoyle. A society columnist noted her attendance at a February 2002 staging of *The Vagina Monologues,* starring Rita Moreno. The occasion was V-Day, to raise money for programs to stop violence against women. She also showed up at an American Jewish

Committee dinner in September honoring Walter and Douglas Shorenstein, large downtown San Francisco property owners and political patrons. She attended an October 2002 gala at which Elton John was raising money to combat AIDS; guests included producer George Lucas, actress Sharon Stone, and other Bay Area luminaries. She was also at the retirement party for a police lieutenant at an Italian restaurant in North Beach attended by cops and many of the city's political and social elite. Her cultivation of the police came at a crucial time and sent an important message.

That North Beach send-off occurred as Hallinan's relations with San Francisco police, which were never good, had unraveled over an episode the San Francisco press dubbed "Fajita-Gate." A few off-duty officers had demanded a man give them his fajita. He refused and a fight ensued. Hallinan prosecuted the officers and police department brass, alleging a cover-up. The case collapsed, as did Hallinan's political support.

None of the gossip items mentioned Harris with a date. She had become private about her personal life, though *Jet* magazine ran a photo of her at a Hollywood event with television talk show host Montel Williams. Harris, shutting down speculative chatter about her private life, told the *Chronicle,* "I was at that event. And his arms were around my waist." Nothing more was written or said publicly about any relationship, though Williams has occasionally contributed to Harris's campaigns.

By 2000, there was public speculation that Harris would run for office, perhaps city attorney when the incumbent, Louise Renne, stepped down or, more likely, district attorney. Hallinan was increasingly vulnerable. For one thing, Mayor Brown was publicly feuding with him, accusing him of failing to prosecute street corner drug dealers. The *Chronicle* editorial page described Hallinan in August 2000 as "hardly a figure of respect" and that he "continues to compile a record of baffling and outrageous judgments." That same editorial cited the uproar caused when Hallinan selected Darrell Salomon as his chief deputy, noting that it led to the departure of "respected veterans" and "the best and brightest legal minds," Kamala Harris included. So it was not surprising that Harris saw an opening to make her first run for office.

High society and Democratic politics blend

in San Francisco, and Harris was getting close to the people who have given the Bay Area its well-deserved reputation for being a cash machine for Democratic candidates. Harris had joined the board of WomenCount in 2000. Then a fledgling organization based in San Francisco that was devoted to increasing voting among women, WomenCount has grown into a national fund-raising force for women running for every office, from school board and city council to governor and vice president of the United States. In 2002, Harris got involved in another organization, Emerge California, a sort of boot camp for women who want to learn how to run for office. Andrea Dew Steele, a political organizer who helped create both WomenCount and Emerge California, got a call from Harris in the fall of 2002.

"Okay. I am ready to run. What do I do?"

Steele invited her to come to her apartment on Ashbury, near the corner of Haight, up four flights of stairs. Over wine and cheese, they typed out Harris's biography, and Steele asked Harris for her contacts, the people who would form the foundation of her base of volunteers and donors. She stored them in a Filofax planner, which in 2002 was basically a notebook. As time went by, the notebook had to be replaced by a PalmPilot.

To show she was a serious candidate, Harris needed to raise money. Steele knew people who could help with that. She worked as a political adviser to Susie Tompkins Buell, a woman who is a quintessential California success story. She was twenty-one and working in a Lake Tahoe casino when she picked up a hitchhiker, Doug Tompkins. They married in 1964, created the iconic North Face and Esprit clothing lines, and split up in 1989. Susie Tompkins had not been particularly interested in politics but had heard talk about a young presidential candidate named Bill Clinton. On a drive from Tahoe to San Francisco, she decided to stop at the halfway point, in Sacramento, and attend a fund-raiser for the Arkansas governor hosted by real estate developer Angelo Tsakopoulos. As retold by the *Los Angeles Times,* she was so moved by Clinton's description of the crushing poverty he saw on the campaign trail, and his vision of how maybe, after twelve years of having Ronald Reagan and George H. W. Bush in the White House, an enlightened Democratic administration could help, that she wrote a $100,000 check the next day. Through Bill Clinton, Susie Tompkins met

Hillary Clinton and the two became dear friends. Susie Tompkins and Mark Buell, friends from high school, reconnected and got married in 1996. Susie Tompkins Buell founded WomenCount and gave the first $10,000 to Emerge California.

Steele's first order of business as a fundraiser was to arrange for Harris to talk to Mark Buell, a real estate executive who had long been involved in San Francisco politics and was no fan of Hallinan's. Buell had viewed Harris as a "socialite with a law degree," he once told a reporter. But over a burger at the Balboa Cafe, one of the restaurants owned by Gavin Newsom, Harris convinced him that she was a serious prosecutor with a vision.

"Once I was convinced that Kamala was real, I told her, 'Not only will I be on your finance committee, I will chair it,' " he said.

Mark Buell convened a meeting at his wife's and his apartment in Pacific Heights in February 2003. Harris, Steele, and a few others were there, including her sister, Maya Harris, and Maya's husband, Tony West. The setting was spectacular even by San Francisco standards. Out one bay window, guests could see the Golden Gate Bridge, the Marin Headlands, and the Pacific Ocean. From other windows, they saw the

San Francisco skyline, the Bay Bridge, Sather Tower at UC Berkeley, and south past San Francisco International Airport. The Buells and their apartment occupy a singular space in Democratic politics. Senators, governors, and others — including Speaker Nancy Pelosi, the Clintons, and Barack Obama before he was elected to the U.S. Senate — have all made the pilgrimage to the Buells' twelfth-floor penthouse.

Like that parade of politicians, Harris could appreciate the view. But she was not there to gaze upon the city lights or to watch the sailboats on the bay.

7
Severing Heads. Figuratively.

Californians weren't paying much attention to the race for San Francisco district attorney in the fall of 2003. They, like most voters in the state, were focused on an only-in-California story, the campaign to recall California's Democratic governor, Gray Davis. Not that Davis was the draw. The one attracting all the attention was his leading challenger for the office, Arnold Schwarzenegger, the former Mr. Universe and international movie star, who made the announcement of his candidacy during an episode of *The Tonight Show with Jay Leno.*

Recall petitions regularly are filed against governors. That's the right of the citizenry under a 1911 state constitutional amendment allowing for recalls and initiatives, a Progressive Era notion intended to give people the final say over their governance and serve as a check on the power of moneyed interests. Gray Davis committed no malfeasance. But the state was in the midst of a budget crisis and had endured infuriating rolling blackouts from 2000 through 2001. Fairly or, more likely, unfairly, Davis got much of the blame.

The cost of qualifying measures for statewide ballots runs well into the seven figures. Darrell Issa, a San Diego County Republican congressman who made a fortune in the car alarm business, dearly wanted to become governor. But after spending $1.87 million to gather the hundreds of thousands of voter signatures to qualify the recall, Issa ultimately realized he didn't have a chance against Schwarzenegger. Fighting back tears, Issa announced he wouldn't run.

But 135 others did, including perennial candidates, a porn star, the little-known California Democratic lieutenant governor, the opportunistic Republican politician Tom McClintock, the diminutive child star Gary Coleman (who was well past his prime), and Arianna Huffington, who later founded the *Huffington Post*.

Schwarzenegger, the one to beat, overcame a front-page exposé in the *Los Angeles Times* in which women said he groped them, and on October 7, 2003, he became the center of the political world by unseating Davis.

■ ■ ■ ■

Kamala Harris had invited her boss, City Attorney Louise Renne, out to lunch in 2002. As Renne recalled it, Harris said:

"I am thinking about running for DA."

"Go for it," Renne replied.

Renne promised to help in any way she could. She also warned that incumbents are tough to dislodge, especially the one she was seeking to unseat, her former boss Terence Hallinan, with the legendary Hallinan name. Harris was thirty-eight at the end of 2002 when she announced her first run for public office.

"TODAY'S VOICE FOR JUSTICE," her website read.

She listed the reasons she was the ideal person to replace Hallinan: She would be a competent manager. She would improve conviction rates, which were far below the statewide average. Where Hallinan "refused to prosecute serious drug dealing of crack and heroin," she would bring drug cases as part of an effort to clean up the streets.

"Perhaps the most alarming of all is the now irreparable animosity between the police department and the district attorney's office — which should be working together to fight crime instead of fighting each other."

As Harris would learn, keeping all those promises would be tough, especially the one about ending the animosity between the district attorney's office and the police.

But first, she had to win.

Mark Buell, her fund-raising chairman, was there to help, recalling that it wasn't a tough sell. Harris was an attractive, energetic candidate who was quick on her feet, clearly part of a new generation of leaders for a city that needed a political makeover. When she talked to someone, she would make eye contact and not be scanning the room looking for some more important person to talk to. She made everyone she talked to feel as if he or she were the most important person in the room.

"She is a good politician. She knows how to fit in in most situations," Buell said.

In a blitz of meetings, fund-raisers, and phone calls in the final six weeks of 2002, Harris raised $100,560. In keeping with campaign finance restrictions in San Francisco, individual's donations topped out at $500. The haul was impressive for a first-time candidate and clearly sufficient to prove she was a serious challenger. It was a family affair: sister Maya Harris, brother-in-law Tony West, and, of course, her mother, Shyamala, each gave her $500. Early donors included many of the swells she would have met in society gatherings: members of the Pritzker family, whose wealth came from the Hyatt Hotel chain; Getty family members; Charles Schwab from the investment house that bears his name; and the Fisher family of Gap fame. Attorneys disenchanted with Hallinan also gave heavily.

"I was tired of the old people running San Francisco. She was one of the new faces," John Keker, one of the most successful trial and criminal defense lawyers in San Francisco, said. In 1989, Keker had led the prosecution of fellow marine Oliver North for his role in the Iran-Contra scandal, in which the Reagan administration sold arms to Iran to raise money to fund right-wing contras fighting a leftist regime in Nicaragua. "Kamala projected decency and compassion. You would turn a room over to her, and she would connect with people."

Mindful that she not come off as a creation of Pacific Heights or fancy downtown attorneys, Harris sought to show that she would look out for people who needed honest law enforcement the most. She placed her campaign headquarters in the middle of the troubled Bayview district, a world apart from $10 million penthouse views and the glistening Financial District. Volunteers painted slogans on one wall of the headquarters: A NEW VOICE FOR JUSTICE. THIS IS OUR TIME. TIME FOR A CHANGE. Harris promised to elevate the prosecution of domestic violence and to protect children who were trafficked.

"We were trying to reimagine what the office could be," Debbie Mesloh, one of Harris's longtime friends and first campaign workers, as well as her campaign spokeswoman, said.

Harris often arrived at the headquarters before sunrise. Shyamala was a constant presence, pitching in wherever needed. Maya and Tony were there, too. In a Norman Rockwell touch to this family affair, Harris and her volunteers would grab ironing boards and cart them to bus stops and sidewalks outside grocery stores, where they would unfold them to create instant desks onto which they'd stack *Harris for District Attorney* brochures. Harris had the enthusiasm, charm, and charisma that attracted volunteers and made them want to bring their best.

In her first television interview as a candidate, Harris spoke of her admiration for the Hindu goddess Kali, a mythological warrior who protects innocents by slaying evil. In a classic depiction, Kali holds the decapitated head of a demon, has a necklace of severed heads, and wears a skirt of bloody arms. Harris also noted that Kali is a mother figure.

Laura Talmus, Harris's professional fundraiser, witnessed that maternal side of Harris. On many Saturday mornings, Talmus would arrive to volunteer with her daughter, Lili. Lili was nine and stood out in any crowd. She was smart, perceptive, precocious, read voraciously, and laughed easily. She also had Apert syndrome, a rare genetic disorder that caused her face and head to be misshapen. When she saw Lili, Harris would make eye contact, ask about her day or week at school, and thank her for her help.

Lili and her mom would head off with their ironing board and brochures and set up outside the supermarket on Nob Hill across from the Hyde Street cable car line. On days when Lili was not quite motivated to hand out brochures, she'd stay in the headquarters, under Shyamala's wing, stuffing envelopes or doing whatever other chores Shyamala assigned to her.

"She just beamed in Kamala's presence," Talmus recalled.

■ ■ ■ ■

In February 2003, Harris spoke to the first group of women who were going through the candidate boot camp she and Andrea Dew Steele helped create, and that Susie Tompkins Buell helped fund, through Emerge. The training was for an array of down-ballot offices but also, the *Chronicle* noted, "the ones who fantasize about running for president someday." That story noted San Francisco had never elected a woman as district attorney.

"There is absolutely a double standard you need to be aware of," Harris was quoted as telling the women. "Being a woman that some would consider attractive carries its own baggage. People assume you're not substantial. It's why it's so important to talk to as many people as possible, and keep conveying what you stand for."

And this: "If you've stepped out in life, you will have enemies. It's not the end of the world — and sometimes it's even good. Women should feel entitled to public office; we belong in the position of being decision-makers."

For much of the race, Harris trailed the men, incumbent Hallinan and Fazio, the more conservative candidate. They both brought up Harris's ties to Mayor Brown.

Harris understood her vulnerability: some voters had grown tired of Willie Brown's machine. He had provided too many jobs to cronies, among them Paul Horcher, the Republican assemblyman who crossed his party in 1994 by casting a vote for Brown for Speaker. Under his leadership, the city also awarded contracts to firms that hired his friends as lobbyists. The *Chronicle* reported that the FBI was investigating city hall for much of his tenure. Though few indictments came of the effort, Harris, a candidate who promised reforms and a unit that would focus on public corruption, made a point of distancing herself from Brown, telling *SF Weekly* that her relationship with him, now eight years in the past, was her "albatross."

If there was any doubt that they were over, she pointedly told *SF Weekly,* "I refuse to design my campaign around criticizing Willie Brown for the sake of appearing to be independent when I have no doubt that I am independent of him — and that he would probably *right now* express some *fright* about the *fact* that he cannot control me.

"His career is over; I will be alive and kicking for the next 40 years. I do not owe him a thing."

Fazio, realizing that Harris was closing the gap, continued to play the Willie Brown card, this time in a mailer sent to women. It was Halloween weekend, days before the first Tuesday after the first Monday in November.

"I don't care if Willie Brown is Kamala Harris's ex-boyfriend," the mailer said, quoting a woman. "What bothers me is that Kamala accepted two appointments from Willie Brown to high-paying, part-time state boards — including one she had no training for. . . ."

Harris quickly answered by recording a robocall warning voters of a "trick" they'd be receiving in the mail and explaining that she used her positions on the boards to provide benefits to gay couples and to help keep a hospital open. Harris was showing herself to be deft at the art of political war. She edged out Fazio for the second spot and would face Hallinan in the runoff in December.

To the outside world, San Francisco is probably best known for its bustling Chinatown, the coffeehouses of North Beach, the Golden Gate Bridge, and cable cars, or maybe the lost souls who have no place to sleep other than sidewalks, freeway underpasses, and vacant lots. It is all of that. But insiders also know that San Franciscans play a hard brand of brawling politics. Politicians who make it in San Francisco know how to win. It's no coincidence that some of the nation's toughest current and former players — including Speaker Nancy Pelosi, Willie Brown, Senator Dianne Feinstein, Governor Gavin Newsom, John and Phillip Burton, former senator Barbara Boxer, and Kamala Harris — all have San Francisco roots.

No San Francisco race would be complete without sharp elbows being thrown. As Harris and Hallinan campaigned, Kimberly Guilfoyle, then married to mayoral candidate Gavin Newsom and on leave from the district attorney's office, threw one Harris's way, dishing to the *Chronicle* that Harris had tried to block her return to the office in 2000.

"The bottom line is she didn't want me there," Guilfoyle said. Her ploy was to suggest that Harris had tried to impede the progress of a successful law-and-order prosecutor. Indeed, in 2001, after Harris had left the office, Guilfoyle gained notoriety as one of two prosecutors in an especially awful case against two lawyers who had kept two one-hundred-plus-pound Perro de Presa Canario dogs named Bane and Hera while the animals' owner, an Aryan Brotherhood member nicknamed "Cornfed" who was both their client and adopted son, served time in prison. Cornfed had bred the beasts to guard meth labs, and they were vicious. One of the lawyers had the dogs on leashes when they broke free and mauled to death a university lacrosse coach in the hallway outside her apartment. Guilfoyle and her partner on the case won convictions, and Guilfoyle caught the attention of cable news bookers. That ultimately led her to the conservative world of Fox News, a divorce from Newsom, and, in time, a relationship with Donald Trump Jr.

In the meantime, Harris succeeded in brushing off Guilfoyle's claim. To the contrary, Harris said, she wanted to help Guilfoyle. In the end, Guilfoyle couldn't touch her, and Harris found a smart way across the finish line.

In San Francisco, winning candidates don't run to the right. It's not a winning strategy. But some do find nuanced ways to seem less to the left than their opponents. That was Harris's path. In the runoff against Hallinan, she promised reforms but also appealed to Fazio's voters, many of whom were, if not conservative, at least less liberal than Hallinan's supporters. The *Chronicle* endorsed Harris on December 7, 2003, under the headline "Harris, for Law and Order."

Harris did not list Willie Brown's endorsement in any of her campaign material. But Brown, loyal to old friends and willing to help talented Black candidates, was helping behind the scenes and using his clout to open doors for Harris. That included access to his donors. But it was Harris's job to close the sale. Many of her donors previously backed Hallinan, but politics had turned Harris's way. With his fund-raising choked off by the upstart, Hallinan used $50,000 of his own money to keep his campaign afloat. By Election Day, she had raised almost three times what Hallinan raised, $1 million for that first election, virtually all of it in $500 increments. Many donors who gave to that campaign remain contributors to this day.

Brown made a brief appearance at Harris's victory party: "It is obviously a gender victory. It is obviously an ethnic victory. But it was her competence that defeated Terence Hallinan," he said.

Harris won by a 56 percent to 44 percent margin and received more votes than any other candidate in San Francisco that day, including the newly elected mayor, Gavin Newsom.

In early 2004, after the votes were counted and the new guard was sworn in, the *San Francisco Chronicle* reported that one of Willie Brown's protégés, Mohammed Nuru, a top official in the public works department, passed word that members of a city-funded street cleaning crew known as the San Francisco League of Urban Gardeners, or SLUG, should vote for Newsom. Nuru told reporters he had campaigned for both Newsom and Harris on his own time and denied pressuring anyone. Reports of such irregularities weren't new in San Francisco. The new mayor and the new district attorney promised to clean up the town. The San Francisco city attorney, the California secretary of state, and the newly elected district attorney all said they would look into the allegations. Nothing came of it.

Harris emerged from the swampy, back-stabbing politics of San Francisco with some scars. She also learned, Kali-like, how to figuratively sever a head or two. Her skill and charisma, her intelligence and grit, and her willingness to fight hard set her apart.

In time, Californians would see more of that.

8
Officer Down

In her 2003 campaign for San Francisco district attorney, Kamala Harris promised voters that she would never seek the death penalty, no matter how heinous the crime. She faced the first test of that pledge three months after taking the oath of office. Her decision affected her career for years to come.

At about 9:30 p.m. on April 10, 2004, San Francisco police officer Barry Parker eased an unmarked gray Crown Victoria past a liquor store selling discount beer and wine at the corner of Third Street and Newcomb Avenue in the Bayview district. His partner, Isaac Espinoza, was in the passenger seat.

"Woo, woo," a spotter shouted, signaling to others doing illicit business that police had arrived.

Cable cars didn't run to the Bayview–Hunters Point district. It was a different city from the one that tourists and the fancy people of Pacific Heights see. In Bayview–Hunters Point, gangs owned many streets to the point that people took to calling parts of it a "war zone."

Two young men seemed startled when the Crown Vic pulled close. One of the men wore a peacoat, though the evening was warmer than normal. Espinoza shined a flashlight onto the man's face. He kept walking. The officers, dressed in plain clothes, stopped and got out of their car.

"Hey, let me talk to you," Espinoza said.

"Stop. Police," he said twice, maybe seven feet away.

The man turned, pulled an assault rifle he had been hiding under his coat, and, in five seconds, fired no fewer than eleven times. Espinoza, shot in the gut and thigh, never had time to unholster his weapon.

"Officer down," Parker, wounded in the ankle, radioed.

Espinoza, twenty-nine years of age, the father of a three-year-old girl, had been on the force for eight years and was a volunteer on the anti-gang detail. By 10:00 p.m., two days before the seventh anniversary of his wedding to Renata Espinoza, Officer Isaac Espinoza had bled to death.

Police, working through the night, found the AK-47 two blocks away. A block beyond that, they found a discarded peacoat with weed in a pocket and an identification card reading David Lee Hill, age twenty-one.

On the night of the crime, a friend gave Hill a ride across the bay to Oakland and then to the apartment of a man in the East Bay suburb of San Ramon who had supplied the gun. That man encouraged Hill to turn himself into a hospital emergency room and evidently tipped the police. Hill was physically unharmed but began acting strangely, talking incoherently, slamming his forehead into a door, and wetting himself. Police, having been tipped, arrived at the hospital, guns drawn, and cuffed him, bound his ankles, checked him for gunshot residue, and drove him to the San Francisco jail.

Police believed Hill was a member of the Westmob and probably was planning to shoot a rival from the Big Block gang, perhaps in retaliation for a murder that happened in February. Hill's attorney, Martín Antonio Sabelli, later would argue that he was on the street looking to buy marijuana, that the assault weapon was for protection, and that he did not know Espinoza and Parker were cops.

"To hesitate is to die. To hesitate as a gang member is to die. To hesitate as a gang member on rival turf in the Bayview at night is to die," Sabelli would tell jurors at the trial in 2007.

On Easter Sunday 2004, officers left flowers near where Espinoza was shot. Neighborhood kids drew a picture of a police car on the sidewalk, the *San Francisco Chronicle* reported, with an inscription: "Best wishes to our SFPD / Our Best Cops / Love, Victor, Richard, Matthew, Lucy, Sam." District Attorney Harris helped oversee the investigation from behind the scenes. Mayor Newsom, who took office on the same January day as Harris, was mostly attracting attention for issuing marriage licenses to same-sex couples, but he also was attentive to the rising number of violent crimes in the city.

There were eighty-eight homicides in San Francisco in 2004, nineteen more than the year before, and San Francisco County would gain the distinction of having the highest homicide rate in California that year.

"It's so utterly unnecessary. My heart goes out to the family," the *Chronicle* quoted the new mayor as saying when he visited the scene of the April 10 crime on Easter.

Under California law, cop killers can be subject to death sentences. But three days after Espinoza died and before his funeral, San Francisco's new district attorney, a death penalty opponent, followed through on her campaign stand by announcing she would not seek death for Hill. Harris did not investigate the question of whether a capital crime could have been charged. Nor did she take a more expedient position of waiting until after the funeral. Instead, she made clear from the start that she would stay true to her word. For that, she would pay a price.

Police officers in San Francisco and around the Bay Area were outraged. Chief Heather Fong attacked Harris's decision: "We, the command staff of this department, urge in the strongest possible terms that this capital murder case be prosecuted to the fullest extent, and that the death penalty be sought upon conviction, as permitted by law."

The *San Francisco Chronicle* could find no other instance in which prosecutors failed to seek the death penalty against a cop killer. In the capital city of Sacramento, forty-three of eighty members of the assembly, including several Democrats, signed on to a resolution urging that California attorney general Bill Lockyer and the U.S. attorney investigate the matter and intervene if necessary, though the resolution never got to the floor for a vote. It died without a hearing in the Assembly Public Safety Committee, chaired by Harris's friend, Assemblyman Mark Leno, a fellow San Francisco Democrat. That spared Harris some embarrassment. But Lockyer, who supported the death penalty at the time and was a potential candidate for governor in 2006, let Harris know that he was contemplating exercising his authority to take control of the case. He ultimately didn't.

Cops from across the state rode their motorcycles to San Francisco for Officer Espinoza's funeral on the Friday after his murder. Thousands filled St. Mary's Cathedral in the middle of the city.

Harris and Senator Feinstein, who had received campaign support from police unions over the years, greeted each other amicably moments before the start of the service. Harris took her seat in the front pew. Other dignitaries sat nearby, as did Officer Espinoza's widow, Renata.

The San Francisco Police Officers Association had endorsed Harris's candidacy, aware that she opposed the death penalty. But Gary Delagnes, the labor organization's president, spoke at the funeral: "Isaac paid the ultimate price. . . . And I speak for all fellow officers in demanding that his killer also pay the ultimate price." That must have stung Harris. But it got worse when Feinstein stood to speak.

As a teenager and young woman, Feinstein contemplated pursuing an acting career. Although she gave up the theater for politics, she retained a flair for the dramatic. At St. Mary's Cathedral, the senior U.S. senator from California discarded her prepared remarks.

"This is not only the definition of tragedy, it's the special circumstance called for by the death penalty law," Feinstein told the audience, as quoted by the *Chronicle.* One Democrat from San Francisco had turned on another in her moment of vulnerability, in a Catholic church. It was an extraordinarily brutal twist even by San Francisco standards.

"You could feel the shock. That's the closest word," Lockyer, who was in attendance, recalled.

Many in the crowd, especially the cops, stood and applauded Feinstein; Harris stayed seated. After the service, Feinstein told reporters that she would probably not have endorsed Harris in her campaign for district attorney if she had known of Harris's opposition to capital punishment, not that Harris had hidden her stand.

Feinstein had her own history with the death penalty and had played it very differently. As a candidate for governor in 1990, Feinstein appeared before partisans at the California Democratic Convention, a decidedly liberal group, and proclaimed her support for the death penalty. It was, she said then, "an issue that cannot be fudged or hedged." Party activists booed her. But knowing the vast majority of Californians supported the death penalty at the time, Feinstein and her campaign handlers used the 1990 episode in campaign ads portraying her as strong and tough and showing that her Democratic rival, Attorney General John Van de Kamp, was a death penalty opponent. The ads, like the boos she elicited, served their purpose. She won the Democratic gubernatorial primary, though law-and-order Republican Pete Wilson defeated Feinstein that November. Feinstein won her Senate seat in 1992 and has been elected five times since, including in 2018. In that 2018 campaign, Feinstein, facing a challenge from the left in a state that had become increasingly liberal, declared that she no longer supported the death penalty.

The attacks on Harris that day and in the days to come would not be the last she endured over her decision. For months, officers would shun Harris by turning their backs when they saw her in the Hall of Justice. Harris made it clear that she would neither fudge nor hedge on the issue, explaining her decision in an op-ed in the *Chronicle* two weeks after Officer Espinoza's murder:

> For those who want this defendant put to death, let me say simply that there can be no exception to principle. I gave my word to the people of San Francisco that I oppose the death penalty and I will honor that commitment despite the strong emotions evoked by this case. I have heard and considered those pleas very carefully and I understand and share the pain that drives them, but my decision is made and it is final.

When Harris was elected district attorney, she tapped an old acquaintance, Harry Dorfman, to handle some of the city's highest-profile murders. Dorfman, who is now a superior court judge, won a conviction of reputed MS-13 gang member Edwin Ramos, who was sentenced to three life terms for killing a forty-eight-year-old man and his two sons in the Excelsior district.

Harris declined to seek the death penalty in that case, too. Dorfman obtained a first-degree murder conviction on Clifton Terrell Jr. for the robbery-murder of Hunter McPherson, the son of former *Santa Cruz Sentinel* editor and California state senator Bruce McPherson, who would later be named secretary of state by Governor Schwarzenegger.

Dorfman's biggest case, though, was the prosecution of David Hill. Dorfman declined to discuss the office's prosecutorial decisions in the case, and no one can know whether a San Francisco jury would have imposed a death sentence on Hill if he had been charged with murder in a way that qualified him for the death penalty. But it seems unlikely. Hill was young and had never been convicted of a violent crime. San Franciscans long have opposed capital punishment, and juries reflect that opposition.

In any case, in 2007, the San Francisco jury found Hill guilty of second-degree murder, a crime that does not carry with it the death penalty. Jurors did conclude that Hill knowingly shot at a police officer. For that, he was sentenced to life in prison without parole. A state court of appeal upheld his sentence in 2011. Hill is serving it at New Folsom state prison east of Sacramento. He is thirty-seven years of age, eight years older than Isaac Espinoza was when Hill killed him.

9
GETTING "SMART" ON CRIME

Presiding over an urban district attorney's office is not easy, and it was especially tough in San Francisco in the 1990s. Jurors were drawn from a pool of people who were skeptical of authorities, and the justice system itself didn't abide by the basic rules. On Harris's watch, prosecutors had to dismiss hundreds of cases after a crime lab technician was discovered dipping into cocaine seized from suspects. Defense attorneys found that her office had failed to comply with the law requiring that prosecutors turn over to the defense evidence that might exculpate defendants.

But as broken as the office could be, Harris kept making a point of focusing on the people who often were ignored by law enforcement until bullets start flying. The Sunnydale housing projects, far from the breathtaking vistas and charming neighborhoods of San Francisco, is the place to go to best understand how she did that. For decades, the projects ranked as the most dangerous area in the city, and they were never more notorious than the years when Kamala Harris was the district attorney.

"Sunnydale, also called 'The Dale' or 'The Swamp,' is littered with bottles and trash," Leslie Fulbright wrote in a 2008 special report for the *Chronicle*. "There is no landscaping, just overgrown grass and clumps of weeds. There are dirty diapers in trees. Cockroaches and mice run around inside. Some sinks are so moldy, they are black."

Graffiti covered the walls of its 785 units, dozens of which had been boarded up, although that didn't stop squatters from taking up residence.

Sunnydale was ruled by street gangs. The city attorney's office responded with anti-gang injunctions, and the feds hit the project's shot callers with Racketeer Influenced and Corrupt Organizations (RICO) actions.

As district attorney, Harris tried her own approach. She repeatedly said she rejected notions of being tough on crime or soft on crime. She professed to being "smart on crime." In addition to prosecuting cases that police brought to her deputies, she tried

intervention and, on more than one occasion, ventured into Sunnydale at night, accompanied by her top gang prosecutors, emergency room doctors from San Francisco General Hospital, and, wisely, a police escort.

It was kind of a "scared straight" approach.

The sessions would be attended by as many as fifteen young "at-risk" men in the project's community room. Harris would give a short introductory speech, followed by a presentation by the doctors who showed the audience members what it looked like when shooting victims came into the emergency room with their stomachs blown open by gunshot wounds. Then her prosecutors took the floor to explain to the gathering what people might expect in terms of years behind bars if they were caught and convicted for the carnage captured in the photographs. The point of it all was to stay out of trouble in the first place, Harris would say.

Harris also instituted a program aimed at diverting first-time nonviolent offenders from a life in crime by dismissing charges if they enrolled in job training in what she called the Back on Track program. Such efforts were not without political risks, as she

would find as she began running for California attorney general.

The *Los Angeles Times* detailed the 2008 case of a Back on Track participant who used an SUV to run into a woman whose purse he had snatched. The man was an undocumented immigrant. Harris had to backtrack, promising to exclude from the program people who could not legally work in this country. The woman survived, and the man was kicked out of the program and tried for assault with a deadly weapon.

Then there were the truly private times that the public would never see. Matthew D. Davis tells the story of his neighbor Naomi Gray, an elderly Black woman who long had been involved in city politics and was "over the moon" when Harris was elected district attorney in 2003. Naomi had a stroke and was hospitalized at the city-run nursing home Laguna Honda. Davis remembers thinking one rainy night how lonely she must have been. On the spur of the moment, he called Harris. She picked up the phone. He asked if she knew Naomi.

"Of course I do," Harris answered.

Davis told her it would mean the world to Naomi if she would send a card.

"What are you doing right now?" Harris

asked, surprising Davis.

They quickly made arrangements to meet in thirty minutes at Laguna Honda. Davis walked Harris to Naomi's room. Harris sat down at her bedside and held her hand. Davis stepped outside, giving the young district attorney and old woman privacy. Harris came out about twenty minutes later.

"There were no crowds of potential voters. Just me in a quiet hallway," Davis said. "We said goodnight and I watched Kamala hustle off to some meeting or event. Naomi passed away a few days later."

After Joe Biden picked Harris to be his running mate and Donald Trump called her "mean" and "nasty," Davis felt compelled to reveal the story in a Facebook essay. It was one of the ways Harris behaved when no one in particular was watching.

Harris used her position as district attorney to shape state policy, sponsoring legislation in her first year, 2004, to increase sentences for sexual exploitation of children. The legislation, carried by then senator Leland Yee, a San Francisco Democrat, redefined prostitution. Children who are bought and sold no longer would be called prostitutes. They were to be called what they are: exploited and victims. Johns and pimps would face longer prison terms for trafficking children. The bill passed without a no vote, and Governor Schwarzenegger signed it into law.

"It's finally in black and white, legislated, that adults cannot buy children for sex," Harris said at the time.

Yee's career came to an ignominious end in 2015 when he pleaded guilty to federal corruption charges, including gun trafficking and trading legislative action for campaign donations, in a case involving Chinatown gangster Robert "Shrimp Boy" Chow, who was the "dragon head" of an international triad. He served five years in prison. Although there was no hint of his shady dealings in the bill Harris sought, the charges against Yee showed that the city's politics could often veer to the seamier side. District Attorney Harris had promised to crack down on public corruption, but there were no major prosecutions during her tenure.

As part of her "smart on crime" approach, Harris turned to the unlikely issue of elementary school truancy. Harris cited statistics showing the vast majority of homicide victims age twenty-five and younger were high school dropouts. Most prison inmates also were high school dropouts. The problem, she concluded, had its roots in elementary school. Some children were missing seventy or eighty days a year. To combat it, she and a judge created a truancy court in San Francisco. Harris, who patterned her effort after one created by the Alameda County district attorney, rarely used a hammer. But when parents appeared at the Hall of Justice, a prosecutor was on hand to make clear that the threat of sanctions was real. Between 2005 and 2009, she and San Francisco school officials said, habitual truancy among elementary school students was cut by half.

In 2010, as she ran for California attorney general, Harris took the issue statewide, turning to a longtime friend and ally, Senator Mark Leno of San Francisco, to push legislation establishing that parents could be charged with a crime for habitually failing to see to it that their elementary and junior high school–age children showed up for class. The penalty could be a $2,000 fine and up to a year in jail.

"There is a very direct connection between public safety and public education," Harris told a reporter. "It's much cheaper to focus on getting that elementary school student to school than it is prosecuting a homicide."

The concept did not sit well with the Left.

Civil libertarians and defense attorneys opposed it. Their argument had a certain logic: a parent who was in jail would have a tough time forcing his or her kid to show up to class. And did the law really address the root cause of truancy? Nonetheless, the bill passed and was signed into law. "I just want these kids to go to school, and I'm prepared to be the bad guy," Harris said at the time.

As attorney general, Harris produced annual reports detailing the problem. The first report showed 29 percent of elementary school children were habitual truants. That had dipped to 25 percent when she issued her final report. A handful of counties did send parents to jail. On the presidential campaign trail in 2019, Harris took heat from the Left for the legislation she championed and said she regretted that any parents were jailed. Harris's successor, Attorney General Xavier Becerra, quietly stopped issuing the truancy reports once he took office. But California law still allows prosecutors to charge parents of elementary school kids who are habitual truants with crimes.

10
Harris and Obama

In September 2004, her first year as San Francisco district attorney, Kamala Harris, always scouring the political landscape, co-hosted a fund-raiser at the Four Seasons Hotel for a fellow traveler, an Illinois state senator from the South Side of Chicago who worked for a small law firm and taught constitutional law at the University of Chicago. His name was Barack Obama.

Obama already knew to come to San Francisco, an important stop for any Democratic politician on the rise. The year before, Susie and Mark Buell had hosted an Obama fund-raiser and their aide had made sure Harris and Obama met. The 2004 event was the first of many times the two rising stars helped each other. Obama was about to win a U.S. Senate seat representing Illinois and had become a huge draw after he stirred the nation at the 2004 Democratic National Convention with the speech in which he said, "There is not a liberal America and a conservative America. There is the United States of America. There is not a Black America and a White America and Latino America and Asian America. There's the United States of America."

The March following the Harris fund-raiser for Obama, the newly elected senator returned the favor, headlining a fund-raiser for Harris at the North Beach nightclub Bimbo's 365. The crowd stood shoulder to shoulder.

The comparisons between Harris and Obama were unmistakable, if facile: they are biracial, smart, and attractive; both accomplished attorneys; and both reflective of the new face of the Democratic Party, if not the nation itself. The May 2006 edition of *Ebony* magazine named them both as being among the "100+ Most Influential Black Americans." Her photo was number five; his was number sixty-seven.

In February 2007, District Attorney Harris, looking beyond San Francisco, traveled to frigid Springfield, Illinois, for Obama's launch of his presidential campaign. By March, she had become the most prominent elected official in California to endorse

Obama.

"That was probably not the right political calculation at the time," said Buffy Wicks, who was Obama's chief California organizer in 2007 and later joined his White House staff. Wicks, now a member of the California State Assembly, noted that California in 2007 and 2008 was Hillary Clinton territory. The former First Lady and senator had locked up many of the major endorsements early, including San Francisco mayor Gavin Newsom, Los Angeles mayor Antonio Villaraigosa, and Senator Dianne Feinstein.

Obama made his first presidential campaign stop in California in March, drawing a crowd of twelve thousand outside Oakland City Hall, the same location where, as a U.S. senator, Harris would announce the start of her presidential candidacy in 2019. "I am so psyched," District Attorney Harris, sitting in the front row, told political reporter Carla Marinucci, then of the *San Francisco Chronicle*. "The energy, the diversity . . . people are excited, and it's not just about Barack. It's about them."

That night, Harris was among the sponsors of a fund-raiser at the Mark Hopkins Hotel in downtown San Francisco that would raise $1 million. Obama was on a fund-raising blitz during which he amassed an astonishing $25.7 million in the first quarter of 2007, nearly matching Clinton's haul and making clear that his candidacy was anything but quixotic. Obama was not likely to defeat Clinton in California. But Harris's task was to serve as Obama's surrogate. So there she was, speaking on his behalf, stumping up and down the state, spending a weekend in early December in Salinas, telling local Democrats who were taking a straw poll that Obama was mounting "one of the most extraordinary presidential campaigns in our lifetime." Obama won that straw poll.

In San Francisco, left-leaning voters did not hold the controversy over the Officer Isaac Espinoza case and issues at the crime lab against Harris, and she ran for reelection in November 2007 without opposition. That hurdle out of the way, the newly reelected district attorney traveled to Des Moines to knock on doors for Obama in the frigid days of December leading up to the Iowa caucuses, spending New Year's Eve there. On January 3, 2008, the night of the Iowa caucuses, I stood not far from her in Hy-Vee Hall in Des Moines as she listened to Obama promise "a nation less divided and more united."

In the California primary a month later, Obama carried San Francisco, but Clinton won the state easily, 51.5 percent to 43.2 percent, ensuring that the race would continue for months. Clinton's California campaign manager was Ace Smith, who would soon become Harris's chief strategist.

When Harris ran for president, a *Politico* reporter asked her about carrying on Obama's legacy.

"I have my own legacy," she told the reporter.

11
The Mad Dash

On the night of November 4, 2008, Kamala Harris joined hundreds of thousands of deliriously happy people who crammed into Chicago's Grant Park for the celebration of her friend's historic election.

"Change has come to America," President-elect Barack Obama told the throngs in Chicago and the millions who watched on television and over the internet.

There was speculation that Obama would find a place for Harris in Washington, and she was thinking about making that her next move. On November 12, 2008, eight days after Obama was elected president, and just eleven months into her second term as San Francisco district attorney, Harris made up her mind. Capitalizing on the Democrats' euphoria over Obama, Harris declared her intention to run for California attorney general in 2010. I wrote that day that she "long had focused on running for attorney general, the state's chief law enforcement officer and a post that can serve as a steppingstone to the governor's office."

District Attorney Harris, accompanied by her chief strategist Ace Smith, spent the day of her announcement giving interviews to Los Angeles television reporters explaining why she was running. At the end of the day, they stopped to visit Mayor Antonio Villaraigosa at Getty House, the mayor's residence in the Hancock Park neighborhood, not far from downtown Los Angeles. They lingered a little too long. Smith checked his watch and realized they had no time to get to Bob Hope Airport in Burbank. The driver sped, weaving through traffic. Once they got to the airport, Harris took off her high heels and they dashed, got through security, and rushed to the gate as the door was about to close. Once in their seats, Smith turned to Harris, smiled, and said, "That's how the campaign is going to be." They'd run like crazy, and when it looked like they weren't going to make it, they'd run a little harder and slip by with the thinnest of margins to spare. She got the message. It would be a wild ride.

Luckily for her, Smith had special insight into the office of attorney general, having managed Jerry Brown's run for the office in

2006. But it went deeper. He was an infant when his father, Deputy Attorney General Arlo Smith, was assigned to help bring an end to the saga of Caryl Chessman, the Red Light Bandit, who was executed in 1960 after being convicted of kidnapping and rape of women on a Los Angeles lovers' lane. Chessman had written memoirs while on San Quentin's death row and had become the focus of the movement to abolish capital punishment. Arlo Smith served three terms as San Francisco district attorney until his defeat in 1995 by Terence Hallinan. In 1990, young Ace helped run his father's campaign for California attorney general. Arlo lost to Republican Dan Lungren by 28,906 votes out of more than seven million cast.

Harris's announcement two years ahead of the election had become one of her ways of campaigning: come out early, big and bold, with the goal of paring down the field of likely Democratic primary opponents. Within a month of Harris's announcement in 2008, California Republican leaders were at work devising a plan of attack against her, having created what they called the "AG Rapid Response Team." Internal emails show they hoped to recruit crime victims, Republican district attorneys, a credible

Democrat to challenge Harris, and the police. Police unions usually backed Democrats. But Harris continued to pay a political price for her decision not to seek the death penalty against the killer of Officer Isaac Espinoza. In early 2009, the San Francisco Police Officers Association leaders informed Harris that the union would under no circumstances endorse her. In solidarity with San Francisco officers and in remembrance of Officer Espinoza, other police organizations were also lining up in opposition.

Heading into the 2010 election, Republicans believed they could win the office of attorney general. The team assembled to devise the strategy included two Republican operatives, former California Republican Party chairman George "Duf" Sundheim and Sean Walsh, who was one of Governor Pete Wilson's top aides and later Wilson's business partner.

Wilson got his start in politics at age thirty-three by winning an assembly seat in San Diego in 1966, the year Reagan was elected California governor. San Diego, a navy and marine town, had a large defense industry and was reliably Republican at the time. Wilson was an ex-marine and lawyer who became San Diego mayor for three terms from 1971 to 1983 and a U.S. senator in 1983 when Reagan was president. In 1990, Wilson defeated former San Francisco mayor Dianne Feinstein to become governor, succeeding another Republican, George Deukmejian. That was when California was a swing state. It's not now, in no small part because of Wilson's politics.

Governor Schwarzenegger, a Republican, started his administration in 2003 by veering to the right. But by his 2006 reelection campaign, he had moved to the middle, and he became a warrior for alternative energy and against climate change. Schwarzenegger explained the brutal truth at a 2007 California Republican Party convention in the desert resort town of Indian Wells: "In movie terms, we are dying at the box office. We are not filling the seats."

Reporters covering the event described an almost silent reaction. The party that had produced Richard Nixon, Ronald Reagan, George Deukmejian, and Pete Wilson was out of step with California voters on gun control, the environment, abortion, same-sex marriage, and, especially, immigration. Latinos, the fastest-growing segment of California's population, turned against the GOP after Wilson won his 1994 reelection by becoming a champion of Proposition

187, an initiative that promised to end all government-funded services to undocumented immigrants, including public schooling and nursing home care. It was, at its core, an attack on new Americans and their families. The California Republican Party has been on a downward slide ever since. By 2010, it had become a rusting hull; a mere 31 percent of the voters registered as Republicans. Now that it's the party of Donald J. Trump, GOP registration is below 25 percent in California.

With visions of reviving the party, Wilson recruited statewide candidates for the 2010 election: a young Black man for secretary of state, a Latino for lieutenant governor. Silicon Valley billionaire Meg Whitman led the ticket by running to succeed Schwarzenegger as governor. She would spend $159 million, most of it from her own pocket. For attorney general, Wilson recruited Steve Cooley, the three-term district attorney from Los Angeles County.

In approach, demeanor, and appearance, Kamala Harris and Steve Cooley could not have been more different. San Francisco District Attorney Harris promised to bring innovation and reform to the criminal justice system if she were elected attorney general in 2010. She would defend the environment, consumers, and marriage equality. Harris, now age forty-six, clearly intended to ascend as high as she could. Los Angeles County District Attorney Cooley promised to defend the death penalty and traditional marriage. He was sixty-three and was running for the final office he would hold. He would be tough to beat, but first he needed to get past the primary.

Kamala Harris was going through a rough patch as the race was beginning, though none of it was public at the time. She and Maya had been making sure that their mother, Shyamala, made it to her chemotherapy sessions. Harris recounted in a 2018 *New York Times* op-ed an incident when her mother was hospitalized, near the end:

> For as long as I could remember, my mother loved to watch the news and read the newspaper. When Maya and I were kids, she'd insist we sit down in front of Walter Cronkite each night before dinner. But suddenly, she had no interest. Her mighty brain decided it had had enough.
>
> She still had room for us, though. I remember that I had just entered the race for California attorney general and she asked me how it was going.

"Mommy, these guys are saying they're going to kick my ass," I told her.

She rolled over and looked at me and unveiled the biggest smile. She knew who she'd raised. She knew her fighting spirit was alive and well inside me.

On February 11, 2009, the rock of the family, the scientist who studied cancer and sought its cure, and the woman who more than anyone else raised and shaped two strong and accomplished women, died of cancer in Oakland. In the months and years ahead, friends would notice Harris's eyes welling up at the important milestones in her life when someone mentioned her mom.

District Attorney Harris had used her experience as a prosecutor to her benefit in her campaign. But her record in San Francisco was complicated. When Mayor Villaraigosa endorsed her early in her 2010 run for attorney general, he declared, "Kamala has spent her entire professional life in the trenches as a courtroom prosecutor, and she has raised conviction rates in her community to the highest in 15 years."

Journalist Peter Jamison, then writing for *SF Weekly,* dug into the San Francisco district attorney's statistics and found that

Harris based her statement on plea deals reached with defendants. Plea agreements are, of course, an important part of the criminal justice system. But when Harris deputies took serious crimes to trial, conviction rates were significantly below the statewide average.

Prosecutors at the San Francisco Hall of Justice had an especially tough day on February 9, 2010. A jury wrongly convicted one man, and a separate jury, after deliberating for only one day, acquitted three gang members of the murder of two rivals in a trial that had lasted five months. Harris was not directly involved in either case, but both happened on her watch.

In the trial that led to the acquittal, defense lawyers found that DNA evidence was mishandled for one homicide and testimony from the key witness was inconsistent. One of the defendants had a broken right hand in a cast and yet purportedly was able to jump a fence in an escape. And although he was right-handed, he was accused of firing the shots. The quick not-guilty verdicts raised questions about the prosecutor's decision to bring the charges.

"They should only bring cases they ethically believe they can prove beyond a reasonable doubt," attorney Kate Chatfield, who represented one of the three men, said.

On that same day, a separate jury returned a guilty verdict against Jamal Trulove in the shooting death of his friend Seu Kuka in 2007 in a Sunnydale housing project at the south end of the city. Trulove wept as the verdict was read — for good reason, as it was later shown.

Trulove was an aspiring rapper who had appeared on a reality television show, the VH1 series *I Love New York 2.* An eyewitness claimed she was 100 percent sure that Trulove committed the crime. The lead prosecutor contended that the witness was testifying despite facing retaliation and possible death, and she had been relocated and given money to cover her expenses. District Attorney Harris didn't prosecute the case but echoed her deputy, praising the "brave eyewitness who stepped forward from the crowd." A judge sentenced Trulove to fifty years to life in prison. Trulove's conviction would count as a statistic that would buttress Harris's claim of increasing felony convictions. But years later, the truth emerged.

Trulove's appellate lawyer had become convinced of his innocence. In January 2014, with Harris as attorney general, a state court of appeals reversed Trulove's conviction, concluding that the San Francisco "prosecutor committed highly prejudicial misconduct" and that the yarn about the witness testifying despite fearing for her life "was made out of whole cloth." In March 2015, two months after Attorney General Harris announced her candidacy for U.S. Senate, a new jury in San Francisco acquitted Trulove of all charges. The matter wasn't over. Trulove, who had spent eight years behind bars, sued the police and city, though not Harris, alleging officers framed him, and a federal jury awarded him $14.5 million in 2018. In March 2019, as Senator Harris was running for president, the San Francisco Board of Supervisors settled the Trulove case by awarding him $13.1 million.

"Kamala Harris tried to be progressive. I very much appreciate that," Marc Zilversmit, Trulove's appellate attorney, said. "At a time when being progressive on crime was a third rail, she put some of these good ideas into practice. There was a lot more that she could have done."

As she ascended to higher office, Harris would point to her experience as a prosecutor and her successes. It was her calling card. But the job cut both ways, and the wrongful conviction of Jamal Trulove haunts her time as San Francisco district attorney.

Harris ultimately faced five Democratic opponents in the primary, all of them men. The more men, the more likely a merry outcome for the one woman in the race. The five guys would eat into one another's sources of support, and Harris would stand out. One potential female candidate was Jackie Speier, a Democratic congresswoman from Hillsborough, south of San Francisco, who let it be known in early 2010 that she was thinking of running. As a young congressional aide, Speier accompanied her boss, Congressman Leon Ryan, to Guyana in 1978, as he investigated Jim Jones and his Peoples Temple cult. Ryan was assassinated on that trip, and Speier was wounded in a series of horrific events that led to a mass suicide and murder of more than nine hundred people. Speier still carries lead in her body from that attack. In the California State Legislature and in Congress, Speier built a reputation as a maverick who stood up to banks over such issues as interest rates and consumer privacy. Those positions resonated in the wake of the Wall Street crash of 2008, the Great Recession, and the home foreclosure crisis, which hit California especially hard. But soon after Speier's name was floated, Harris's campaign disclosed that she had raised $2.2 million for the attorney general's race, an impressive sum that would be tough for a candidate just starting out to match. Speier opted to remain in Congress.

Money matters in any campaign, especially in down-ballot state races, which attract much less media attention and voter interest than races for governor or U.S. senator. Harris had no independent source of wealth and certainly didn't inherit a fortune from her mother's modest estate. Her most worrisome primary opponent was the self-funding former Facebook attorney Chris Kelly. Kelly, a first-time candidate, ultimately spent $12 million through the June primary, double what Harris spent in the entire race.

Harris brought with her advantages: she had run twice in the meat grinder that is San Francisco politics, had name identification in the Bay Area because she regularly was on the evening news and in the *Chronicle,* and was the only prosecutor among the six Democratic primary candidates.

Significantly, Harris's internal polling reflected a shift in public attitudes. Voters who had approved the harsh three-strikes law in 1994 were turning away from the lock-'em-up philosophy of Pete Wilson and were open to an alternative. Having laid out her philosophy of diversion, education, drug treatment, and rehabilitation in her book *Smart on Crime,* Harris portrayed herself as a prosecutor who supported criminal justice reform.

"People saw the prison system as a revolving door, and people weren't getting corrected," Ace Smith said. "It was perhaps the first major election where someone ran on that idea of criminal justice reform."

Harris got a boost in October 2009 when the reform-minded Los Angeles police chief William Bratton, the most popular person in law enforcement in Cooley's home county, endorsed her. It was the most significant law enforcement endorsement she would receive and helped validate her credentials as a law enforcement official.

The good news was tempered by tragedy.

Lili Smith, the precocious girl with Apert syndrome who helped stuff envelopes and hand out brochures in Harris's first district attorney's race, had turned fifteen, an age when appearances and fitting in become all-important. In the Marin County schools she attended, other kids didn't bully or tease her. But they did ignore her and she was becoming socially isolated. She and her parents, Ace Smith and Laura Talmus, decided to try a boarding school, Scattergood Friends School in rural West Branch, Iowa. There, she was finding community and acceptance, and excelling.

She had been reading the autobiography of Cherie Blair, the wife of former British prime minister Tony Blair, after having finished the biography of United Farm Workers cofounder Dolores Huerta. On October 9, she called her mom and left a message saying they'd speak in the morning.

That night, she had a seizure and died.

Harris was spending time off the campaign trail when she got a call from one of Smith's partners, Dan Newman, telling her of Lili's passing. Ace Smith and Laura Talmus were important parts of Harris's political operation. But they were also part of her tight circle of friends. Harris quickly got on a flight to San Francisco to sit shivah with Lili's parents at their Marin County home.

Nothing is worse than the loss of a child. But Talmus and Smith turned their grief into good by creating a charity, Beyond Differences, which develops curriculum used in schools nationwide to help combat social isolation. They also learned something about Harris's way of caring. In the years since Lili's death, Harris has not missed calling on birthdays and Mother's Days and has been available to help raise money for the cause of Beyond Differences in Lili's name.

On primary night, June 8, 2010, Harris piled up huge margins in San Francisco and Alameda Counties and won in Los Angeles County. Statewide, she beat her nearest opponent by more than two to one; Chris Kelly placed third.

Steve Cooley's primary fight was tougher.

His main challenger was John C. Eastman, the dean of Chapman University's Dale E. Fowler School of Law in Orange County and a former clerk to Justice Clarence Thomas. Eastman's chief strategist, Frank Schubert, had overseen the "Yes on Proposition 8" campaign to ban same-sex marriages in 2008. Eastman supported that measure. Later, he would be one of the lawyers who filed briefs before the Supreme Court urging that the so-called traditional marriage initiative be deemed constitutional, and would become chairman of the National Organization for Marriage, the main organization devoted to ending same-sex marriage.

Eastman, the Tea Party favorite in California, attacked Cooley over his government pension, citing a calculation that Cooley, who had thirty-six years of Los Angeles County service, could receive an annual pension of $292,000. With the attorney general's pay, Cooley could be collecting $425,000 if he won. Pensions were a raging issue at the time, especially in Southern California. Authorities were investigating Bell, a poor Los Angeles County town of thirty-seven thousand populated by immigrants, where city leaders were looting the treasury. The city administrator collected an annual salary of $787,637 and stood to collect a huge pension. The Bell scandal was front-page news. Cooley was not doing anything wrong. Indeed, his office was overseeing the corruption investigation of Bell. Eastman ultimately placed a distant second. But the issue of Cooley's pension did not go unnoticed.

12
Change Comes to California

Attorneys general go by the initials AG. People who seek the office know the truth: AG stands for "aspiring governor." San Francisco district attorney Kamala Harris undoubtedly was interested in running for an office beyond attorney general — perhaps governor, or U.S. senator. Los Angeles County district attorney Stephen Cooley, for his part, had no apparent interest in running for any office beyond attorney general.

The son of an FBI agent, Cooley was a sad-eyed, gray-haired man who looked like he had seen it all, and he had. At least, he knew the awful things people could do to other people, a brutal reality reflected in certain statistics. Between the time he took office as Los Angeles district attorney in 2000 and 2010, when he ran for California attorney general, Cooley's deputies obtained death sentences against fifty-nine men and three women, more than half of all murderers sentenced to death during that period in California. In San Francisco, it had been more than twenty years since anyone had been sentenced to death.

To the public and reporters covering him, Cooley came off as authentic, a prosecutor to the core. He took a progressive stand by urging the softening of California's extreme three-strikes sentencing law, and he seemed to be about as nonpartisan as politicians come. He also made news by regularly bringing public corruption cases against shady Southern California politicians, an issue that played well with editorial boards. Most endorsed Cooley over Harris, including mine, the *Sacramento Bee.*

"Against almost any other opponent, she would easily win our endorsement," the *Bee* opined in an editorial that I took the lead in writing. "But because of his standing in the law enforcement community, Cooley has greater potential to spark a much needed overhaul of California's sentencing system and to take bold action against public officials who abuse the public trust."

Cooley, citing Harris's refusal to seek the death penalty against the shooter of Isaac Espinoza, emphasized his support for capital punishment and Harris's opposition. Officer Espinoza's parents and widow endorsed

Cooley, and police unions ultimately spent $1.5 million to elect Cooley.

Cooley's support of and Harris's opposition to the death penalty undoubtedly resonated in some parts of the state, but not in the Bay Area where Harris was especially strong. Harris blunted the attack by saying she would enforce the law, her personal opinion notwithstanding. This matched a long tradition of prosecutors in California who personally opposed the death penalty but enforced it nonetheless. For example, John Van de Kamp, a former public defender, was attorney general in the 1980s, and although he was a moral opponent of capital punishment, his deputies repeatedly defended death sentences and the death penalty itself before the state supreme court.

Cooley was the front-runner, and pundits bet on him winning. Garry South, one of the most accomplished strategists of his time, predicted Harris would lose to Cooley and enumerated the reason for his thinking at a forum at the University of California, Irvine: "When you have a woman who is a minority, and who is anti–death penalty, who is the district attorney of wacky San Francisco."

That was four strikes, and it was the

conventional wisdom.

Events were breaking Cooley's way. In September, Los Angeles County sheriff's deputies arrested eight Bell city officials. Cooley was the one who announced the charges, telling the *Los Angeles Times:* "This, needless to say, is corruption on steroids." Even former attorney general Bill Lockyer, a Democrat, predicted Harris would lose, though he had endorsed her and donated to her campaign. Cooley outraised Harris between the June primary and the November general election by more than $500,000 and was receiving far more money than Harris from donors from outside California. That was a clue that the race was taking on broader significance.

Cooley recalled that his campaign strategist explained the politics of the race: "This is not about Kamala Harris running for attorney general. It is all about her being vice president." Cooley dismissed the notion.

Cooley may have been underestimating Harris. But savvy Republican strategists weren't. In October, the Virginia-based Republican State Leadership Committee stepped in, and suddenly the race for California attorney general became nationalized. Its chairman, Ed Gillespie, had been a top strategist for President George W. Bush and was a former Republican National Committee chairman. The committee spent more than $1 million on a pointed statewide television ad in which Renata Espinoza criticized Harris for failing to seek the death penalty against her husband's killer.

The content of the ad had little to do with the motive for airing it. Republican strategists were saying that the GOP saw Harris as a potential national candidate and wanted to end her career before she could step onto the national stage. They also believed a Republican attorney general in California could serve as a bulwark against the Obama administration.

The next attorney general surely would have to take a stand on the Affordable Care Act, President Obama's signature domestic policy achievement, either by suing to unravel it or by defending it in court. The Republican State Leadership Committee raised more than $30 million that year, much of it from the health insurance industry and other groups critical of the health care law. Harris promised to do whatever she could to defend the ACA, also known as "Obamacare." Cooley was noncommittal.

In the years to come, Republican attorneys general from Texas and other red states would take the lead in lawsuits to invalidate the health care act, which covers nearly forty million Americans. Under Harris and her successor, Xavier Becerra, California has led Democratic states in defending the law. Answering the Republican State Leadership Committee's effort, Obama came to California to help Harris, further elevating the profile of the race. Obama told a Los Angeles audience that she was his "dear, dear friend" and headlined a fund-raiser for her in the wealthy enclave of Atherton, south of San Francisco. She was the one state candidate for whom he raised money in the 2010 election.

As Election Day neared, Meg Whitman and other Republicans faltered. That left Cooley as the one Republican with a decent chance of winning. To lock in that victory, Cooley's San Diego–based campaign manager, Kevin Spillane, turned to one of the Republican wisemen, Joe Shumate, a strategist who had advised Pete Wilson, John McCain, Arnold Schwarzenegger, and Russian president Boris Yeltsin in a campaign depicted in the film *Spinning Boris* (the trim actor Liev Schreiber played Shumate, a man who was extra-extra large). Shumate, a pioneer in the use of computer analysis to microtarget voters, planned to place ads aimed at voters in specific media markets. By October 1, time was running short, and Shumate wasn't answering his phone, which was unlike him. Spillane became alarmed and called a friend to check on him. He was in his Sacramento apartment, dead of a heart attack. The ads he envisioned never aired.

It's a fact of California politics that while most Californians live in Southern California, Northern Californians are more attuned to politics and vote in greater percentages. That benefited Harris. She and her campaign team also knew how to throw a punch, as they had demonstrated many times. Under the headline "Corruption Fighter Accepted Many Gifts," the *Chronicle* detailed gifts of Scotch whisky, wine, cigars, and Lakers tickets Cooley had accepted. The gifts became an ad attacking Cooley. But the big attack was yet to come.

Cooley agreed to one debate, held on October 5, 2010, at the UC Davis School of Law. The two candidates showed themselves to be smart, quick, deft, and very different from each other.

Harris made it clear she would refuse to defend Proposition 8, the initiative approved in November 2008 that banned same-sex marriage and led to litigation that went to the California and U.S. Supreme Courts. As attorney general, Jerry Brown refused to defend it, as did Governor Schwarzenegger. That left the proponents of the initiative to hire their own lawyers and defend it. On August 4, 2010, U.S. District Judge Vaughn Walker struck down Proposition 8, ruling that it "cannot withstand any level of scrutiny under the Equal Protection Clause." If she were elected, Harris said, she, too, would refuse to defend it.

"Now that Proposition 8 has been found to be unconstitutional by a federal district court judge, we should not use the precious resources of the State of California to defend a law that is unconstitutional. I agree with that decision and I support it," Harris said at the October 5 debate.

Cooley countered that voters had spoken and their will "should be defended by the California attorney general whether the attorney general believes in it or not." Schwarzenegger and Attorney General Jerry Brown were "abandoning their responsibilities" by refusing to defend the state, Cooley said.

They clashed over the environment, too. In 2006, Schwarzenegger signed landmark legislation intended to combat climate

change by requiring that Califorı
reduce greenhouse gas emissions
state had taken such a step. The
in time impose added costs on c
ies, food processors, factories of
and gasoline, with a goal of pe
people to find alternatives. In
companies and coal producers
main funders of a $10 million cam
an initiative endorsed by the C
Republican Party that would have k
measure by delaying its execution.
took no stand on the initiative. Ha
an out-front opponent. More than t
attacked Cooley for failing to state h
tion.

"I don't think we can be selective
what we choose to render an opinion
or not based on perhaps what it mig
us in terms of political risk," Harris
the debate. Turning to Cooley, she
little deeper: "Take on some risk. Yo
do it."

Later, Harris would not follow her
counsel. Once in office, she refused to
stands on ballot measures. But in 2010
was on the side of the electorate. The
and coal-backed measure failed, recei
less than 39 percent of the vote.

Their differences over marriage equa

ıate change, and the death penalty aside, most telling moment of the debate came ɛn one of the questioners, Jack Leonard, the *Los Angeles Times,* asked Cooley ether he would collect the attorney ıeral's pay and "double dip" by taking Los Angeles County pension if he were win on November 2, 2010. The issue was ught with political risk. Cooley should ve assumed the question would come up, ːer Eastman had raised it in the primary d since Cooley's own office was prosecut- g officials from the city of Bell. He was rthright, if abrupt: "I earned it, thirty- ght years of public service. I definitely ırned whatever pension rights I have and I ill certainly rely on that to supplement the ːry low, incredibly low salary of state at- ɔrney general."

Harris, seeing the answer for the blunder ıat it was, responded, "Go for it, Steve." Vith a "gotcha" laugh, she added, "You've arned it; there's no question."

Harris had been spending her time in Los Angeles, trying to chip away at Cooley's ɔase, campaigning across the city with a ɣoung African American aide, London Breed, now the mayor of San Francisco. With the election less than a month away, Harris poured all her money into an ad buy

in the Los Angeles television market. The focus of the ad: Cooley's answer on the pension question. The attack was withering and had its intended effect.

In 2010, the year of the Tea Party, a red wave washed over the nation. Republicans made historic gains in state houses and in the U.S. House of Representatives. But the wave stopped on the eastern slope of the Sierra Nevada. Jerry Brown easily defeated billionaire Meg Whitman. Only the Harris-Cooley race was in doubt. On election night, Cooley declared victory. The *San Francisco Chronicle* had a "Dewey Defeats Truman" moment, running an online headline declaring Cooley had won. Cooley even handed out ATTORNEY GENERAL COOLEY lapel pins. But California's secretary of state takes weeks to count mail-in and provisional ballots. In the six most-populous Bay Area counties, Harris beat Cooley by almost two to one, by 533,500 votes. In Los Angeles County, which should have been Cooley's stronghold, Cooley lost by 315,000 votes.

When all the 9.6 million-plus votes were tallied at the end of November, Harris had won by 74,157 votes. She became the first woman, the first Black person, and the first person of Indian descent to become California's top cop. Change had come to California.

13
Attorney General Harris

On one of her first days in office, Attorney General Kamala Harris held a reception in the seventeenth-floor corner suite of the California Department of Justice headquarters in Sacramento. No cameras, no press, just her, some cookies and punch, and the staff. Veteran prosecutors, Department of Justice agents, custodians, and cafeteria workers came. It was the first time many of the staffers had been in the corner suite or shaken the hand of an attorney general. It was a hopeful, friendly, professional moment. For the first time in thirty years, the department would be led by a lawyer who had significant courtroom experience. She coached them on the pronunciation of her name, *comma-la,* and told them how honored she was to be holding an office once held by Earl Warren. She repeated the receptions in branch offices in San Diego, Los Angeles, and San Francisco.

Harris entered a California Department of Justice that had a staff of 4,996 people and a budget of $732 million. It was far larger than any law firm in the state, larger than any other state justice department, and second in size only to the U.S. Department of Justice. The state Department of Justice has one of the largest police forces in the country, and its forensic scientists operate one of the nation's most sophisticated crime labs.

Old-time deputy attorneys general — DAGs as they're called — are a skeptical bunch. They have seen attorneys general come and go, mostly going on to run for governor. Each successive attorney general seemed to care less about the office he held than the office he would later seek; he knew the office was a stepping-stone. Certainly, Harris had ambition. That could be good. But maybe she would be engaged.

She was and she wasn't.

As attorney general, Harris showed herself to be both innovative and cautious. Depending on the issue, she was bold or she held her fire. She took strong stands or she stood mute on the important criminal justice issues of the day. On occasions when she might have led, she remained behind. In other instances, she was a trailblazer. As for her management style, veterans recall little personal direction from her. She was rarely seen at the department's Sacramento headquarters, preferring to remain in the branch offices near her home in San Francisco and later in Los Angeles, the cities where the most voters and donors were located.

In the end, she would make her name in California and raise her profile nationally by taking stands against banks and for-profit colleges that bilked their students, and in defense of child victims of human traffickers. She used her prosecutorial discretion to file tough-to-win cases and she rejected what might have been high-profile cases. She did not, for example, prosecute alleged foreclosure law violations against OneWest Bank, then owned by Steve Mnuchin, who went on to become the Trump administration's Treasury secretary. As detailed by the *Intercept* in 2017, her deputies recommended the prosecution in 2013. But Harris concluded that there was not enough evidence to warrant the resources it would take to bring the case. She left to her successor major unfinished cases.

As so often happens to politicians, events beyond her control forced her hand.

Her predecessor, the newly elected governor Jerry Brown, had been governor for two terms thirty years earlier and understood the intricacies of the state better than any living politician. In the best of times, Brown was tight with a buck. These were not the best of times. More than one million Californians lost their jobs in the Great Recession, and many more lost their homes and savings in the mortgage crisis. The statewide unemployment rate climbed to 12.6 percent, but it was much worse in parts of the Central Valley and rural expanses of the state. For the first time since 1938, Californians' collective income actually dropped. Tax payments to Sacramento fell 24 percent. Unlike the federal government, which can print money, California, like other states, must balance its budget each year. The state faced a $27 billion budget shortfall in 2011. Brown and legislators had no choice but to cut spending and make structural changes to the state government to balance what was a $127 billion budget. Having come from the office that Harris was entering, Brown knew what it needed and what it could get by without. He trimmed $37 million from the Office of Attorney General's budget in that first year and $75 million in the following year. The cuts would fall hardest on a public employee labor union that had endorsed Brown's opponent in the 2010 election. Harris, caught off guard, had to scramble to save jobs and manage the cuts; there would be no money for expansion. Big ideas would have to wait, though they would come eventually.

The California Department of Justice includes the Division of Law Enforcement, with agents who combat major crime, organized crime, transnational gangs, and major drug rings. The department's attorneys are responsible for defending consumer rights, protecting the environment, and enforcing antitrust law. Much of the department's work is workaday. Deputies defend the state against lawsuits and provide counsel to myriad boards and commissions. Criminal division deputies defend convictions secured by county district attorneys in state and federal courts. An elite group of veterans defended death penalty judgments.

Dane Gillette had worked in the office for almost four decades, moving from line deputy to coordinator of death penalty cases for the entire office to chief of the criminal division. Raised primarily in the Central Valley cities of Fresno and Madera, Gillette was the Republican son of Republican parents and grandparents, though he changed his registration to "no party preference" after becoming disenchanted with the

GOP during Trump's presidency. As death penalty coordinator, Gillette oversaw each of the thirteen executions carried out between 1992 and 2006 in California. Harris's view of capital punishment was well known. But Gillette never felt that she tried to interfere on a death penalty case.

"She understood the issues," he said. "Sometimes, if she didn't understand it as well, she would ask questions. You could talk the talk with her."

Harris could be tough on her staff, abrasive and brusque. She also could be slow to make policy calls. In December 2013, Gillette was seeking her approval to file a petition seeking U.S. Supreme Court review of a case raising the issue of whether police improperly interrogated a murder suspect, after he initially had invoked his right against self-incrimination. The appellate court had tossed out the confession. The deadline to appeal was approaching. Figuring Harris would agree with him, and having not heard from her, he filed the petition. She called him at home shortly before Christmas, as she was preparing a holiday dinner, and told him she disagreed with his call and would not have appealed the decision. Chastened, he offered to resign. She brushed off his offer but asked that it never happen again. With a wish of good holiday cheer, she said her goodbye. One-on-one, she was at her best, he thought.

When Gillette retired the following year, Harris surprised him by coming to his send-off dinner, lingering at his table and talking with his wife and kids. It was an act of graciousness not soon forgotten.

One of the California Justice Department's busiest units is the one that defends the state's massive, thirty-four-institution prison system. Lawyers for prisoners had been suing the state over conditions in the prisons for decades. Federal courts consistently were siding with prisoners against the state. As attorney general, Jerry Brown had fought the cases. But the court losses, coupled with the financial crisis and a prison system that cost the state $10 billion a year and rising, were forcing action. In May 2011, five months after Harris and Brown took their new offices, the U.S. Supreme Court in a 5–4 decision concluded that California prisons violated constitutional protections against cruel and unusual punishment. The prisons housed 173,000 prisoners at their most crowded, twice the number of inmates they were designed to hold.

The decision was written by Justice Anthony Kennedy, the one Californian on the court and an appointee of President Reagan. At one prison, Kennedy wrote, fifty-four men shared a single toilet. At another prison, an incarcerated man complained of untreated pain for seventeen months before finally succumbing to testicular cancer. A psychiatric expert reported observing an inmate who had been held in a cage for nearly twenty-four hours, standing in a pool of his own urine, nearly catatonic. Prison officials had no other place to put him.

"As a consequence of their own actions, prisoners may be deprived of rights that are fundamental to liberty," Kennedy wrote. "Yet the law and the Constitution demand recognition of certain other rights. Prisoners retain the essence of human dignity inherent in all persons. Respect for that dignity animates the Eighth Amendment prohibition against cruel and unusual punishment."

It was among the most important decisions ever rendered on the subject of punishment and incarceration, and it had far-reaching implications for California. The state led the nation in mass incarceration. It built twenty prisons in a twenty-year span, and the number of prisoners quintupled in that period to 173,000. Now that the state had lost before the highest court in the land, California would need to reverse itself. Brown was pushing legislators to realign the criminal justice system so that far fewer people went to prison and to institute an array of changes that would reduce the prison population to 120,000. It was Brown's push, not Harris's. The new attorney general deferred to the governor on the fundamental issue of incarceration.

Brown was getting some much-needed outside help: David W. Mills, a wealthy investor, civil libertarian, and Stanford Law School professor, and New York billionaire George Soros, a Holocaust survivor from Hungary who had advocated for an array of measures to reduce prison population together spent $1 million to place a measure on the 2012 ballot that would soften the hardest edges of California's three-strikes sentencing law. Their campaign strategists, Ace Smith, Sean Clegg, and Dan Newman, were the same ones who managed Harris's winning race for attorney general.

Under the initiative, Proposition 36, repeat felons no longer would be sent to prison for twenty-five years to life for drug or property crimes, such as shoplifting. Instead, the crime would have to be violent or serious. About three thousand people serving life sentences under the three-strikes law would gain the right to petition the courts to be released.

They were people like Shane Taylor, a sometimes homeless drug user from Tulare County, a Republican part of the Central Valley represented by Congressman Devin Nunes. Taylor's past crimes included convictions for two burglaries when he was a teenager and stealing a checkbook to buy a pizza. One day in 1996, the former pizza thief was drinking beer with friends at a reservoir, Lake Success, outside the small town of Porterville, when police pulled up, searched him, and found 0.14 grams of methamphetamine, an amount equal in size to a tenth of a sugar packet. Superior court judge Howard Broadman, following the letter of the law, sentenced Taylor to twenty-five years to life for possession of the tiny amount of meth. Broadman wasn't one to second-guess himself. But the sentence weighed on him.

"Shane Taylor was a mistake," Judge Broadman said.

Taylor became one of many exhibits in the campaign to soften the nation's harshest three-strikes law. Another was the repeat felon who got a twenty-five-to-life sentence for stealing a pair of gloves from a Home

Depot. A third was a mentally ill man who was sentenced to twenty-five to life for possessing a stolen computer worth about $200. There were thousands more like them.

Given Harris's self-portrayal as a criminal justice reformer, voters might have benefited from the California attorney general's counsel. Los Angeles County District Attorney Cooley endorsed the measure. Harris, however, took no stand. Her stated reasoning was that her deputies wrote the blurb summarizing the measure for voters and that her deputies might have to defend the measure in court. She argued that if she were to take a stand for or against ballot measures, she would put her deputies and her office in an awkward position as they carried out their official duties. It was a position that she took on other ballot measures throughout her time as attorney general.

But there are many political reasons to not take stands on ballot measures. What if a third striker got out and committed a horrible crime? That would make for an attack ad in some future campaign. It was much easier to duck the issue. Some of Harris's predecessors found ways to balance the needs of being lawyerly and politically engaged. For instance, Dan Lungren, the attorney general in 1994, supported the original three-strikes initiative and built his 1994 reelection campaign around his endorsement of the initiative, well aware that his deputies would be defending the new law in the appellate courts after it passed. Unlike Harris, Lungren saw no conflict between his official duties defending a law in court and his role as a political leader responsible for letting voters know where he stood on a measure of significant public importance.

The measure to roll back the three-strikes law passed in a landslide, receiving almost 70 percent of the vote. Since its passage, about three thousand third strikers have been released from prison. Relatively few have returned, and none for homicide. One who didn't return was Shane Taylor.

Harris failed to take stands on several other criminal justice initiatives during her tenure, including one promoted by Gavin Newsom when he was California's lieutenant governor, to reduce sentences for drug offenses and property crimes, and one by Governor Jerry Brown, giving hope for parole to felons serving long sentences if they follow prison rules by taking classes and learning a trade. Harris, the lifelong opponent of capital punishment, also declined to take stands on initiatives to abolish the death penalty during her time as attorney general in 2012 and 2016. They failed by relatively narrow margins. Nor did she take a stand on a third measure, one sold to voters in 2016 as a way to hasten executions. Dane Gillette, the retired chief of the criminal division, cowrote the initiative. It passed, though the promised executions never occurred. Like all death penalty laws, the measure to speed up executions became entangled in litigation. Over the decades, Californians repeatedly voted for the death penalty. The state has by far the largest number of condemned inmates of any in the Union. But because of court decisions and opposition from Democrats who control state politics, California probably will never carry out another execution.

14
The Relic

Capital punishment was a relic when Kamala Harris took office as attorney general, not the sort of issue that a self-styled progressive prosecutor who was smart on crime would want to dwell on. But during the 2010 campaign, Harris promised to enforce the law as it stood, despite her opposition to the death penalty. That meant she would allow her deputies to do their jobs, which was to defend death judgments in state and federal courts. It was a futile effort.

The death chamber at San Quentin State Prison had been inactive for nearly five years when Attorney General Harris took office in January 2011. The prison sits on a slight rise on the north shore of San Francisco Bay. It had grown into a small, walled-off city of four thousand people since it opened in 1852. Within its walls, nearly seven hundred condemned men live in three high-security sections, built in 1913, 1930, and 1934. Collectively, they're known as death row. The prisoners would have multimillion-dollar views if they had windows that faced the outside world. They don't. No fewer than 59 of the men were sixty or older in 2011, and 145 men had died of natural causes, suicide, homicide, or drug overdoses. Most of the condemned men reside in East Block, a huge warehouselike building. Inside is a structure five tiers high, sixty cells to a tier. Cells are not quite fifty square feet. There's a Mickey Mouse clock on the wall of the guards' station, above a sign that reads THE HAPPIEST PLACE ON EARTH.

Capital punishment was dysfunctional in California long before Harris became attorney general. More than nine hundred men and women had been sentenced to death since capital punishment was reinstated in 1977. Some had their sentences overturned. A few walked out free. For most, appeals lasted for decades, and the result was that only thirteen men had been executed at San Quentin between 1992 and 2006.

In 2006, Michael Morales was on the verge of being executed for the 1981 rape and murder of a Lodi high school senior, Terri Winchell, when his lawyers persuaded U.S. District Judge Jeremy Fogel, an appointee of President Clinton, that the state's lethal combination of drugs could cause undo pain, in violation of the Eighth Amendment prohibition against cruel and unusual punishment. Under the protocol established by the California Department of Corrections and Rehabilitation, prison officers were supposed to knock out the condemned inmate by injecting sodium thiopental, a fast-acting barbiturate. Then pancuronium bromide was to be pumped into the person's veins, inducing paralysis. Finally, potassium chloride was to be administered, which caused death by cardiac arrest.

Morales's lawyers presented evidence suggesting insufficient amounts of the barbiturate were used in past executions. If the inmates were not in a deep sleep, they could have suffered excessive pain when the other drugs were injected. Exactly what happened during each execution was not clear because record keeping was shoddy. But one man, who was sentenced to death after ordering murders while he was in prison, had to be injected twice with potassium chloride. Robert Lee Massie, the last San Franciscan executed, might have been conscious and felt pain when the second and third drugs were administered in March 2001, records suggested.

As the lethal injection case dragged on, U.S. District Judge Cormac J. Carney, an appointee of President George W. Bush, considered the case of Ernest Dewayne Jones. Jones had been on death row for nineteen years by 2014, having been sentenced to death for the 1992 rape and murder of his girlfriend's mother. Carney had seen enough. In a twenty-nine-page order issued in 2014, he detailed the many steps entailed in the death penalty system, tracing a typical case through state and federal courts and back again. He noted how few condemned inmates were executed and how many had died of other causes. At the time, the state would have to carry out more than one execution a week for fourteen years in order to empty death row. And California had no approved execution protocol.

"Inordinate and unpredictable delay has resulted in a death penalty system in which very few of the hundreds of individuals sentenced to death have been, or even will be, executed by the State," he wrote. "It has resulted in a system in which arbitrary factors, rather than legitimate ones like the nature of the crime or the date of the death sentence, determine whether an individual will actually be executed. And it has resulted in a system that serves no penological purpose. Such a system is unconstitutional."

Carney concluded that the death penalty was unconstitutional because no one was being executed. If his order stood, it could mean the end of capital punishment in California. Attorney General Harris had a choice. She could have decided that Judge Carney was correct and not appealed, as part of an effort to put the death penalty system out of its misery. That would have cheered death penalty abolitionists. But her deputies would have been outraged and she would have faced protests from death penalty supporters. She would not have been true to her promise during the race for attorney general that despite her personal opposition, she would enforce the law and defend capital punishment.

Harris decided to appeal the case, explaining the decision in a brief press release, saying the ruling was "not supported by the law." Most interesting, her statement added that Carney's ruling "undermines important protections that our courts provide to defendants."

Some California Department of Justice

deputies had no idea what protections for defendants she was talking about. Nor did lawyers for death row inmates. On its face, Carney's ruling undermined no discernible protection for defendants. But Harris was thinking steps ahead. If she refused to appeal, she assumed, county district attorneys who supported capital punishment would have stepped up to pursue the appeal on their own. In time, the case could have reached the U.S. Supreme Court. There, a majority of justices had shown impatience for repeated appeals. She was concerned that the justices would have concluded that, indeed, there were too many impediments to executions and that states needed to more efficiently execute inmates. Carney's ruling could have ultimately undermined efforts to abolish the death penalty. The state appealed Carney's ruling to the U.S. Ninth Circuit Court of Appeals, which called Carney's ruling "novel" and reversed it in 2015. That meant capital punishment would remain the law of California. Until, that is, Gavin Newsom stepped in.

On March 13, 2019, two months after being sworn in as Jerry Brown's successor, Governor Newsom called a press conference to announce that he was taking the dramatic step of imposing a moratorium on executions. No one would be executed as long as he was governor. Newsom underscored that order by directing that the death chamber be disassembled, its various parts trucked to a warehouse. At the time, California had 737 condemned inmates; one was from San Francisco.

By then Harris was a U.S. senator and a newly announced candidate for president of the United States, and this freed her from what she saw as the constraints of being attorney general. On the day of Newsom's announcement, Senator Harris issued a press release praising the governor's action and called the death penalty "immoral, discriminatory, ineffective, and a gross misuse of taxpayer dollars." The following day, she told reporters that she wanted a moratorium on the federal government's use of the death penalty.

Newsom's executive order did not abolish the death penalty. Nor did it empty death row. A constitutional amendment making it the law and approved by voters in 1972 remains in place, though it is like a zombie. As of this writing, California has 691 condemned men and 20 condemned women. Their sentences are in limbo. None will die at the hands of the state so long as

Newsom is governor. They will age, h ever, and succumb to other causes. Betwe June 24 and July 29, 2020, as the nov coronavirus ripped through San Quentir thirteen death row inmates died, equal tc the number of people executed at San Quentin between 1992 and 2006.

Harris's hands-off approach to death penalty cases may have cost her during her 2019 presidential run. One line of attack by her Democratic opponents was that she had not insisted on DNA testing that might have exonerated a death row inmate, Kevin Cooper.

Cooper has been on death row since 1985 for the 1983 massacre of four people in their home in Chino Hills, east of Los Angeles. Doug and Peggy Ryen (both forty-one), their daughter, Jessica (ten), and an overnight guest, Christopher Hughes (eleven), had been hacked to death. The Ryens' eight-year-old son, Joshua, survived, though his throat had been slit. The murder scene sickened the most hardened detectives and shocked Southern California.

Cooper had been serving a four-year prison term for burglary when he escaped from the California Institution for Men in Chino shortly before the murders took place

and holed up in a home 126 yards from the Ryens' home. He claimed his innocence from the start, that he was in the wrong place at the wrong time. In the decades since the murders, there have been six attorneys general, and deputies under each of them have defended Cooper's conviction. Much of the legal battle has been over DNA. For decades, his lawyers had been requesting that DNA testing be conducted so that he could prove his claim. That request has been public dating back to at least 2000, when the Riverside *Press-Enterprise* produced a 3,700-word exposé raising questions about Cooper's conviction.

As the Riverside paper reported, Joshua Ryen said he thought there were three killers and that they were either White or Latino, and Jessica Ryen had blond hairs clenched in her hand. Cooper is Black. A bloodstain on a hallway wall could prove or disprove his innocence, his lawyers contend.

"They'd rather execute an innocent man than admit that they made a mistake," Cooper told the *Press-Enterprise* in 2000.

In January 2004, the month that Harris took office as San Francisco district attorney, Governor Schwarzenegger refused to grant clemency to Cooper. Cooper's

execution was set to take place at a minute past midnight on February 10, 2004, a Tuesday. On that Monday, after Cooper had been moved from his cell to a holding cell near the execution chamber, an eleven-judge panel of the U.S. Ninth Circuit Court of Appeals intervened and blocked his execution. That decision placed Cooper's case on hold. His lawyers and deputies and the attorney general have spent years since then battling over DNA testing.

On May 17, 2018, *New York Times* columnist Nicholas Kristof wrote a 3,500-word piece detailing the many questions about Cooper's conviction and singled out Governor Jerry Brown, who as attorney general declined to require DNA testing, and Kamala Harris, who also had failed to act:

> It appears that an innocent man was framed by sheriff's deputies and is now on death row in part because of dishonest cops, sensational media coverage and flawed political leaders — including Democrats like Brown and Kamala Harris, who was California's attorney general before being elected to the U.S. Senate. They both refused to allow advanced DNA testing for a black man convicted of hacking to death a beautiful white family.

After the column was posted online, Kristof reported, Harris called and said, "I feel awful about this," and issued a statement urging Brown to allow for the testing. On Christmas Eve 2018, shortly before the end of his time in office, Brown agreed to order testing, though his order fell short of the full testing Cooper's lawyers sought. In 2019, Governor Newsom issued an order expanding that testing.

In the months that followed, investigators found that blood samples were missing or had so degraded that they were inconclusive, with the exception of one bloody towel discovered not far from the Ryens' home. DNA showed it was not Cooper's blood. Cooper's lawyers hope for a pardon from Newsom, or an order for a new trial. Although Harris didn't act when she was attorney general, Senator Harris did react to Kristof's report by calling on Governor Brown to order testing.

"That was a big break for us," Norman C. Hile, Cooper's attorney, said. "I am very grateful for what she did."

As of this writing, Cooper remains in prison. He was twenty-five at the time of the crime; he's sixty-two now.

15
WEDDING BELLS

At first, Kamala Harris was a bit player in the historical march that led to the legalization of same-sex marriage in America. It was Gavin Newsom who took center stage and became the hero of the marriage equality movement during his tenure as mayor of San Francisco. In the days leading up to Valentine's Day weekend of 2004, Newsom generated international attention, much approbation, and plenty of criticism by decreeing that the city and county of San Francisco would recognize same-sex marriage.

Harris, the newly inaugurated district attorney, was en route to the airport when she saw the crowd lined up outside city hall, stepped out of her car, and was quickly deputized to help officiate.

"We stood together performing marriages in the hallway, crowded into every nook and cranny of City Hall," Harris wrote in her autobiography, *The Truths We Hold.* "There was all this wonderful excitement building as we welcomed the throngs of loving couples, one by one, to be married then and there. It was unlike anything I had ever been a part of before. And it was beautiful."

Harris and Newsom were young stars on the rise, occupying a similar political space and attracting many of the same benefactors. News accounts from that time described their relationship as chilly. One day, they might find themselves running against each other. In the meantime, Newsom knew how to make headlines. On January 20, 2004, twelve days after his swearing-in as mayor of San Francisco, he attended President George W. Bush's State of the Union address, the guest of his hometown congresswoman, Nancy Pelosi, then House minority leader.

"Our nation must defend the sanctity of marriage," Bush told Congress, raising the prospect of a constitutional amendment that would define marriage as being between a man and woman.

As Newsom's aides later told the story, the new mayor decided then that he was going to challenge societal norms by directing them to take the necessary steps to issue marriage licenses to same-sex couples. The idea was bold, to be sure, but hardly unique. Already, there was a public effort afoot in San Francisco to legalize same-sex marriage.

In 2003, Assemblyman Mark Leno, Harris's friend and ally and a San Francisco Democrat who is gay, was working with lawyers at Equality California, the LGBTQ rights organization and a leading advocate of marriage equality, on legislation that would, they hoped, lead to legalization.

On January 15, 2004, the *Bay Area Reporter,* a publication aimed at the LGBTQ community, broke the news that Leno would introduce the legislation in Sacramento. It would be the first in the nation and almost certainly would gain national attention. Its chance of success was slim. Party leaders urged Leno to wait. But Leno pressed ahead, delivering the bill to the assembly clerks on February 12, 2004. The date was significant. It was National Freedom to Marry Day, a day on which same-sex couples would go to their county clerks seeking marriage licenses, be turned away, and then protest.

Newsom was about to take an action that would relegate Leno's bill to a footnote. On that same day, citing the California constitutional right that grants everyone equal protection, Newsom directed county officials to begin issuing marriage licenses to same-sex partners. As word spread, hundreds of couples wearing wedding dresses, tuxedos, shorts, T-shirts, and jeans converged on the gilded Beaux-Arts city hall. Some flew in from other parts of the country.

Gavin Newsom had cemented his status as a social justice pioneer.

Fellow Democrats, including Massachusetts Democratic congressman Barney Frank, who is gay, and Senator Dianne Feinstein, one of Newsom's predecessors, were aghast.

"Too much. Too fast. Too soon," Feinstein said at the time.

John Gibson, then a Fox News host and a former San Francisco newsman, called Newsom "San Francisco's gay-marriage mayor," noting thousands of same-sex couples had been hitched and describing it as "a marriage lollapalooza."

At the time, California law defined marriage as being between one man and one woman. That was the result of an initiative, Proposition 22, approved by voters on March 7, 2000, by a 61–39 percent margin. Significantly, Proposition 22 created a statute, not an amendment to the California constitution, and that would prove to be its undoing later in the litigation.

But first, the California Supreme Court, citing that statute, acted to halt same-sex marriages on August 12, 2004. The court did not reach the question of whether marriage was a right. Instead, the justices issued a narrow ruling, concluding that if local officials could ignore the state law on marriage as a violation of the Fourteenth Amendment, they could just as easily ignore laws banning, say, assault rifles as violation of the Second Amendment. The justices' reasoning:

> If every public official who is under a statutory duty to perform a ministerial act were free to refuse to perform that act based solely on the official's view that the underlying statute is unconstitutional, any semblance of a uniform rule of law quickly would disappear, and constant and widespread judicial intervention would be required to permit the ordinary mechanisms of government to function. This, of course, is not the system of law with which we are familiar.

That decision would not be the last word. Appeals would continue for a decade. San Francisco district attorney Kamala Harris had no part to play then, but that would soon change.

Before the court put a stop to the same-sex marriages in 2004, about eighteen thousand couples had gotten married in California. From across the state and nation, attorneys filed briefs in what they thought would be the defining case on marriage equality. District Attorney Harris was not among those attorneys; it was not part of her purview. Her job was to prosecute criminals, not defend the actions of the mayor or the county clerk who issued marriage licenses.

The state constitutional question reached the California Supreme Court in May 2008. Chief Justice Ronald George was waiting. George had sworn in Harris as district attorney on January 8, 2004, with her mother, Shyamala, proudly looking on. No one could question George's law-and-order credentials. As a deputy attorney general in the early 1970s, George defended California's death penalty statute before the California Supreme Court, and it was Governor Ronald Reagan who first appointed him to the bench. As a superior court judge in Los Angeles in 1981, George assigned Republican attorney general George Deukmejian to take over the prosecution of Angelo Buono for ten rape-murders in what was known as the "Hillside Strangler" case, after Los Angeles County district attorney John Van de Kamp concluded that Buono's cousin and accuser, Kenneth Bianchi, was an unreliable witness and refused to proceed. Buono was convicted and died in prison in 2002. Republican governor Pete Wilson appointed George chief justice in 1996.

On May 15, 2008, George issued a 221-page decision for the majority in the 4–3 decision. "In view of the substance and significance of the fundamental constitutional right to form a family relationship, the California Constitution properly must be interpreted to guarantee this basic civil right to all Californians, whether gay or heterosexual, and to same-sex couples as well as to opposite-sex couples." Proposition 22 created a statute that violated the California constitution. It was an unequivocal victory for marriage equality.

Religious conservatives had other ideas. The National Organization for Marriage, the Church of Jesus Christ of Latter-day Saints, the Knights of Columbus, and Catholic bishops, among other advocates of what they called "traditional marriage," had paid petition circulators to gather 1.12 million signatures of registered voters. Two weeks after the state supreme court issued its ruling in the Proposition 22 case, California election officials announced what would become Proposition 8. That new proposition, which qualified for the November 4, 2008, ballot, would overturn the California Supreme Court decision by amending the California constitution to read: "Only marriage between a man and a woman is valid or recognized in California."

The "Yes on Prop. 8" campaign, which banned same-sex marriage, raised and spent more than $43 million. Playing on fears that same-sex marriage would be harmful to children, the money paid for ads in which a little girl comes home from school and tells her horrified mom, "Mom, guess what I learned in school today? I learned how a prince married a prince."

"Teaching about gay marriage will happen unless we pass Proposition 8."

District Attorney Harris spoke out against Proposition 8. Her sister, Maya Harris, then director of the ACLU of Northern California, was directly involved in the campaign to defeat it. Maya Harris and leaders of Equality California selected the campaign team and raised $42 million toward the effort; the ACLU of Northern California delivered more than $2 million.

Newsom and the mayors of San Diego and Los Angeles campaigned against Proposition 8. Feinstein lent her voice to the opposition, as did Senator Boxer and Governor Schwarzenegger. The California Teachers Association gave $1.3 million toward its defeat. Hollywood figures, including David Geffen, Brad Pitt, and Ellen DeGeneres, gave $100,000 each, as did Silicon Valley leaders including Google cofounder Sergey Brin.

On election night 2008, Democrats had much to celebrate. They gained twenty-one seats in the U.S. House of Representatives, enough to make Nancy Pelosi Speaker. Democrats in the U.S. Senate gained a filibuster-proof sixty seats. Most important, Barack Obama became president. In California, Obama trounced Senator John McCain, the Arizona Republican, by a 61–37 percent margin. But California remained many states.

More than 75 percent of voters in San Francisco voted against Proposition 8. But a majority of voters in forty-two of California's fifty-eight counties, including the population centers of Los Angeles, Orange, and San Diego Counties, supported the measure. Proposition 8 was approved 52.3 to 47.7 percent.

"We canvassed the entire state of California, one on one, asking people face to face how do they feel about this issue," Frank Schubert, the "Yes on Prop. 8" strategist, told the *Los Angeles Times*. "And this is the kind of issue people are very personal and private about, and they don't like talking to pollsters; they don't like talking to the media, but we had a pretty good idea how they felt and that's being reflected in the vote count."

Opponents headed to court.

Attorneys general are obligated to defend the laws of the state, regardless of their philosophical views. But there are exceptions.

Attorney General Jerry Brown, an opponent of Proposition 8, figured out a way to thread the needle, reminiscent of how his father, Pat Brown, and Attorney General Stanley Mosk refused to defend Proposition 14, the 1964 initiative that repealed California's fair housing law.

In a 111-page brief filed at the end of 2008, Jerry Brown urged the California Supreme Court to overturn Proposition 8. His argument: Marriage is protected as part of the inalienable rights to liberty and privacy, both of which are embedded in

California's constitution. The power to amend the constitution, as happened with Proposition 8, could not be wielded in ways that invalidate an inalienable right.

For Brown, there was a political advantage to not defending Proposition 8. Brown was planning to give up the attorney general's office and run for governor in 2010, reclaiming the office he had held as a young man from 1975 to 1983. He was taking a stand that would insulate him against a challenge from the left by Mayor Newsom, who was considering running for governor.

Brown's decision had an immediate impact on the court case. With the state abandoning Proposition 8, its defense shifted to the initiative's supporters. They chose as their advocate Kenneth Starr, then dean of Pepperdine University School of Law in Malibu, whose yearslong inquisition into President Clinton led to the president's impeachment over him lying about an affair he had with White House intern Monica Lewinsky.

Starr's side carried the day, initially. By a 6–1 margin, in another decision by Chief Justice George, the California Supreme Court upheld Proposition 8 on state constitutional grounds, though the justices also held that the marriages of the same-sex couples who wed during the window when the unions were clearly legal remained valid.

George left little doubt about how he viewed the issue. In a speech to the American Academy of Arts and Sciences in Cambridge, Massachusetts, on October 10, 2009, George cited a lesser-known initiative that was overwhelmingly approved on election night 2008, directing farmers to provide fowl and other farm animals with larger cages and pens: "Chickens gained valuable rights in California on the same day that gay men and lesbians lost them."

The real fight was taking place in the federal courts, where judges would determine whether the California constitutional amendment created by Proposition 8 violated the U.S. Constitution. Jerry Brown was leaving the attorney general's office for the governor's suite. The next attorney general would decide whether to follow Brown's lead and leave Proposition 8's defense to its supporters or defend the law.

That's where Kamala Harris came in. It would take another two years, but she would prevail, and marriage equality would become a reality in California.

But there were a few detours on the way. As it happens, California's Proposition 8 did not, in the end, form the basis for the U.S. Supreme Court's final word on same-sex marriage. That came in 2015, when the justices in a 5–4 decision in *Obergefell v. Hodges* affirmed marriage equality as a constitutional right. The majority opinion author, Justice Anthony M. Kennedy, wrote: "No union is more profound than marriage, for it embodies the highest ideals of love, fidelity, devotion, sacrifice, and family. In forming a marital union, two people become something greater than once they were." But as it often is, California was once again ahead of the rest of the nation.

Upon taking office in January 2011 as attorney general, Harris, like Brown, refused to defend Proposition 8. More than that, she argued against it, filing a brief on February 27, 2013, with the U.S. Supreme Court urging that the law passed by California voters be struck down.

"To be clear," Harris's brief said, "Proposition 8's singular purpose was to prevent same-sex couples from marrying, and its only function was to stigmatize the relationships of gay and lesbian families. There is absolutely no legitimate or rational state interest in doing so. Proposition 8 is therefore unconstitutional."

With Attorney General Harris unwilling

to defend the law, the initiative's proponents were left to defend it. That case came to be known as *Hollingsworth v. Perry,* named for Dennis Hollingsworth, a Republican legislator from a conservative part of San Diego and Riverside Counties who was an advocate of traditional marriage.

The U.S. Supreme Court rejected Hollingsworth's argument on June 26, 2013, concluding he and the organizations that were challenging Proposition 8 didn't have standing. They weren't directly affected by same-sex marriages. Only the state was. Two days after the Supreme Court ruled, the U.S. Ninth Circuit Court of Appeals based in San Francisco issued an order opening the way for the marriages to resume in California.

Kris Perry and Sandy Stier, mothers of four sons between them, were first in line. They had wanted to get married in San Francisco in 2004 when Mayor Newsom ordered that marriage licenses be issued to anyone, no matter their sexual orientation. When courts had put a halt on same-sex marriages, the Berkeley couple sued in the case that came to be known as *Hollingsworth v. Perry.* Once the Ninth Circuit cleared the way for marriages to resume, Perry and Stier rushed to San Francisco City Hall. A crowd gathered to witness the ceremony. Attorney General Harris tweeted, "On my way to S.F. City Hall. Let the wedding bells ring! #Prop8."

On June 28, 2013, on the balcony outside the mayor's office, Harris performed the marriage ceremony for Perry and Stier. One of Perry's grown sons was the ring bearer.

"By virtue of the power and authority vested in me by the State of California, I now declare you spouses for life," Harris declared. The ceremony lasted four minutes and thirty seconds. It was eons in the making.

16
THE DAMNED PHOTOS

At a Safeway shopping center in Tucson, Arizona, Jared Lee Loughner, a schizophrenic twenty-two-year-old man who had been kicked out of community college because of his erratic behavior, pulled out a legally purchased Glock 9mm semiautomatic pistol with a thirty-round magazine, fired it until it ran empty, and reloaded with another thirty-round magazine. When he was finished, six people were dead and Congresswoman Gabrielle Giffords was shot in the head. That was on January 8, 2011.

Two days earlier, Kamala Harris had been sworn in as California attorney general. As San Francisco district attorney, Harris was an advocate of getting firearms off the city's streets. Now, she was looking to set a marker firmly on the side of statewide gun control. The terrible Tucson massacre refocused public attention on gun violence and on people who should be prohibited from possessing firearms. Thankfully, a predecessor had created a law that she could build on.

Bill Lockyer was the Democratic leader of the state senate when he decided to run for California attorney general in 1998. Lockyer, a gun control advocate, faced a Republican who opposed the California state law that banned assault weapons. Lockyer built his campaign around that contrast. To shove that point home to voters, Lockyer aired an ad that used television news footage of the bloody 1997 shootout in North Hollywood, in which two bank robbers armed with assault weapons battled Los Angeles police for forty-four minutes, injuring eleven officers. Police were so outgunned that some of them went to a gun shop during the bloody showdown so they could borrow seven AR-15–style rifles and two thousand rounds of ammunition.

At one time, California voters may have opposed gun safety laws. Not any longer. Lockyer's election proved that a strong stand on gun control was good politics. In the years to come, the legislature would pass many more gun safety laws. By any measure, California became one of the toughest — if not the toughest — gun control states in the nation.

In 2001, Attorney General Lockyer came up with the idea of merging databases: One data set included the names of people who were registered gun owners. The other was of convicted felons, people who had committed domestic violence, and individuals who had been adjudged by courts to be so mentally ill that they needed to be held against their will. Based on their criminal past, abuse of spouses, or psychiatric problems, they were not legally entitled to own firearms. Lockyer's thought was to create a law that would allow authorities to use the merged database to identify people who could not legally own guns and seize those weapons.

To author the bill, Lockyer turned to his friend California state senator Jim Brulte, a bear of a man, a brilliant political strategist, and a Southern California Republican. With Brulte as the author, the bill passed without a single no vote. Even the NRA supported it, though it quickly thought better of that position and its representatives have been trying to undermine the bill ever since, without success.

Lockyer's legislation created the inelegantly named Armed and Prohibited Persons System (APPS). Its clunky name notwithstanding, it's one of the most far-reaching pieces of legislation ever sponsored by a California attorney general.

When Kamala Harris became attorney general in January 2011, there were an estimated eighteen thousand "armed and prohibited persons" in California who possessed as many as thirty-four thousand guns. The California Department of Justice had detailed eighteen agents to carry out the mission of removing guns from those individuals. She wanted to double the number of agents. The issue was cost.

California was in the throes of a budget crisis and carried a $27 billion deficit. Governor Jerry Brown and the legislature were looking to cut spending. There would be no money for expanding any program. But Harris had an important ally, Senate Budget and Fiscal Review Committee chairman Mark Leno. Leno had grown up in Milwaukee, moved to New York as a young man (where he considered becoming a rabbi), and settled in San Francisco in 1981. There, he opened a sign shop and met the love of his life, Douglas Jackson. Leno was by his lover's side when he died of AIDS in 1990. Leno and Harris had met during Willie Brown's run for mayor in

1995, and they often would have lunch in the years that followed. In 1996, they got decked out in their finest evening clothes for the San Francisco Symphony's opening night, and he had the high honor of being a guest at a Harris family Thanksgiving at Shyamala's home. Mayor Brown appointed Leno to fill a vacant seat on the San Francisco Board of Supervisors. With Brown's support, Leno ran for and won state assembly and senate seats, serving for fourteen years until he was termed out in 2016.

In Sacramento, Leno took on hard issues: the annual state budget as budget committee chairman, battling chemical manufacturers to ban toxic flame retardants in furniture, crossing many businesses to push to raise the minimum wage to $15, and requiring police to obtain warrants before searching phones — 161 laws in total by the *Los Angeles Times*'s count. Always civil and gracious, Leno was a liberal who never forgot his core but could find common ground with Republicans. Harris could not have had a better ally in the legislature.

In 2011, Leno carried legislation to come up with special funding for the program, earmarking money collected by the state when people purchased guns. Harris, testifying on behalf of the legislation, said it would

"protect innocent Californians by takin guns out of the hands of those prohibited from owning them." The gun lobby no longer supported the program, but politics had turned. The gun lobby had little clout in the California capitol. The legislation passed on a party-line vote in the Democratic-controlled legislature.

Harris was able to assign thirty-three agents to the program, not nearly enough. The thirty-three agents could clear twenty-five hundred cases a year. But three thousand new prohibited persons were added to the list each year. The backlog of "armed and prohibited persons" had grown to more than nineteen thousand by the end of 2012.

Then, on December 14, 2012, Adam Lanza, wielding an AR-15–style Remington assault rifle and Glock and Sig Sauer pistols, slaughtered twenty children and six educators at Sandy Hook Elementary School in Newtown, Connecticut. In California, legislators reacted by introducing several new measures to combat gun violence. Harris decided to revisit the Armed and Prohibited Persons System.

I spent a cold January night five weeks after the Sandy Hook slaughter riding with a dozen California Department of Justice

agents as they went about what struck me as an extraordinarily difficult and dangerous job: persuading ex-felons, people with a history of severe mental illness, and wife beaters to give up guns that, by law, they are not legally entitled to own.

Attorney General Harris encouraged the ride-along, hoping that what I wrote as a columnist for the *Sacramento Bee* would help generate support in the legislature for a proposal she was contemplating to significantly expand the only-in-California law that allowed for those guns to be seized. As for me, I was just looking for something to write.

At the northeast end of Stockton, a hard-luck part of town, a Justice Department agent wearing a bulletproof vest beneath his black uniform knocked on the door of a small tract home belonging to a man who had suffered his share of tough times in his sixty-five years.

The man, who lived alone, opened the door a crack. As I wrote at the time, he was the registered owner of eight handguns. Separate records showed that authorities deemed on two occasions that he needed to be held in locked psych wards because he was a danger to himself or others.

The agent didn't have a warrant to search

the man's house. His goal was to talk his way in and, with the man's consent, leave with his guns. The man told the agent he had no guns but agreed that the agent and his partners could come in and see for themselves. A half hour later, they emerged with two revolvers, six bolt-action rifles, and a crate filled with one thousand rounds of ammunition. The guns were kept in closets and under furniture. He seemed clueless that he had them.

"I'd say he is more of a danger to himself," John Marsh, the special agent in charge of the unit, told me at the time. "He definitely has his bad days."

The agents knocked on ten doors in Stockton on one night and eleven more on a second night in Sacramento and the suburb of Elk Grove. Agents seized twenty-four pistols, rifles, and shotguns. On a final stop in Sacramento, they knocked on the door of a man who had been convicted of assault with a firearm years earlier. After talking their way inside, they found a loaded revolver, a loaded shotgun, and eight other rifles and shotguns, plus ammunition. They took him to Sacramento County jail, where he would be booked on charges of being a felon in possession of guns and ammunition.

"You have the sense you're saving lives," Marsh said at the time. "You're preventing them from killing themselves or someone else."

Harris hoped to double the number of agents, with the goal of clearing the backlog in five to seven years. She was quick to get behind new legislation by Leno. This time, the state would specify that $24 million collected from the fee levied on people who purchased guns would be used to provide additional funding for the program. The bill zipped through the legislature in a mere four months with only a smattering of no votes. The gun lobby objected, but it was all but defanged in California.

The contrast between what happened after Sandy Hook in Sacramento and what didn't happen in Washington was stark. With the encouragement of Harris in the aftermath of Sandy Hook, Congressman Mike Thompson, a Democrat from Napa Valley, a Vietnam War veteran, and a hunter, introduced legislation to provide federal funding to states that wanted to establish the Armed and Prohibited Persons System. Harris lobbied for the bill by sending a letter to Vice President Biden seeking the administration's support. She and an aide testified on its behalf in Congress. But on Capitol Hill, the progun lobby is dominant and so, like all the other measures that were proposed in the weeks and months after the Sandy Hook massacre, Thompson's bill never materialized.

In California, Harris did not eliminate the backlog of prohibited people who possess firearms, though it wasn't for lack of effort. There were 18,268 armed and prohibited persons on the list in 2011 when she took office. That number grew to 21,249 in 2014, the year of her reelection, and dipped to 20,483 in 2016, her final year as attorney general.

When she makes her case for gun control, Harris talks about "the damned photos." Legislators, or members of Congress who hesitate to vote for gun control bills, should be required to look at "the damned photos" of children who have died by gunfire.

"Babies. Babies. Babies," she says in speeches.

17
Mortgage Meltdown

In much of the country, the worst of the Great Recession was ending in January 2011 when Kamala Harris took office as attorney general, but not in California. Unemployment in the Central Valley exceeded 16 percent, more than 10 percent of California homeowners were seriously delinquent on their mortgages, and nearly a third of California homeowners owed on their homes more than those homes were worth.

The ways in which Harris confronted that crisis and the human toll it took in her first thirteen months in office defined much of her tenure as attorney general, formed the foundation of her public image as a leader, and shaped her future.

"As Attorney General of California, I took on the five biggest Wall Street banks during the financial crisis. We won $20 billion for California homeowners and together we passed the strongest anti-foreclosure law in the United States of America," Harris posted on her Facebook and Twitter accounts. It is her calling card. The statement is true. As is her way, it is also complicated.

Months before Harris was sworn in, state attorneys general, the U.S. Justice Department, and five big lenders — Bank of America, Wells Fargo, JPMorgan Chase, Citigroup, and Ally Financial (formerly GMAC Mortgage) — had been negotiating a settlement over one aspect of the housing crisis. The issue initially involved "robo-signing," a pernicious practice by which banks foreclosed on homes without verifying the details related to any delinquency in payments. This rubber-stamp process came about based on how subprime mortgages were bundled into securities and resold to investors. As demand for those securities increased, lenders peddled more loans to unsophisticated homebuyers. Too many of them didn't understand the terms and could not afford the payments when adjustable interest rates ballooned. The bubble burst and the economy crashed. As the foreclosure crisis worsened, loan servicers foreclosed on some people who were not seriously delinquent or owed little on their mortgages and never should have lost their homes.

When Harris arrived in office, Iowa attorney general Tom Miller was leading negotiations to settle the robo-signing case on behalf of the fifty attorneys general. From the outside, it seemed, Harris was slow to engage. In reality, she began meeting with top advisers on the issue immediately. Her first public engagement occurred in March 2011, two months after her inauguration, at the National Association of Attorneys General meeting in Washington, D.C. In her autobiography, she writes that she concluded that the investigation was incomplete and that any settlement amount being discussed would not be based on any math she understood. California, which was home to seven of the ten cities with the worst foreclosure numbers, would get $2 billion to $4 billion — crumbs on the table. Rather than attend the afternoon session of the meeting, Harris ducked out, seeking to make a point that she was not pleased with its direction. That afternoon, she decided to launch her own investigation, though she was not ready to formally withdraw from the negotiating team. She was, however, beginning to separate herself from the Obama White House, which had been pushing for the deal, and breaking from her brother-in-law, Tony West. Although he was not directly involved in the negotiations, West was the third-ranking member of the Justice Department.

"They seemed to be under the misimpression that I could be bullied into submission; I wasn't budging," Harris wrote.

Miller, meanwhile, concluded that New York attorney general Eric Schneiderman was actively undermining the settlement and cut him from the team. Schneiderman answered by vowing to undertake his own investigation and flew to San Francisco in an effort to enlist Harris in his effort. The meeting spanned two days. Harris asked lots of questions and clearly grasped the politics and the policy. At the end, she kept her opinions to herself. The Occupy Wall Street movement was under way, as the Left took a page from the Right's Tea Party movement by demonstrating its anger at the people at the top of the economic ladder, the top 1 percent. Occupy spread to Oakland and San Francisco and to college campuses. In September 2011, Harris traveled to New York, where Schneiderman helped pull together a campaign fund-raiser for her. As negotiations continued, Harris faced pressure from the Left. MoveOn.org was demanding that she hang tough against the banks. The influential Los Angeles

County Federation of Labor, AFL-CIO, wrote a letter urging that she abandon the talks. A new organization, Californians for a Fair Settlement, was agitating for Harris to hold out. At first glance, Californians for a Fair Settlement seemed to have sprung up organically. In reality, Schneiderman's chief of staff, a political organizer named Neal Kwatra, created the group. Significantly, Lieutenant Governor Gavin Newsom, Harris's sometimes rival, sometimes friend, and potential competitor for higher office, signed on to a letter by Californians for a Fair Settlement, calling the Miller deal "deeply flawed." The *Los Angeles Times* quoted from the letter and included a list of the signatories on September 30, 2011.

On that same date, a Friday, Harris announced that she was pulling out of the talks, this after state attorneys general and the U.S. Department of Justice had worked for almost a year on a deal with the five largest lenders. Knowing that her decision could affect stock prices, she waited until the markets had closed before making her decision public.

"After much consideration, I have concluded that this is not the deal California homeowners have been waiting for," Harris said in a letter to U.S. associate attorney general Thomas J. Perrelli and Miller of Iowa.

Dane Gillette, chief of the criminal division, said Harris's deputies worried that her brinkmanship would leave California without anything. Harris quoted Governor Jerry Brown, her predecessor as attorney general, as telling her he hoped she knew what she was doing, suggesting he doubted her strategy.

"The banks were furious that I was causing trouble. The settlement was now in doubt. But this had been my goal. Now, instead of merely noting my concerns, the state attorneys general and the banks would have to answer them, too," she wrote.

Harris had allies, most notably Delaware attorney general Beau Biden, the son of then vice president Joe Biden.

"There were periods, when I was taking heat, when Beau and I talked every day, sometimes multiple times a day. We had each other's backs," Harris wrote. It was a relationship that would affect the future course of her life and career. Joe Biden referred to her friendship with his son when he chose Harris to be his running mate.

In meetings with her staff, Harris often spoke of the people they were fighting for, the ones who were not in the rooms where decisions get made. In this instance, those people were the ones who lost their homes or who stayed while homes all around them were abandoned, and neighborhoods deteriorated.

On January 23, 2012, state attorneys general met in Chicago with Shaun Donovan, the Obama administration's secretary of the U.S. Department of Housing and Urban Development. Obama, running for reelection, clearly wanted a deal, and his top aides were engaged in making it happen. Word leaked to the press about a possible $25 billion national settlement. Harris skipped that meeting and issued a statement restating her position that she wanted to retain authority to prosecute mortgage lenders who broke the law.

If anyone was missing her message, on the same day Donovan and other attorneys general were meeting in Chicago, Harris drove to Stockton, a city of three hundred thousand south of Sacramento. It is the self-proclaimed "Asparagus Capital of the World," although farmers years ago found they could grow it cheaper south of the border. Stockton also was the epicenter of the housing crisis in California and would go bankrupt in June 2012.

In Stockton, she met with Jose R. Rodriguez, president and CEO of the nonprofit El Concilio, which counsels families facing crises. He introduced her to people affected by the meltdown: a couple in their forties who could not pay their mortgage because construction work had dried up, another couple who bought their house with an adjustable rate mortgage thinking they would be able to refinance before the higher rates kicked in, and a couple in their sixties who could no longer work and lost their home when they couldn't get their mortgage adjusted.

"The reality," Rodriguez told me at the time, "is that for some of these folks, it is not going to get better. The number of people we see crying, I have never seen anything like this."

As Edward-Isaac Dovere wrote in the *Atlantic,* Schneiderman sat by Michelle Obama at President Obama's State of the Union address on January 24, 2012. That might have given the impression that he was aligned with the White House's desire to finalize the deal. Harris had declined that invitation, not wanting to suggest that she was finished with negotiating.

On February 9, 2012, Harris announced the deal she had struck on behalf of California: "Hundreds of thousands of homeowners will directly benefit from this California commitment." The agreement with the lenders ensured "homeowners actually see a benefit that will allow them to stay in their homes, and preserved our ability to investigate banker crime and predatory lending." She placed the value of the deal at $20 billion. A month later, the Obama administration announced the nationwide settlement, which included the California piece that Harris had detailed.

In the end, as she later explained it, the banks provided California $18.4 billion in debt relief and $2 billion in other financial assistance. In total, 84,102 California families received reductions on their first or second mortgages.

"This issue has never been about anything other than allowing homeowners, hard-working people, to be able to stay in their homes," Harris said during a February 2012 news conference announcing the settlement.

However, many Californians who received assistance under the settlement did not stay in their homes, as the *Los Angeles Times*'s Phil Willon later reported. About half of the $18.4 billion in debt relief given to California homeowners was through short sales,

$9.2 billion. The banks took a loss because homeowners sold their houses for less than they owed. But they would need other places to live. When the housing market recovered, they would see no benefit.

Author and journalist David Dayen, who has written extensively about the mortgage crisis for the *Intercept,* characterized the settlement as a bank bailout, "protecting legally exposed mortgage fraudsters while doing little to prevent evictions."

"For the banks, the settlement was cause for celebration," Dayen writes, adding, "The actual impact made barely a dent in their profits. And they got a broad release from prosecution, putting their intense legal exposure behind them."

Although housing prices have risen, particularly along coastal California, much of the state has not fully recovered from the mortgage meltdown. No politician, no matter how tough or skilled, could have put all the pieces back together from the Great Recession and its housing disaster. Matt Levin, the housing reporter for the Sacramento-based nonprofit news organization CalMatters, reported that as of 2018, California had 450,000 more single-family homes used as rentals than it did a decade earlier. Who owns all those rentals? Mainly

Wall Street firms that swooped in and bought homes at cut-rate prices in foreclosure sales.

After settling with the banks, Harris turned her attention to the legislature, putting the weight of her office behind the legislation that came to be called the California Homeowner Bill of Rights. Senator Mark Leno carried the legislation.

It sought to ban the practice of robo-signing, to ensure homeowners received clear notices that they were at risk of losing their homes, and to require that lenders provide a single contact for distressed homeowners so they would not have to repeat their stories each time they called. One effect would be that homeowners facing foreclosure would get several more months to work out a compromise.

First, it had to get past California state senator Ron Calderon, a Southern California Democrat who was chairman of the banking committee and often sided with banks. Calderon became the swing vote on a special conference committee established to work out the details of the legislation. As a result, every lobbyist for every bank would need to deal with Calderon.

"I would make all my best arguments and

it was like talking to a brick wall," Leno said, referring to Calderon.

Harris spent time walking the halls of the capitol, stopping in the offices of legislators. Although several ducked her, the bill ended up passing by a wide margin in the assembly and more narrowly in the senate. Harris credits legislative leaders with helping push the bill through to a final vote. Leno, loyal to Harris, sees it differently:

"She made it happen. The whole game changed when Kamala got involved. The attorney general was not going to not get her way."

Ron Calderon ended up voting for the bill. Two years later, Ron Calderon, along with his brother Tom Calderon, a former legislator, were indicted on federal corruption charges related to other legislation. They were convicted and sent to prison.

18
PHENOMENAL WOMEN

In September 2012, Kamala Harris was given the honor of a prime speaking slot at the Democratic National Convention in Charlotte, North Carolina. Barack Obama was in a close race for reelection against former Massachusetts governor Mitt Romney. Harris's goal was to help her friend win. But she and her political staff also thought the speech could be her breakout moment on the American political stage, much like the speech Obama gave in 2004 that catapulted him into the nation's consciousness.

After stepping onto the stage for her run-through and looking out into what soon would be a full Spectrum Center, she told the *Chronicle*'s Joe Garofoli, "It was incredible. It was humbling." She paused. "I couldn't help but think, 'If only my mother could see me.' " She was nervous. Who wouldn't be? Her speech would precede one by Bill Clinton.

Harris and her team wrote a speech that, while not on the level of Obama's speech in 2004, was strong. It was a tailored version of one she had been giving to audiences in California, which was still recovering from the Great Recession: "If you really want to know what this election is all about, come west. Visit the forest of foreclosure signs. Witness the mountains of family debt. Talk to the thousands of good families stuck without a path out or a way up.

"Go to Stockton, California, America's foreclosure capital."

The speech praised President Obama and Vice President Biden for standing up to Wall Street and scorned Mitt Romney for siding with bankers. Then the speech pivoted, flipping the phrase coined during the time that huge financial institutions needed to be bailed out because they had become "too big to fail."

"I'll tell you what's too big to fail.

"I say it's our middle class that's too big to fail.

"I say it's the American dream of home ownership that's too big to fail.

"It's the promise of a universal free quality public education that's too big to fail.

"Our young people — the next generation

— they're what's too big to fail.

"Environmental protection is too big to fail.

"And, Democrats, it's our vision of an inclusive society that's too big to fail.

"Marriage equality is too big to fail!

"The rights of women are too big to fail!

"Our immigrant communities are too big to fail!"

The speech was a humdinger and might have left the audience cheering and on its feet. But it was never given.

Harris deferred to the Democratic National Convention managers, who provided her with a speech that was filled with talking points, none of them her own and none of them inspired. Shortly after beginning, her aides noticed that vast numbers of delegates at the Spectrum Center stopped paying attention and started talking among themselves. At one point, she stumbled over the words that had been given to her.

What was supposed to have been her big moment in the spotlight went unnoticed. Her aides knew it was terrible. If Kamala Harris brought it up with anyone, her staff was not aware of it. However, Maya, in front of others, rebuked some of her sister's staffers, as if they were responsible for the speech foisted on Attorney General Harris by Democratic National Convention staff. They weren't.

Kamala Harris's tight-knit family is made up of exceptionally high achievers. Maya, two years younger than Kamala, is her sister's confidante and political adviser. Aides to Harris know never to get between her sister and her. If Kamala Harris has to choose, she'll always choose Maya.

During campaigns, Kamala and Maya would talk several times a day. Often, a call with Maya was the first of the day and the last at night. Their sense of humor is similar and the sound of their laugh is all but identical. They're brilliant, detail oriented, tough, and competitive, sometimes with each other in the ways big and little sisters can be.

While Kamala was away at Howard University in Washington, D.C., Maya, still a teenager living with her mother in Oakland, had a daughter, Meena. Meena is as close to a daughter as a niece can be to Kamala. Kamala Harris provided *Politico* with a rare, if brief, glimpse into her personal world, recalling being in law school and coming home to help toilet train Meena: "I would come home and we would all stand by the toilet and wave bye to a piece of shit." Maya, her daughter in tow, graduated from the University of California, Berkeley, and Stanford Law School. According to a story told by Maya, young Meena was playing hide-and-seek with a law student, Tony West. That's how Maya and her future husband met.

Tony West was president of the *Stanford Law Review,* and had worked on presidential campaigns since he was a boy, starting with Jimmy Carter in 1976. He ran unsuccessfully for the California State Assembly in 2000, with Maya as his campaign treasurer. In 2004, he was enthralled by Barack Obama's speech at the Democratic National Convention and, along with his sister-in-law, worked on Obama's 2008 presidential campaign. West went on to head the civil division of the Obama administration's Justice Department and rose to become associate attorney general, the third-highest-ranking Justice Department official. After the Obama years, West worked as counsel for PepsiCo. More recently, he has been general counsel for Uber. In that role, he has battled organized labor's efforts to force Uber and similar gig economy companies to hire workers as full employees, rather than independent contractors. Kamala Harris took the side of labor, not Uber.

Maya became executive director of the ACLU of Northern California, one of the nation's largest ACLU affiliates. In that role, she helped organize the ACLU's campaign against Proposition 8, the 2008 initiative that banned same-sex marriages for a time. As the 2008 election neared, Maya got hired at the Ford Foundation in New York, a position that allowed her to oversee millions of dollars in grants. Later, she became a policy adviser to Hillary Clinton during Clinton's 2016 presidential campaign.

Her daughter, Meena, graduated from Stanford University and Harvard Law School and is a part of Harris's political organization. Meena is married to an executive at Facebook, Nik Ajagu; she writes children's books, was an executive at Uber, and is a founder of Phenomenal Woman Action Campaign, a reference to the poem by Maya Angelou: "Now you understand / Just why my head's not bowed. / I don't shout or jump about / Or have to talk real loud."

Meena's version of "Phenomenal" is a cross between a political organization and a clothing brand; it sells T-shirts and sweatshirts with various inspirational phrases. One is I'M SPEAKING, the line "Auntie Kamala" repeated to great effect during her debate in October 2020 with Vice President Mike Pence.

19
"Just a Dude"

It was a typical California Democratic Party convention on the weekend of June 1, 2019. Outside the Moscone Center convention hall in downtown San Francisco, not far from Kamala Harris's condo, a group of men wore bright white pants with red paint splattered on the crotches. They were demonstrating against circumcision. Sex workers, some dressed as dominatrices, called for the decriminalization of their craft.

Inside, Speaker Nancy Pelosi, the icon of the Democratic Party in the age of Donald J. Trump, got heckled for being too soft on the president, and an animal rights activist with a man bun burst onto the stage and grabbed the microphone from Kamala Harris, then a presidential candidate who was talking about gender pay inequity. If she was taken aback, she didn't show it. She had a look of bemusement and didn't move.

As he started to mansplain about the need

to rescue chickens or some other farm animals from slaughter, Karine Jean-Pierre, who was interviewing Harris at the Move On.org event and was a fraction of the man's size, threw herself between the candidate and the guy, and tried to wrest the microphone back.

Then Douglas C. Emhoff, a Century City entertainment lawyer dressed in a blue blazer, jeans, and a HARRIS FOR PRESIDENT T-shirt, leaped onto the stage, his lips curled in fury. Along with buff security staffers, Emhoff muscled the man offstage. Emhoff didn't punch the guy, but he looked as if he might.

Brooklyn born and New Jersey and Los Angeles raised, Emhoff is Kamala Harris's husband. When they met in 2013, he was a hardworking attorney managing the Los Angeles office of an international law firm, Venable LLP, representing corporate and entertainment industry clients. He had a son and a daughter from a previous marriage, is a decent golfer, a Lakers fan, and was a middle-aged guy trying to navigate the dating scene. Like many Californians, he paid little more than passing attention to politics. Emhoff contributed a grand total of $5,800 to Los Angeles politicians and $650 to California state politicians in the

2000s. The state donations went to two candidates seeking state assembly seats. Neither won. Through a payroll deduction, Emhoff donated $100 a month to his law firm's federal political action committee, an obligatory amount, given his leadership role in the firm, and $100 toward John Kerry's 2004 presidential campaign; he was hardly a big political spender.

As a lawyer, Emhoff defended clients fending off allegations of breaches of consumer privacy, an ad firm in a suit by Taco Bell over the use of a chihuahua in an ad campaign, movie studios in a pay dispute with workers, and Merck in class action lawsuits over a drug that allegedly made users' thighs brittle.

At Venable, Emhoff represented a Los Angeles company that buys rights to viral videos and that accused another L.A. company of violating its copyright on such classics as "Gorilla Teaches Toddler How to Use Her Middle Finger," "Broken Urinal Shoots Out Water," "Physics Teacher Gets Hit in the Nuts," and the unforgettable New York subway scene captured in "Rat Takes Pizza Home on the Subway." The case settled.

For obvious reasons, dating was complicated for Kamala Harris. She had to be careful about her choices, and her work first as district attorney of a major city and then as the attorney general of California was all-consuming. Some guys might have found dating the top cop of the state of California a bit intimidating. Whatever relationships she had stayed private.

Emhoff recalls their story in a video posted on the internet by Chasten Buttigieg, the husband of former South Bend mayor and Democratic presidential candidate Pete Buttigieg. Here is what happened:

Chrisette Hudlin, a decadeslong friend of Harris's, and her husband, filmmaker Reginald Hudlin, had gone to Emhoff seeking his counsel on a knotty legal issue. At the end of the session, Chrisette asked Emhoff whether he was single.

"Why are you asking?" Emhoff replied.

Chrisette had a single friend she had known for thirty years, she explained. Emhoff asked who it was.

"Kamala Harris," Chrisette replied.

"How do I know that name?" Emhoff asked.

Chrisette jogged the lawyer's memory — the California attorney general.

"I said, 'Oh my god, she's hot,' " Emhoff told Chasten Buttigieg.

Chrisette gave Harris's number to Emhoff, warned him that it was confidential, and told him not to mess it up, or else the Hudlins would take their legal business elsewhere. Harris writes in her autobiography that Chrisette called Harris to tell her about this guy she had met: "He's cute and he's the managing partner of his law firm and I think you're going to really like him."

That night, Emhoff texted Harris from a Lakers game. She came down to Los Angeles that weekend.

"I was like just a dude as a lawyer," Emhoff told Buttigieg, "and then I met Kamala on a blind date set up by legendary filmmaker Reginald Hudlin." In other words, it was a typical L.A. love story.

The relationship blossomed under the radar. Even some of Emhoff's good friends were taken by surprise. In the small world of corporate L.A. law, for instance, attorney Ron Wood would see Emhoff at Peet's Coffee in Brentwood and in the lobby of the Century City high-rise where they worked. Both were divorced and single fathers, and they bonded at lunch and over drinks about the complexities of the dating scene, the pressures of corporate law, and the loss each felt not being able to go home at the end of their days and on weekends to be with their children. "Like a lot of career divorced single dads, he took his family obligations seriously," Wood said.

One day in 2014, Wood and Emhoff were waiting in line at one of their regular lunch spots, a grab-and-go Chinese place, when Emhoff showed off the engagement ring he had been given by his fiancée. He had proposed to her, but the couple decided to both wear rings. His was nothing fancy. But the engagement was big news and it came out of nowhere. Emhoff had kept the relationship that quiet. Wood was even more floored when Emhoff told him the name of his fiancée. Wood, a Howard University alumnus, is friends with Harris from their college days. They had kept in touch in the years since, and Wood had been among her campaign contributors. In the weeks ahead, after the engagement became public, he'd bump into Emhoff and Harris when they came into Peet's, sweaty after their spinning class. "In a world of eight billion, how do they collide?" Wood wondered. But the more he thought about it, the more it made sense. Both are leaders in their own worlds — smart, active, and accomplished. "It seemed entirely right."

Harris had a test for Emhoff before the deal was sealed. She remembered that her first campaign finance chairman, Mark Buell, once said you could learn a lot about a person's character by playing golf. So she assigned him to play a round with Emhoff. Buell chose Mayacama golf course, an exclusive club in the Sonoma County wine country. Emhoff could swing a club. But that wasn't the point. "He was the sweetest guy," Buell said. Clearly, he had passed the test.

Harris and Emhoff were married on August 22, 2014, in a private ceremony at the Santa Barbara County Courthouse, a beautiful mission-style building that is a favored Southern California wedding venue. Harris's sister, Maya, officiated. Harris writes in her autobiography that she placed a garland around his neck, an Indian tradition. Emhoff, who is Jewish, stomped on a glass, as is tradition.

They were both forty-nine; he was born seven days before his bride. After the wedding, Harris and Emhoff had a party for their San Francisco–based friends at the Presidio Officers' Club. "She looked truly very happy," said Erin Lehane, a supporter and friend who also works for the State Building and Construction Trades Council of California.

Emhoff, the second husband, is stepping down from his law firm, DLA Piper. When he worked there, he didn't lobby. But the firm's Washington lobby arm represents defense contractors, health insurers, entertainment conglomerates, and many more.

Starting in 2014, people could see him on the Harris campaign trail; he was a regular presence in 2016 and 2019, too. Someone tweeted a video of him dancing at the 2019 San Francisco Pride parade in a convertible as Harris laughs at what Emhoff calls "these dad moves with my dad bod." In 2020, he was on a far bigger stage, stumping for the Biden-Harris ticket. The *Washington Post* described him as "the evolved hubby" who has "become one of the unexpected breakout figures in the 2020 campaign, a headliner in the unconventional, pandemic-plagued race for the White House."

Emhoff's children, Cole and Ella, are named for the jazz greats John Coltrane and Ella Fitzgerald. Ella Emhoff introduced Harris at the Democratic National Convention. They call Harris "Momala." Harris, the proud stepmother, places that term of endearment on the bio of her @Kamala Harris Twitter account.

The guy with the man bun was escorted out of the Moscone Center. It being San Francisco, he made himself available for media interviews. I took a pass.

20
WOMAN IN A HURRY

The question was not whether Kamala Harris would win a second term as California attorney general in 2014. The question was whether she'd serve out that second term.

"I hope so," she told me in August 2014, being coy.

Kamala Harris was in a hurry. People had been assuming that Harris would run for governor in 2018 or the U.S. Senate in 2016 if Barbara Boxer retired. What if a Senate seat should open? "I have not thought about that." I can't say I fully believed her. She was moving fast.

In 2014, no Democrat dared challenge Kamala Harris in her bid for a second term. Her Republican opponent, Los Angeles lawyer Ronald Gold, built his campaign to become California's chief law enforcement officer around his view that marijuana should be legalized. That prompted Debra J.

Saunders, then a *San Francisco Chronicle* columnist, to call him "Acapulco Gold." Gold spent less than $130,000 on his campaign and received no discernible support from the California Republican Party.

Harris, who had long supported medical marijuana, dismissed a reporter's question about what she thought of legalizing the commercial sale of weed with an incongruous laugh. Although she later embraced the notion, the commercial sale of marijuana was not the issue that would sway the 2014 race for attorney general. And in her first four years, Harris had shown herself adept at not taking stands when doing so was not politically necessary.

One example is gambling. In California, attorneys general are responsible for overseeing gambling. Sixty-one Indian tribes in the state own sixty-three casinos that generate a combined $8 billion a year; another eighty-eight card rooms produce $850 million in annual revenue. The state lottery generates $2.5 billion a year. Altogether, California almost matches Nevada for being the biggest gambling state in the country.

During Harris's tenure, legislators considered legalizing internet poker and sports wagering. Indian tribes, among the largest campaign donors in California, were split.

Card-room owners and horse-racing interests liked the idea, so long as they could get a piece of the action. Harris said she was studying the question in 2014. The issue pitted moneyed interests and potential campaign donors against each other. She never did take a stand. The issue remains unresolved.

For years, Harris had been decrying elementary school truancy, saying habitual absences would haunt vulnerable kids for the rest of their days. But she did not publicly voice her opinion during the 2014 campaign on an issue that affected many children who attended California's tougher schools: tenure. The powerful California Teachers Association, among her supporters and campaign donors, supported protecting teachers with tenure. But in 2014, a state judge ruled that California's teacher tenure rules violated the civil rights of poor students, reasoning that younger teachers are assigned to the schools with the biggest number of them and are the first to receive layoff notices.

"Substantial evidence presented makes it clear to this court that the challenged statutes disproportionately affect poor and/or minority students," Judge Rolf M. Treu wrote in an opinion that President

Obama's education secretary, Arne Duncan, praised. Harris's deputies appealed the ruling on behalf of the California state superintendent of public instruction, and the lower court ruling was overturned in 2016 as Harris was running for U.S. Senate.

So Harris took positions when she needed to and when those stands might help her politically. But she also understood one of the truths of politics. Whenever a politician takes a stand, she or he risks alienating someone. With virtually no competition in 2014, Harris didn't have to take stands on the issues she chose to avoid, and she didn't.

Harris had done plenty to deserve a second term. She had extracted concessions from banks to help homeowners crushed by the mortgage crisis. She filed lawsuits to enforce environmental laws by requiring that polluting businesses not open unless they could limit emissions that would damage the lungs of people living nearby, invariably in poor and minority communities. One of the suits protected kids attending an elementary school in Long Beach from the exhaust emitted by diesel-powered trains.

She sought to enforce privacy laws, in a state where the tech industry is dominant, and would do much more of that in her second term. She vastly expanded the number of records that were readily accessible to the public on the California Department of Justice website related to deaths in police custody.

She established a solicitor general's unit within the Office of Attorney General to argue cases before the U.S. Supreme Court and the California Supreme Court. That bothered some of the most senior and skilled deputies who looked forward to the intellectual challenge of arguing their own cases. But experts believe the unit improved the quality of the state's appeals.

Certainly, she could have done more. Some advocates believe she didn't go hard enough after police brutality. But she was mindful of who she is, a Black woman who opposed the death penalty and had infuriated police before. She knew she needed law enforcement's buy-in to make any sort of long-lasting change. She worked to neutralize police opposition by not missing the funeral of an officer who died in the line of duty. She also traveled to local police agencies to present awards for their heroic work.

Harris spent $3.6 million on her reelection campaign, and she had $1.3 million left over for a future candidacy. By piling up huge margins in the Bay Area and Los Angeles County, she won with 57.5 percent of the vote. Perhaps in an indication that she had failed in her first four years in statewide office to connect with Republican bastions and Southern California suburban counties, Harris won only twenty-six of the state's fifty-eight counties against a lackluster opponent.

On January 5, 2015, Tani Cantil-Sakauye, the state's chief justice, administered the oath of office to Harris for her second term, and Cantil-Sakauye's role that day captured the evolution of California and its political leaders. Her mother emigrated from the Philippines, and young Cantil-Sakauye lived with her parents for a time next to a brothel in an alley in Sacramento. She put herself through college by waiting tables and dealing blackjack in Reno, became a prosecutor and trial court judge, and was elevated to the position of chief justice by Governor Schwarzenegger. She was a Republican but would quietly quit the party after watching the confirmation hearings of Supreme Court justice Brett Kavanaugh.

Addressing the modest crowd at the Crocker Art Museum in downtown Sacramento, Harris spoke in ambitious terms about her state and the leaders it produced:

"People around the country look to California. They look to us, to see what change looks like. They look to us, to see what innovation can be. They look to us, because we are unburdened by what has been and instead are inspired by what can be."

Harris listed her proudest achievements: going "toe-to-toe against an army of the highest-paid hired guns the Wall Street banks could put on retainer" to wrest $20 billion for California homeowners and helping create the California Homeowner Bill of Rights. During her first four years, she said, California Department of Justice agents seized twelve thousand pounds of methamphetamine and took twelve thousand illegal guns off the street.

"I promise you this: in my next term, we're going to double down," Harris said. "I am going to use the power of this office to lift up the next generation of Californians."

She set out an agenda that included protecting unaccompanied minors who arrive at the southern border after fleeing Central America and confronting the "crisis of confidence" in law enforcement. She promised to use her new eCrime Unit to "prosecute online predators that profit from the extortion, humiliation and degradation of women by posting images without their consent." She planned to create the Bureau of Children's Justice and pledged a continued focus on combating elementary school truancy.

"It's time to say that in the State of California it is a crime for a child to go without an education," Harris declared.

That was on January 5, 2015. But Kamala Harris was a woman in a hurry.

Ten days later, Harris announced her next step.

21
Joe Biden Gives Harris a Hand

Three days after Kamala Harris took the oath of office for her second term as California attorney general, Senator Barbara Boxer announced that she would not be running for reelection in 2016, opening a seat that had been occupied since 1992. That was on January 8, 2015, a Thursday.

On Saturday morning, Kamala Harris arrived early at the downtown San Francisco office of her campaign team, which was made up of Ace Smith, Sean Clegg, and Dan Newman. They had serious business to discuss. They took their places at the conference table, which was fashioned from old oak seats salvaged from California Memorial Stadium on the campus of the University of California, Berkeley, when it was retrofitted to protect against the Hayward fault line that runs directly beneath it. The conference room walls were decorated with drawings by Thomas Nast and covers from

Harper's Weekly dating to the Lincoln administration and *Puck,* the late nineteenth- and early twentieth-century magazine devoted to political humor and satire. Its Shakespearean motto: "What fools these mortals be!"

Harris had wanted to run for governor once Jerry Brown retired in 2018. People around her envisioned her becoming the first woman to govern the nation's largest state. Fellow San Franciscan Gavin Newsom wanted to run for governor, too, having toyed with the possibility of challenging Brown in 2010. Harris had administered the oath of office to Newsom for his second term as lieutenant governor earlier that week. She also thought she could have beaten her "frenemy" if he ever ran against her. But with Boxer retiring, she considered instead a different political prize.

Harris wanted to know what impact she could have as one of one hundred senators. She wanted to know how she could best represent the folks who, as she was wont to say, aren't in the room, the people who need a hand, immigrants, people of color. Although she supported Hillary Clinton's 2016 presidential run, Harris was part of the Obama wing of the party, not the Clintons', and the House and Senate were in

Republican hands. Harris was trying to imagine herself as a member of the minority party at the bottom rungs of the seniority ladder.

In recent decades, Jimmy Carter, Ronald Reagan, Bill Clinton, and George W. Bush had emerged from gubernatorial offices to become president. But Senators John Kerry, Barack Obama, John McCain, Hillary Clinton, Bernie Sanders, and others showed that this launching pad was not the only way to go. American politics had become nationalized, one of many unfortunate consequences of the diminution of state and local news organizations and their concomitant reductions in statehouse and city hall coverage. For all the power a governor had, especially one in California, the media were focused on Washington, as were voters.

The consultants told the tale of two politicians from Massachusetts. Did Harris see herself as a leader in the mold of Senator Elizabeth Warren, who regularly drove national discussion, or Governor Deval Patrick, who, for all his talent, was little known beyond the Bay State?

As a senator who had spent time as a district attorney and an attorney general, Harris could have an outsized impact on the confirmation of justices to the Supreme

Court. In 2015, no one could have guessed how the 2016 presidential election would turn out. But a bright and ambitious senator from California could find herself in Iowa and New Hampshire testing presidential waters sooner rather than later. Harris took it all in and went home to think it through with her husband, sister, and Tony West.

On that Sunday evening, Newsom told Harris he wasn't going to run for the Senate seat and made that decision public on Monday, all but announcing that he would run for governor in 2018. On that Tuesday, eight days after being sworn in for her second term as attorney general, Harris made her announcement. She was running for the U.S. Senate. And as is her way, she made it loud. She raised no less than $92,452 on that first day. Her team spun the story line that she was unbeatable, and it was believable.

"She has been dubbed the female Obama. She cooks. She goes to the gym in a hoodie," the *Guardian* wrote. "She views lawyers as heroes and takes on mortgage companies the way Elizabeth Warren takes on Wall Street."

On the day of Harris's announcement, Senator Warren issued a statement calling her a "smart, tough, and experienced prosecutor who has consistently stood up to Wall Street." Senator Cory Booker asked his Twitter followers to go to a website where they could donate to Harris. Senator Kirsten Gillibrand called her "exactly the kind of leader we need in the Senate." All three would compete with Harris for the 2020 presidential nomination. For now, they were all part of a team.

In 1992, Barbara Boxer ran for the Senate seat held for four terms by Alan Cranston, while Dianne Feinstein ran for a second seat held by a Republican appointed to serve out the term of Pete Wilson, who had defeated Feinstein in the 1990 gubernatorial contest. Boxer and Feinstein both faced stiff competition: Democrats included Gray Davis, who would become governor in 1998; Lieutenant Governor Leo McCarthy; and an influential Los Angeles congressman, Mel Levine. In 2015, voters might have expected a high level of interest in the state's first open U.S. Senate seat in a generation. And sure enough, there was no shortage of ambitious politicians.

Democratic members of Congress from Southern California — Adam Schiff, Xavier Becerra, and Loretta Sanchez — all were thinking about running, as was San Francisco hedge fund billionaire and climate change activist Tom Steyer, a Democrat. Steyer could have funded the race on his own. As Meg Whitman and other wealthy candidates found, however, Californians have not been kind to self-funding candidates. Steyer thought better of it. Becerra and Schiff were little known outside the Beltway.

Former Los Angeles mayor Antonio Villaraigosa considered a candidacy, too, and would have been a tough opponent. He is a deft campaigner, has a million-dollar smile, was a staunch Clinton backer, and had taken stands that would have appealed to many Californians.

He and Harris also were friends, having met in 1995, during Villaraigosa's first term in the assembly. For a time, they spoke regularly. Villaraigosa was touched by how Harris would end the conversations by telling him in a sisterly way that she loved him. Assembly Speaker Willie Brown was on his way out of Sacramento in 1995 but saw a bit of himself in Villaraigosa and acted like a mentor. Villaraigosa grew up in East Los Angeles, the son of a single mom and an alcohol-angry father who was never around. Young Antonio would put cardboard in his shoes when the soles developed holes. He dropped out of high school and got arrested for a brawl in a restaurant, but he found a teacher who believed in him, went to UCLA, then law school, and got a job with the teachers' union in Los Angeles. In 1994, he was elected to represent part of downtown Los Angeles and emerged as one of the assembly's most liberal members, pushing for gun control and higher taxes on wealthy Californians when neither issue was popular.

He rose to become Assembly Speaker before terming out and moving back to Los Angeles, where he was elected the city's forty-first mayor in 2005. For a time, Villaraigosa's campaign consultants included the same San Francisco–based crew that represented Harris. As Villaraigosa contemplated entering the Senate race, Willie Brown urged him to express his fealty to Harris instead. "His loyalty and his relationship with her should be so valuable, and he should, in my opinion, see it as an opportunity to demonstrate that," Brown said. And Villaraigosa's former mentor added, "I am hopeful that his candidacy will be rewarded with a statewide office — at some point."

Brown was telling Villaraigosa, then sixty-two, that he should stand aside for Harris and wait his turn, whenever that might come. It was a fundamentally offensive notion, given what Villaraigosa had achieved in a state where Latinos account for 40 percent of the population.

But having been mayor of the nation's second-largest city, Villaraigosa preferred being chief executive. Like Newsom, he wanted to be governor. For Villaraigosa and the other Southern Californians, the decision came down to ability to raise money, polling, and a basic fact about the California electorate: although California's population is in Southern California, Northern California Democrats have an edge, because people in the Bay Area turn out in greater percentages to vote. (Villaraigosa did run for governor in 2018 against Newsom, without Harris's support.) Putative opponents all thought better of running against Harris, with one exception.

On May 14, 2015, five months after Harris entered the race, Loretta Sanchez, a ten-term member of Congress from Orange County, announced she was running. On paper, Sanchez could have been strong. Her story was compelling. She is one of seven kids of immigrant parents and is the sister of another member of Congress, Linda Sanchez. She went to Head Start. Sanchez's hope was that Latino voters and her roots in the population center of Southern California would propel her to the Senate. But as a candidate, she was prone to gaffes.

Early in her campaign, Sanchez used a stereotypical war whoop as she described the difference between Indians and people whose families came from India. She apologized to offended Native American leaders. At a candidates' debate, Sanchez made what she thought was a clever point and broke into an odd dance move called the "dab," made popular at the time by Carolina Panthers quarterback Cam Newton.

Harris reacted with a double take.

On important policy, Sanchez was out of step with California Democrats. In Congress, she sided with gun manufacturers and President George W. Bush by casting a vote to grant gunmakers immunity from lawsuits over their products. It was a bill pushed by the NRA. The result was that manufacturers of weapons used in mass shootings received immunity from lawsuits by surviving family members of those massacres.

Since announcing her candidacy on January 13, 2015, Harris had been busy, locking up endorsements and dialing for dollars. By mid-May, when Sanchez entered the race, Harris had raised $3.977 million — not bad given the federal cap of $2,700 that an individual could give for a single election at the time. The money came from old San Francisco friends, such as Mark and Susie Buell; Wall Street billionaires George Soros and Ronald Perelman; and Hollywood stars, including Barbra Streisand, Rob Reiner, Sean Penn, Kate Capshaw, and Don Cheadle, as well as from attorneys, Silicon Valley venture capitalists, labor unions, and scores of smaller donors. The $3.977 million nearly matched the $4.2 million Sanchez would raise for her entire campaign. Harris's campaign team marveled at the candidate's seeming air of invincibility. But it was short-lived.

Evidently unsure about the issues, Harris dodged reporters through much of early 2015. In April, three months after her announcement, Harris had a huge kickoff in San Francisco. Former Michigan governor Jennifer M. Granholm, Senator Cory Booker of New Jersey, several members of Congress, and city officials were there. But as Carla Marinucci, then of the *San Francisco Chronicle,* reported, the press was denied access. It was a bizarre way to start a campaign.

Although she was running to be a U.S. senator, Harris was not taking stands on international issues such as Russia's invasion of Ukraine, the NATO alliance, or the Middle East, let alone federal issues that mattered to California related to the environment and water. By refusing interviews, she was reinforcing the view among reporters and rivals that she was overly cautious. The situation would get worse later in the year.

Harris's California campaign consultants were adept at winning statewide races. Their stable of winning statewide clients included Jerry Brown, Gavin Newsom, and Harris, among others. Their goal was to have Harris amass millions and to keep spending lean in 2015, saving it for much-needed ad buys as the election approached and voters started paying attention to the race.

The Democratic Senatorial Campaign Committee, run by Washington insiders and working through Maya Harris, had a different vision of what a top-tier California candidate needed. It presented an organizational chart that included a cast of dozens, at an extravagant cost. Word spread that Harris's campaign was overspending. In October 2015, the *Sacramento Bee* reported that Harris's campaign was burning through money as quickly as she was raising it, "spending hundreds of thousands of dollars on mail-fundraising appeals, a large campaign staff anchored in Los Angeles and prominent fundraisers scattered across the country." In November, the *Los Angeles Times* reported on a campaign shake-up. A Californian, Juan Rodriguez, was installed as campaign manager and several staffers from D.C. were axed. Then an anvil fell on the campaign in the form of a December article in the *Atlantic* detailing how Harris's campaign had "splurged on luxury cars, airline tickets, and first-class accommodations." The magazine reported bills totaling $18,000 at such luxury hotels as Washington's St. Regis, the Waldorf Astoria in Chicago, and the W in Los Angeles. The piece cited "anemic fundraising [that] have dimmed her aura of inevitability." Donors were upset that their money was being wasted, and Team Harris feared that after seemingly winning the race in April 2015, the candidate was in danger of losing it. Rodriguez set about imposing discipline, trimming salaries, and reining in spending. In Harris's favor at that moment was the fact that competition, in the person of Sanchez, was thin.

In 2016, Republicans were an afterthought. To have even an outside chance of winning in California, a Republican candidate would have needed the star power of Schwarzenegger or Reagan and the bank account of a billionaire willing to spend $100 million. The national Republican Party was not going to spend a dime in California, knowing that its money could be put to far better use in smaller states where a few million dollars could tip a Senate race.

Under California's primary system, the top two vote-getters in the primary face off in the general election, regardless of their party. Hapless Republicans split their small and shrinking piece of the electorate in the 2016 primary, allowing Sanchez to win the second spot against the clear front-runner, Harris.

To become competitive in the November runoff, Sanchez, as the less liberal Democrat, would need to appeal to Republican voters while not straying too far to the right that she alienated Democrats. Sanchez did win Republican endorsements from former Los Angeles mayor Richard Riordan. He hadn't been in office since 2001. Hugh Hewitt, a radio talk show host for the conservative Salem Media Group, also endorsed her. So did Congressman Darrell

Issa, the San Diego County Republican who infuriated Democrats with his shrill attacks on the Obama administration and an over-the-top investigation into the deaths of four Americans, including Ambassador Chris Stevens, at the U.S. diplomatic compound in Benghazi.

Harris set her sights on winning the endorsement of the California Democratic Party. To do that, she called Vice President Biden and asked that he come to the state party convention in San Jose in February 2016. He did. He opened his speech by singling out Harris, recalling that she had been close to his son Beau, who had died the year before of cancer. Forty-five minutes into the speech, which went on for nearly an hour, Biden got to his main point. It was the same point he would make during the 2020 presidential campaign: "Our people are not the problem. Our politics is the problem. It has grown so petty, so personal, so angry, so ugly." With Biden giving his blessing to Harris, the California Democratic Party endorsed her. President Obama also endorsed Harris. Sanchez blundered by seeking to diminish Obama's endorsement, suggesting in an interview with a Spanish-language television outlet that he endorsed Harris because they are both

Black. No Democratic politician was or is more popular in California than Obama. But her comment was in keeping with her gaffe-prone campaign, to Harris's good fortune.

Entering 2016, there was never much doubt which candidate would win. Harris, meanwhile, had to tend to a demanding day job, running the California Department of Justice.

22
Picking Her Shots

Corinthian Colleges, once one of the nation's largest for-profit colleges, occupies a special place in the shameful history of moneymaking institutions that prey on people seeking an education to better themselves.

Trump University, the for-profit company that Donald Trump created to capitalize on his brand and his *Apprentice* television show, gained its share of infamy as well. As attorney general, Kamala Harris sued Corinthian but not Trump University. Those decisions help illustrate Harris's way of conducting the public's business.

Politicians regularly travel to New York seeking campaign money, just as politicians from New York and other states come to California for money.

Harris, wanting to raise money and build a national profile, made a pilgrimage to

Manhattan in September 2011. Then New York attorney general Eric Schneiderman helped her draw a crowd with the help of a New York lawyer whose practice was built around representing clients with issues before state attorneys general. The trip was political business as usual, or so it seemed. Trump was among the New Yorkers who donated to Harris on that trip, $5,000 dated September 26, 2011. Trump donated another $1,000 on February 20, 2013. His daughter Ivanka Trump added $2,000 on June 3, 2014. The Trump Organization had business in many states, California included, and it made sense to cultivate the state's chief lawyer. Those were the sorts of donations Trump and his family made as they went about their business.

In May 2011, the first news stories appeared that Schneiderman had opened an investigation into the New York–based "university" that bore Trump's name, over allegations that the company peddled overpriced seminars that were all but worthless to people looking to strike it rich in real estate. By August 2013, Schneiderman sued Trump over the practices at the school.

Trump responded by attacking Schneiderman, accusing him of barraging him with requests for campaign contributions.

Trump's claim that there was something nefarious about Schneiderman's solicitations prompted an investigation by the Joint Commission on Public Ethics, a New York State watchdog agency. The case ended without charges in 2015, after Trump descended the gilded escalator in Trump Tower on June 16 and announced his improbable presidential candidacy. Trump and his so-called university settled suits brought by New York and private plaintiffs for $25 million in November 2016, after he won the election.

In her floundering campaign for U.S. Senate in 2016, Congresswoman Loretta Sanchez thought she had an issue with which to sully Harris, the front-runner. Sanchez wasn't wrong on the politics. In 2016 in California, no politician was less popular than Trump. Candidate Trump, meanwhile, fed the narrative that politicians were corrupt, telling followers at his rallies that campaign donations were transactional. In return for donations, he said, politicians would grant favors. "When you have a candidate who says he contributed to political candidates for favors, then you really have to question why Trump contributed twice to Harris when Trump University was coming under scrutiny, and you have to question why Harris accepted the contributions from Trump," Sanchez's campaign spokesman said at the time.

That Sanchez would make the claim was understandable. She needed an issue. Harris has never publicly discussed the case. But the allegation that Harris decided against filing a suit in exchange for $6,000 in campaign donations strained credulity. Between 2002, when she started running for office, and 2016, Harris had raised more than $32 million for her campaigns. An ambitious politician — a prosecutor no less — who aspired to higher office would not have taken a dive on such a case. Besides, if there had been a lawsuit worth filing, Harris would have attracted national attention for suing Trump during the 2016 presidential campaign.

The far more likely explanation for not suing Trump is the obvious one. Relatively few Californians were victims of the Trump University scam. People who fell for Trump's bluster were out some money but weren't made destitute. In 2015, Harris deftly blunted the issue before Sanchez raised it, finding a fitting use for the $6,000 that Trump donated to her. Her attorney general's campaign account recorded a $6,000 donation to the Central American

Resource Center of Los Angeles, a nonprofit organization that assists refugees and immigrants.

In the meantime, Harris had taken aim at a far larger target than Trump's degree-churning operation, one that hurt Californians. Corinthian Colleges was based in the Orange County city of Santa Ana. Its stock was traded on NASDAQ and rose and fell based on its profitability. Its profits depended on its ability to attract students and their ability to take out federally subsidized loans to pay for Corinthian's inflated tuition and fees. Whether those students got jobs or could repay those loans mattered little to Corinthian's shareholders.

In 2007, then California attorney general Jerry Brown extracted $6.6 million from Corinthian to settle claims that it was misleading students. Corinthian promised to reform. Then the Great Recession hit. Operating under various names, Corinthian advertised heavily during *The Jerry Springer Show* and *The Maury Povich Show,* targeting people who had afternoon time on their hands. Its internal documents show Corinthian sought enrollees who were "isolated" and "impatient," had "low self-esteem," had "few people in their lives who care about them," and were "unable to see and plan well for the future." The *Los Angeles Times* reported that Corinthian was one of the big beneficiaries of the crash, as unemployed workers seeking training and a better life bought into the Corinthian promise. The company nearly doubled its revenue to $1.75 billion from the start of the Great Recession in 2007 to 2011.

At one point, Corinthian had twenty-seven thousand students in California and charged them $39,000 or more to obtain an associate's degree, something they could get almost for free at California's public community colleges. Corinthian students would pay upward of $68,800 for a bachelor's degree of questionable utility. A California State University degree could be had for a fraction of that cost. So on October 10, 2013, Harris brought a sweeping lawsuit against Corinthian. It became one of the biggest cases ever brought against a for-profit college, and it crippled and ultimately killed the institution. It also gained the notice of powerful Democrats in Washington, who had been trying to restrict federal subsidies in the form of the student loans that fueled the for-profit college industry, notably Senator Elizabeth Warren, who was among the first national figures to endorse

Harris's Senate run. Corinthian became one of the first targets of the Consumer Finance Protection Bureau, which Warren helped create when she worked in the Obama administration. Warren also was one of a dozen senators who wrote to the Obama administration's education secretary, Arne Duncan, urging that he crack down on for-profit colleges. The letter singled out Corinthian.

"Corinthian Colleges Incorporated represents a risk to students on a scale that could overwhelm the current system of support and safety net provisions for students," the letter said. "Corinthian has shown itself to be one of the worst actors in the for-profit college industry. . . ."

Like almost all for-profit colleges, Corinthian depended on students obtaining subsidized loans to pay the inflated tuition and fees. Whether they got jobs at the end of their studies, the students were on the hook to repay the loans. Two-thirds of Corinthian's students dropped out, and three-fourths of the former students couldn't repay their loan debt, all of which was fodder for Harris's suit alleging that Corinthian was fleecing its students and providing them little benefit.

As the election neared, on March 23,

2016, Harris announced a $1.1 billion judgment. That included $800 million to be repaid to students. By then, however, Corinthian had shut its schools and gone bankrupt. It could not pay. Harris, with other state attorneys general, urged the Obama administration to forgive federal student loans taken out by Corinthian students. Obama's Department of Education agreed. The Trump administration took the opposite tack by seeking repayment, not that many students could ever meet that obligation.

The reason Harris sued Corinthian was clear: people wearing fancy suits in well-appointed suites were taking advantage of powerless victims, many of whom were single parents, veterans, and people of color who had little. None of them were, as Harris would say, in the room where decisions get made.

Critics and some friends say Kamala Harris was overly cautious during her time as attorney general. There is evidence to support that view. However, there is great danger in being too quick to sue or to file criminal charges. Prosecutors have the power to deprive people of their liberty, destroy their reputation, and seize their property. They need to be certain they're right before accusing an individual or a corporation of wrongdoing. Kamala Harris was not quick to wield that power. When she did take a shot by filing a case, she rarely missed.

23
FIGHTING THE FOREVER WAR

On its website, Planned Parenthood's political advocacy arm lists "9 Reasons to Love Kamala Harris."

Some of them: She is unstinting in her defense of access to contraceptives and reproductive health care.

She bested Supreme Court justice Brett Kavanaugh during his confirmation hearing before the Senate Judiciary Committee.

And, in a bit of whimsy, "Dancing. And Drumlines. Enough said."

Harris's stand on the side of abortion rights is well aligned with the vast majority of voters in her home state. But among its forty million residents, California has some of everyone. That includes a man called David Daleiden. From at least his high school days in the liberal college town of Davis, California, Daleiden has been a self-styled warrior against abortion. While in his twenties, between October 2013 and July 2015, he and a partner used phony identities to gain access to abortion conferences and clandestinely videotaped conversations with Planned Parenthood physicians and others. In July 2015, he and an entity he created, the Center for Medical Progress, gained national attention by releasing selectively edited and misleading versions of those videos that supposedly depict Planned Parenthood officials agreeing to the sale of fetal parts.

Daleiden created legal problems for himself. Under California law, it's a crime to surreptitiously record conversations. Both parties must consent to being recorded. Daleiden believes that the law doesn't apply to him because he is a journalist who was seeking to expose illegality.

In the summer of 2015, the forever war over abortion rights ran hot. Planned Parenthood's work — providing reproductive health care to women including contraceptives, reducing teen pregnancy, combatting sexually transmitted diseases, issuing the latest warnings about pesticides that could cause birth defects — became ever more complicated after the release of Daleiden's tapes. They led to inquiries by the Republican-controlled Congress and new demands that Planned Parenthood be sanctioned. In the months that followed there was a wave of threats and violence directed at Planned Parenthood. Clinics were firebombed. Physicians and nurses who provided medical care for women at the clinics feared being assassinated. A Washington man was arrested after offering to pay for the murder of a biotech executive whose California firm was mentioned in the tapes. At a Planned Parenthood clinic in Colorado Springs in November 2015, a gunman raving about body parts killed three people: a police officer, an Iraq war veteran, and a mother of two. Later, he purportedly told police that when he died, he believed fetuses in heaven would thank him for averting abortions.

Daleiden maintained that the violence was not related to his videos. "I don't think the pro-life movement or my videos have anything to do with that — my videos carry a strong message of nonviolence," he told Shawn Hubler, then of the *Sacramento Bee,* in April 2016.

Democrats in Congress, including Jerrold "Jerry" Nadler of New York and Zoe Lofgren from San Jose, came to Planned Parenthood's defense, urging Harris to look into the legality of what Daleiden had done and the subsequent attacks on Planned Parenthood.

"Planned Parenthood is a well-respected and important organization in my community," Lofgren wrote in July 2015. She urged Harris to investigate, saying, "The recent surreptitiously recorded video is the latest iteration of harassment and partisan attacks on Planned Parenthood which have become far too common, and raises serious legal questions that merit an investigation into whether the so-called 'Center for Medical Progress' has broken the law."

Kathy Kneer, who for twenty-four years directed Planned Parenthood's political organization in California, also thought the California Attorney General's Office should investigate. There was, after all, the state criminal prohibition against the secret recording of conversations.

On July 24, 2015, Harris responded to the call from Lofgren and Nadler by issuing a statement saying she would look into the matter. Although she told her staff internally that she worried about the lives of people who worked in the clinics as well as the patients who needed care, she said nothing publicly beyond issuing that statement. There was no press conference.

Planned Parenthood had been among the

Harris campaign's supporters and donors. That might have given the organization a level of access. It didn't, at least not initially. Kathy Kneer didn't have Harris's cell phone number or her personal email address. Going through regular channels, Kneer got an appointment with the California Department of Justice staff and eventually met with attorneys, not including Harris. More silence followed. "They worked at their normal, slow bureaucratic pace," Kneer said.

Threats of violence were not abating, however. Kneer and other Planned Parenthood leaders, concerned about the safety of their staff, worried that local law enforcement was not taking the issue seriously enough. So they again turned to the California Department of Justice. In March 2016, they secured meetings with top officials there.

Emails from that time show that, as a result of the meetings, one of the lawyers from the California Department of Justice would speak at a general meeting of Planned Parenthood staff, set for April 7, 2016, at the Sheraton Grand Hotel in downtown Sacramento.

On April 5, 2016, two days ahead of that gathering, the California Justice Department lawyer Jill E. Habig restated in an email what she was planning to discuss: "ongoing security requests/needs (both as to individual doctors and as to clinics) from your affiliates so we could provide assistance as needed with local law enforcement." She agreed to talk for twenty minutes, with a few minutes for questions. It was to be a small part of the all-day agenda.

As it happened, April 5, 2016, was a momentous day in David Daleiden's life. As he has told and retold the story, he was carrying kitchen trash from his Huntington Beach apartment out to the garbage can when California Department of Justice agents stepped out of an unmarked white van and served him with a warrant to search his apartment. That day, nine months after Harris promised to investigate, they seized Daleiden's computers, hard drives, and documents. Career Justice Department agents who conducted the search are protected by a strong civil service system and their union. As elected attorneys general come and go, they remain, doing their jobs. They're cops, not politicians, although Daleiden and his attorneys allege that the search was directed from the top, Harris.

Planned Parenthood's leaders and top California Department of Justice officials had been trading emails in the days leading up to the search. At least some of the Justice Department officials on the emails knew that the search was being planned. But there were no leaks. Kneer and other Planned Parenthood executives learned of the search only when it became public. "We had no advance word. Not even a hint," Kneer said.

Kneer was, of course, delighted at the turn of events. The release of the Daleiden tapes had been "traumatic," like "gasoline on a fire," Kneer said. Now, nine months after the tapes became public, perhaps the law might be used to protect Planned Parenthood.

The April 7 Planned Parenthood general meeting in Sacramento took place as scheduled. The Justice Department lawyer who spoke made no mention of the search or investigation. Harris did not appear at the event, and she did not hold a press conference to tout the search. There was, instead, more silence. The investigation continued through the summer and fall. No charges were filed against Daleiden during Harris's tenure as attorney general.

As Daleiden's tapes inflamed the abortion wars in 2015, Kamala Harris became one of the lead sponsors of legislation — along with the abortion rights groups Black Women for Wellness and NARAL Pro-Choice California — that was aimed at pregnancy crisis centers. The centers, which operate in California and across the country, are run by conservative Christian organizations. Employees, many of whom are not medical professionals, counsel women against terminating their pregnancies. Called the Freedom, Accountability, Comprehensive Care, and Transparency (FACT) Act, the legislation required that the anti-abortion crisis pregnancy centers post signs informing women of their options. In California, those options include receiving publicly funded abortions.

The signs would read: "California has public programs that provide immediate free or low-cost access to comprehensive family planning services (including all FDA-approved methods of contraception), prenatal care, and abortion for eligible women."

As it stated, the legislation's goal was to "ensure that California residents make their personal reproductive health care decisions knowing their rights and the health care services available to them."

Opponents included the National Institute of Family and Life Advocates, a Virginia organization that "exists to protect life-

affirming pregnancy centers that empower abortion-vulnerable women and families to choose life for their unborn children." "Forcing speech is not the solution," NIFLA, which operates more than one hundred crisis pregnancy centers in California, said in its letter opposing the bill.

Lawyers who work for the California State Legislature and advise lawmakers understood that the legislation raised constitutional issues. But their belief was that longstanding law allowed the government to regulate commercial speech to prevent false, deceptive, or misleading statements, particularly where public health is at issue.

Daleiden's tapes became part of Republican lawmakers' talking points in Sacramento as they tried without success to derail the FACT Act. "Now, we're finding out that maybe a strong motivation for abortion is not to help someone in need . . . but it is maybe to harvest. Maybe there has been a huge conflict of interest and the nation is waking up to it," Senator John Moorlach, an Orange County Republican, said in his speech opposing the legislation.

In their weakened state, Republicans were unable to block any legislation in California. The bill passed easily on a party-line vote, with most Democrats supporting it and

Republicans voting against it.

Harris was often accused of being cautious, but not in this instance. Harris cheered when Governor Jerry Brown signed the legislation into law on October 9, 2015: "I am proud to have co-sponsored the Reproductive FACT Act, which ensures that all women have equal access to comprehensive reproductive health care services, and that they have the facts they need to make informed decisions about their health and their lives."

If she could have looked into the future, or if she had thought of the makeup of the U.S. Supreme Court, Attorney General Harris might not have been quite so enthusiastic.

NIFLA sued, claiming the act violated the free speech rights of the centers by requiring that they post notices that conflicted with their beliefs. The lower courts sided with the state. But after losing in the lower courts, the antiabortion forces appealed to the U.S. Supreme Court. Among the attorneys representing NIFLA was John Eastman, the former clerk to Justice Clarence Thomas who had run for attorney general as a Republican in 2010, the year Harris was elected. On June 18, 2018, in a

5–4 decision authored by Justice Thomas, the court sided with NIFLA.

"Licensed clinics must provide a government-drafted script about the availability of state-sponsored services, as well as contact information for how to obtain them," Thomas wrote. "One of those services is abortion — the very practice that petitioners are devoted to opposing."

That wasn't the end of it.

By law, winning parties in civil rights cases are entitled to attorney fees. In 2019, California attorney general Xavier Becerra settled the claims by agreeing to pay $2 million to attorneys for the antiabortion organizations who had sued over the FACT Act. And in 2019, several of those very same lawyers were in U.S. District Judge William Orrick's courtroom in San Francisco.

There, they were representing none other than David Daleiden. The cause célèbre of the antiabortion movement was fending off a suit by Planned Parenthood alleging that he violated individuals' privacy rights and trespassed when he made his secret recordings. His legal team consisted of no fewer than sixteen lawyers and paralegals, all of them working free of charge to him.

On November 15, 2019, a jury in a federal court in San Francisco awarded Planned

Parenthood $2.2 million, finding Daleiden and his collaborators violated laws against trespassing, fraud, clandestine recording, and racketeering. Daleiden is appealing. He also has sued Harris and the state, alleging they violated his First Amendment rights.

As she ran for the U.S. Senate in 2016, Kamala Harris never did hold a press conference to tout the case against Daleiden. Nor did she file a criminal complaint against him, even though such a filing in California would have been to her political benefit, given public attitudes supporting a woman's right to control her own body. That was left to her successor.

On March 28, 2017, with Harris in the Senate, Attorney General Becerra filed a criminal complaint against Daleiden and an associate for the surreptitious taping. The criminal case against Daleiden is pending. He has pleaded not guilty and contends that he was acting as a journalist seeking the truth. Daleiden has a top-notch criminal defense team. That team includes Steve Cooley, the former Los Angeles County district attorney who ran against Harris in 2010. Cooley contends Harris's actions were corrupt because she is beholden to Planned Parenthood. Daleiden speaks out as well. "It's pretty obvious that the reason that I alone was targeted by Kamala Harris is because I dared to criticize Planned Parenthood and the abortion industry," Daleiden says on a well-produced video.

Kathy Kneer retired from Planned Parenthood in July 2017. What did she think of Harris's role?

"I think she was cautious. Even when you met with her, she didn't say, 'I'm going to be on your side.' She was neutral."

Harris proudly supports a woman's right to choice. But as Kneer saw it, Harris was a professional prosecutor. That was her way.

24
"Go Get 'Em"

Kamala Harris had seen sexual exploitation of children when she worked as a prosecutor in Oakland and San Francisco. She used her position as California attorney general to elevate the issue. Those efforts ultimately would resonate nationally.

"Human trafficking is a modern form of slavery," Harris said in a report issued in 2012, her second year as attorney general. "It involves controlling a person through force, fraud, or coercion to exploit the victim for forced labor, sexual exploitation, or both."

The report pointed out that in the internet age, "the business of sex trafficking, in particular, has moved online." And the report singled out "unscrupulous websites like Backpage.com."

Backpage was, as she and others saw it, the equivalent of an online pimp. It came to dominate the online sex trade. Anyone with a smartphone could gain access to its classified listings and order up a prostitute. It operated in 943 locations and ninety-seven countries, and its revenue exceeded $100 million a year.

Backpage's origin dates to alternative newspapers of the 1960s and 1970s. Like mainstream papers, alternative papers relied on classified ads for much of their revenue. In 2004, Craig Newmark disrupted that business model by offering free classified ads through his Craigslist website.

Michael Lacey and James Larkin were running *Phoenix New Times* and other publications that were part of their Village Voice Media Holdings. To respond to the Craigslist threat, they created Backpage.com. Named for the back-page ads that ran in alternative newspapers, the site was a thinly veiled bazaar for prostitution. Craigslist, under pressure from law enforcement and advocacy groups, shut down its "adult" section in 2010. But Backpage was there to fill the void.

As its revenue grew, Larkin and Lacey lived large, regularly traveling internationally and buying exclusive properties. One hilltop home with a view of the Golden Gate Bridge in San Francisco was recently valued at $13.99 million. A five-bedroom home in St. Helena, in the heart of the Napa Valley wine region, was valued at $3.4 million.

In August 2011, eight months after taking office, Harris was one of forty-five state attorneys general who signed a letter to Backpage's attorney saying they were "increasingly concerned about human trafficking, especially the trafficking of minors." Backpage.com, the law enforcement officials said, was "a hub for such activity." The letter apparently had little if any impact. Backpage's business continued.

In July 2013, Harris was one of forty-nine state attorneys general who signed a letter addressed to key members of the U.S. House and Senate pointing out that the federal Communications Decency Act precluded state law enforcement authorities from carrying out their duty "to investigate and prosecute those who promote prostitution and endanger our children." The Communications Decency Act, signed by President Clinton in 1995, was supposed to protect children from seeing online pornography. It didn't. That's because the Communications Decency Act has shielded Facebook, Twitter, Google, Reddit, and the other corporations that dominate the internet from criminal and civil liability for whatever content gets posted on their sites. That immunity is fundamental to their business model.

Backpage hid behind that same immunity. Its executives contended that they could not be held responsible for the content of the ads. In their 2013 letter to Congress, the state attorneys general cited evidence that the site was used to buy and sell children for men's sexual gratification and for the financial gain of pimps and Backpage itself. One Florida pimp, the letter said, tattooed his name on a thirteen-year-old child's eyelids to show that she was his property.

In the years to come, more details would emerge about victims. A girl sold via Backpage on the East Coast was forced to perform oral sex at gunpoint, choked, and gang-raped. In 2013 and 2014, a fifteen-year-old girl sold through Backpage by her uncle and his friends for $200 an hour was raped in hotel rooms. On June 20, 2015, a girl bought and sold in Texas was murdered by a customer. He tried to cover it up by burning her body.

"Federal enforcement alone has proven insufficient to stem the growth of internet-facilitated child sex trafficking. Those on the front lines of the battle against the sexual exploitation of children — State and local law enforcement — must be granted the authority to investigate and prosecute those who facilitate these horrible crimes," the attorneys general said in that 2013 letter to Congress.

Congress failed to act in 2013. Nor did Congress act the year after that, or the year after that, or the year after that. But Attorney General Harris had a plan.

Maggy Krell graduated from the UC Davis School of Law in 2003 and went to work as a deputy district attorney in San Joaquin County, one of the richest agricultural counties in the richest farm state in America, though one where much farmland has been plowed under for housing developments and strip malls. As a junior deputy district attorney, Krell was responsible for prosecuting prostitution cases. That meant bringing charges against young women accused of prostitution. They seemed so vulnerable. Their stories, she said, "made me sick to my stomach." There had to be a better way.

Krell moved to the California Department of Justice in 2005, working her way up to a unit that prosecutes complex crimes that cross county lines. Many involved mortgage fraud. Those were interesting and important. But her passion involved cases of human trafficking, specifically the sex trade. Over her years in the California Department of Justice, she helped prosecute people who ran bordellos that masqueraded as massage parlors. She brought cases against members of domestic and international gangs who found that, unlike guns or drugs, which could be sold only once, they could sell and resell girls and women. The girls and women had little if any control over their lives. "Every case had a common denominator. It was Backpage," Krell said.

In July 2016, Krell was kayaking with her eight-year-old son on Donner Lake, a postcard-perfect body of water named for the Donner party of pioneers who got caught in the terrible Sierra winter of 1846–1847 and survived by cannibalizing the pioneers who had perished. Her cell phone buzzed, but the number was blocked, so Krell ignored the call.

A few minutes later, Attorney General Harris's chief of staff, Nathan Barankin, sent her a text imploring her to pick up her phone.

The phone buzzed again.

Harris was on the line.

Krell paddled back to the dock and stepped barefoot out of the kayak. Cell reception was spotty, so she climbed a hill to hear better. Harris wanted details about a case Krell had been working on for three years. How many victims were there? Were they minors? Would they testify? What about the law, which in this case would be a particular hurdle? Krell was winded from the climb but answered as best as she could. "I was talking to another prosecutor. She got it," Krell said. "At the end of the call, Harris said, 'Go get 'em.' "

With Attorney General Kamala Harris's backing, Krell prepared to prosecute a case that would test the limits of California state law. She would charge the owners of Backpage.com, a $600 million corporation that used state-of-the-art technology and operated worldwide, with that oldest of vice crimes: pimping.

Krell had started working on the case in 2013, the result of news accounts about Backpage and reports from the National Center for Missing & Exploited Children, which had identified hundreds of suspected instances of children being sold in California using Backpage ads.

It didn't take much effort to prove that Backpage was used for prostitution. She and the agents paid for two Backpage ads: one for a sofa and one for an "escort." One Backpage reader called inquiring about the sofa. Within forty-eight hours, 803 calls came from men seeking the escort's services.

Under Krell's direction, agents also invited women and girls advertised on Backpage to come to a motel room off Interstate 80 in Rocklin, a suburb northeast of Sacramento. Four women who responded were in their twenties. Two girls who arrived were fifteen, one was sixteen, and another was seventeen. One of those girls told about a fifth girl, known publicly only by the initials E.V. She was thirteen, and her picture was on Backpage. In another world, Krell imagined that E.V. would have been batting a piñata at a birthday party with friends. In the world of Backpage, E.V. was following the lead of her seventeen-year-old mentor, bringing money to their pimp. One day, the seventeen-year-old told Krell, their pimp brought them to a clothing store. The thirteen-year-old was so tiny she had to shop in the little-girls' section.

"We never found her," Krell said. "I think about her all the time."

On behalf of the State of California, Krell filed the criminal complaint under seal at the end of September 2016, accusing Backpage's chief executive officer, Carl Ferrer, and its principal owners, Lacey and Larkin, of multiple counts of pimping. She also filed an arrest warrant for Ferrer, Larkin, and Lacey. Authorities were waiting in October when Ferrer stepped off a flight from Amsterdam at George Bush Intercontinental Airport in Houston. Once Ferrer was in custody, they searched Backpage's offices in Dallas.

On October 6, 2016, a little more than a month before Election Day, California unsealed the complaint. Texas attorney general Ken Paxton, whose agents helped California authorities, held a press conference announcing the arrest. Harris issued a press release but held no press conference. Nor was Harris in the Sacramento courtroom on October 12, 2016, when all three defendants were arraigned and numerous reporters, me included, were there. She rarely held press conferences after arrests, and she did not parade defendants before cameras in perp walks.

Parents of exploited children and people who advocate on their behalf filled several pews in the courtroom that day. They had waited years to see the Backpage executives in court. Harris had done something no one else had done. In announcing the charges,

Harris singled out Carissa Phelps, praising her for helping find and counsel child victims. Phelps, an attorney, tells her story of being trafficked when she was a girl in her book, *Runaway Girl*. "Somebody needed to start it," Phelps said of Harris. "To have the California connection is bold. This is the home of tech."

Defenders of Backpage were quick to denounce Harris, accusing her of timing the complaint to coincide with the November 8 election. Although Harris was running for the U.S. Senate, the outcome of that race was hardly in doubt. A poll taken two weeks before the arrest showed Harris ahead of Sanchez by 22 points.

In court, Backpage executives argued that they could not be held responsible for the content of their site. The Communications Decency Act gave them immunity from state pimping laws. To buttress their argument, the defendants' lawyers used Harris's own words against her, as written in the July 2013 letter that she and the other state attorneys general signed urging Congress to amend the Communications Decency Act so states could prosecute websites that advertise the sale of children for sex.

On December 9, 2016, a California state

judge agreed with Backpage's attorneys and dismissed the case. That was not its end, however. In the search of Backpage's offices, agents had amassed a huge cache of documents detailing Backpage's financial transactions. They used those documents to build a case showing that when major credit card companies stopped processing payments for Backpage, Backpage instructed customers to send checks to post office boxes, use cryptocurrency, or make payments to shell corporations. Backpage sought to launder money by using banks in Iceland, Hungary, and the Principality of Liechtenstein, the state alleged.

Harris was a U.S. Senator–elect when on December 23, 2016, Krell, with the outgoing attorney general's blessing, filed a new complaint charging all three with violating state laws that made money laundering a crime. The Backpage empire was unraveling.

Harris's decision to challenge Backpage was not without political risks. Although Backpage was a rogue company, she was attacking an internet company in a state that more than any other had created the internet and was challenging protections provided by the Communications Decency Act. Some of the biggest corporate players in California and many of the state's largest taxpayers depend on protections provided by that law. "This is a frightening abuse of power to harass a company just because Harris doesn't like how people use that company," one commentator wrote, "and because she and her staff can't be bothered to do the actual law enforcement work of using that information to go after the actual lawbreakers. It's shameful."

Harris was a member of the U.S. Senate on August 23, 2017, when superior court judge Lawrence G. Brown in Sacramento vindicated her decision, ruling that California could pursue money laundering charges against Larkin, Lacey, and Ferrer.

In April 2018, Ferrer pleaded guilty to the state money laundering charges and promised to testify against his former bosses, Larkin and Lacey. As of this writing, California's case against Larkin and Lacey is pending; they have pleaded not guilty.

On April 9, 2018, the U.S. Attorney's Office in Phoenix announced a ninety-three-count indictment against seven Backpage executives, accusing them of conspiracy, facilitating prostitution across state lines, and money laundering. The trial is pending, too, and each has pleaded not guilty. Ferrer is cooperating with the feds. The federal case resulted in part from the investigation done in California. "It was always a national case," Krell said. "We needed to file it in California because no one else did."

Federal authorities shut down Backpage in April 2018. New sites have emerged to fill the vacuum. But they will need to be less brazen than Backpage. In April 2018, President Trump signed legislation stating that the Communications Decency Act does not provide immunity to websites that pimp children and that victims and state attorneys general can sue such sites.

25
"I Intend to Fight"

By October 2016, the U.S. Senate race between Kamala Harris and Loretta Sanchez was an afterthought. Harris had led in every poll for more than a year. Not that she needed it, but in the final weeks of the election, outgoing president Barack Obama gave her a final push by appearing on her behalf in a commercial that aired statewide.

"As your senator, Kamala Harris will be a fearless fighter for the people of California every single day," Obama told voters.

California voters were paying far more attention to Donald Trump and his crude remarks recorded in the *Access Hollywood* tape, in which he talked about assaulting women, and FBI director James Comey's letter, in which he announced that he was reopening an investigation into Hillary Clinton's emails.

To the extent they were watching state issues, the ballot was full of provocative initiatives. One would legalize the commercial sale of cannabis. Another would raise tobacco taxes by $2 per pack of cigarettes. A third would make it illegal for people who could not legally own guns to buy ammunition. Two others would either end the death penalty or speed up executions.

Los Angeles Times political columnist George Skelton, who had been covering California campaigns since Pat Brown was governor, wrote a month out from the election that the Harris-Sanchez race was "drawing all the interest of a mosquito abatement board seat. California has had many compelling Senate fights in the past: Boxer–Carly Fiorina. Dianne Feinstein–Mike Huffington. Jerry Brown–Pete Wilson. Alan Cranston–Max Rafferty. But Kamala Harris–Loretta Sanchez? Snore."

Harris could have been forgiven if she was confident that she'd win when she held a luncheon fund-raiser at Boulevard, one of downtown San Francisco's finer restaurants, on October 20, 2016, her fifty-second birthday. Her friend, New Jersey Democratic senator Cory Booker, was a special guest. Harris stood to speak. As she often did, Harris addressed gun control, gun violence, and school shootings.

San Francisco is a city attuned to gun violence like few others. In 1978, Dan White, a former San Francisco cop and firefighter who had quit his post as San Francisco supervisor, evaded detection by climbing through a side window at city hall. He walked into Mayor George Moscone's office, demanding that Moscone reinstate him. When Moscone refused, White pulled out a handgun and shot him four times, killing him. Then White stalked Harvey Milk, the city's first gay supervisor. Stepping into Milk's office, White fired five times. Supervisor Dianne Feinstein, hearing the gunshots and smelling gunpowder, rushed to Milk and checked for a pulse. There was none. Under the city's succession plan, Feinstein became mayor of a city in shock.

Feinstein had been a U.S. senator for six months on July 1, 1993, when, on the thirty-fourth floor of a downtown high-rise less than a ten-minute walk from Boulevard, a failed businessman armed with two Intratec DC9 semiautomatic pistols, a .45-caliber semiautomatic handgun, and hundreds of rounds of ammunition put on a headset to muffle the sound and inexplicably opened fire at a law firm, killing eight people. In the wake of that massacre, Senator Feinstein won passage of a federal assault weapons ban, though that ban expired a decade later.

At Boulevard, Harris spoke to the gathering about police reports she had read detailing the slaughter of "Babies. Babies. Babies."

Then she stopped herself.

"Erin, I am so sorry. I forgot."

Erin Lehane, one of the donors to Harris that day, had brought her daughter, Rose, who was seven, the one kid in the audience.

Harris, who had known Rose since she was a baby, looked her in the eyes and promised that she would talk with her after the event was over. Once the guests started clearing out, Harris pulled two chairs close together, leaned in toward Rose, and asked whether her remarks had frightened her.

Lehane could not hear everything Harris was saying. Rose later told her mom that Harris told her not to worry, that there were so many people who would protect her — her mom, her teachers, the police.

"She tried to be reassuring," Lehane said. "She asked if Rose had questions. She spent a huge chunk of time. There was no camera. There was no press. Nobody knew. She was very human in that moment and wanted Rose to feel safe."

Lehane could see that Harris was keeping her entourage waiting. Staffers were looking impatient. They had other events to attend.

"It was a very human moment for someone who didn't have a lot of time to be human," Lehane said.

Kamala Harris, certain that her race was over in the closing days, began campaigning for other candidates seeking legislative and congressional seats. She was making allies, collecting chits, knowing she'd want to cash them in at some point. Even before votes were cast and counted, there was speculation about her next step.

"Those in the know point to a run for the White House," *San Francisco Chronicle* columnists Phil Matier and Andy Ross wrote on November 6, 2016, two days before the fateful election day.

As polls closed in the East on election night 2016, Harris's campaign staff ordered guacamole, chips, and tapas at a restaurant near the California Department of Justice offices in downtown Los Angeles. All the while, they were looking at their phones, checking the needle on the *New York Times* probability meter, refreshing it, not believing what they were seeing, Harris's press secretary Nathan Click recalled.

"Holy fuck," Sean Clegg, one of Harris's main strategists, said.

Clegg was the first to declare what they all were thinking. Distraught and realizing that the improbable had occurred, Clegg rushed to Harris's election-night venue, Exchange LA, the renovated art deco downtown event space that once housed the Pacific Stock Exchange.

Harris had been at another restaurant with her family and her close friends Chrisette and Reginald Hudlin and their children. As the reality set in, Harris wrote in her autobiography, the Hudlins' son, Alexander, not yet a teen, looked at the soon-to-be senator-elect with tears in his eyes.

"Auntie Kamala, that man can't win. He's not going to win, is he?"

The child's fear hit Harris hard. She hustled to Exchange LA, huddled in an alcove with Clegg and Juan Rodriguez, and tore up the hopeful speech she had written in anticipation of Hillary Clinton's victory.

On that night, some Democratic leaders elsewhere in the country gamely offered to work with President-elect Trump. Not Harris, not on this night. She wasn't wearing a necklace of severed heads like the mythological warrior goddess Harris spoke about in her first run for office thirteen years earlier, but her words, handwritten on scraps of paper, suggested that she was becoming Kali-like. The politician who so often was criticized for failing to take stands threw caution into the trash.

At about 10:00 p.m., Harris took the stage, her husband by her side, with maybe one thousand people watching, many of them in tears and all of them in a state of disbelief. She proceeded to repeat the word "fight" no fewer than twenty-six times in a speech that ran about eight minutes. There was no teleprompter.

"Do we retreat or do we fight? I say we fight. And I intend to fight. I intend to fight for our ideals.

"I intend to fight for a state that has the largest number of immigrants documented and undocumented of any state in this country, and to do everything we can to bring them justice and dignity and fairness under the law and pass comprehensive immigration reform. Bring them out from under the shadows, fight for who we are. I intend to fight.

"I intend to fight for Black Lives Matter.

"I intend to fight for truth and transparency and trust. I intend to fight.

"I intend to fight for a woman's access to health care and reproductive health rights.

"I intend to fight against those naysayers who suggest there is no such thing as climate change."

Harris promised to fight for the civil rights of all people and to fight to defend marriage equality. She pledged to fight for students against loan debt, to fight against Big Oil and science deniers, and to fight for workers' right to collective bargaining and for gun safety laws.

"So, guys, here is the deal. Our ideals are at stake right now. We all have to fight for who we are."

Harris had won that night in a cakewalk, by a 61.6 to 38.4 percent margin. She got 7.5 million votes, winning all but four of California's fifty-eight counties. She received 3.1 million more votes than Trump in California, though 1.2 million fewer than Hillary Clinton's 8.7 million votes.

At the end of Harris's speech, the campaign staff did the obligatory balloon drop, though it was a mistake. No one was in a mood to celebrate. The room emptied quickly. Harris and her campaign team agreed to meet at the campaign office on Wilshire Boulevard the following morning.

That next day, she made some thank-you calls to supporters and began thinking about the committee assignments that would give her the greatest impact. She and her team also decided on her first public appearance as senator-elect. It would be at the headquarters of the Coalition for Humane Immigrant Rights of Los Angeles, an immigrant advocacy organization. Reporters covering the event noticed that she choked up when she recalled children asking whether they'd be deported.

"You are not alone," she told the gathering, "you matter and we've got your back."

Senator Kamala Harris had staked out the posture she would bring with her to Washington. Harris didn't discuss her next campaign that night or the day after. However, her team of consultants could not help but think ahead and contemplate what might come in Campaign 2020.

26
Stepping onto the National Stage

By Election Day 2016, Kamala Harris and her staff were already months into laying the groundwork for the launch of a Senate career that would propel her into the national spotlight.

But those plans were not her idea — they were urged upon her by her staffers. That's because Harris was too superstitious to consider the possibility of victory until after the polls closed. Focusing on anything else, even for a minute, she thought, could trip up a candidate or damage a political career. But by mid-September, she had a comfortable lead over Sanchez. So when her senior advisers talked to a wider circle of supporters, the subject of what would happen after the election came up regularly. In one of those conversations, a senior Obama administration official told Harris directly that not looking past Election Day would be a big mistake and that she needed to ask for committee assignments. Harris responded that she hadn't made those requests because she hadn't yet won. The official tried to explain the ways of Washington: if Harris were to wait, she would find herself at the end of the line.

Superstition notwithstanding, Harris took the official's advice and asked her campaign staffers to begin working on transition matters. They got to work immediately. That included gaming out how to help Harris get on the committees she wanted, especially those that would give her a high enough national profile to deliver on her ambitious campaign promises.

For starters, she wanted to get on the Environment and Public Works Committee. That committee had jurisdiction over water and forest management, vital as the climate changed and critically important to California. Droughts had become prolonged, and Sierra forests and oak and brush in the hills closer to the coast were burning with a ferocity never before seen. Obama had gotten on that committee as a freshman senator in 2005 and enjoyed it very much. Harris was also interested in the Veterans' Affairs Committee, given that California is home to two million veterans.

Above all, she wanted to get a seat on the

Judiciary Committee, because it dovetailed with her skills and experience as a prosecutor and her interest in criminal justice reform. It was also one of the highest profile of all Senate committees. Its hearings frequently were televised. Judiciary also had a notoriously long line of senators coveting seats on it.

In 2016, the conventional wisdom, the polls, and every other signal pointed to a Hillary Clinton presidency. That meant planning not just for the Senate transition but also for how Harris would plug into the machinery of an incoming Clinton administration and the ripple effects that would have across Washington.

Harris had attributes that most other freshman senators lacked, mostly the backing of Obamaworld. Besides helping her make wise transition decisions, top Obama administration officials and other prominent advisers could give her some standing, maybe pull a few strings and set her apart from the rest of the incoming class.

Harris had national visibility already, too, and support from some of the most prominent Democrats around. Ron Wyden of Oregon was one of several senators who had helped with her Senate campaign. Senators

Elizabeth Warren of Massachusetts, Cory Booker of New Jersey, and Kirsten Gillibrand of New York endorsed her on the day she announced.

There was also the issue of money. Washington campaign advisers had told Harris that she needed to raise $40 million to mount a successful campaign, roughly the same amount that Warren had raised in her 2012 race. Her California team knew she would not need that much. Besides, Harris was not an enthusiastic fund-raiser, never fully comfortable asking acquaintances for money. She ended up raising $15 million for the 2016 race and spending $14.1 million on the campaign. But because she came from a state known as a cash machine for Democrats, she could use the leftover cash to tithe to the Democratic Senatorial Campaign Committee for use in other races around the country. Her willingness to help fellow Democrats put her in good standing with Senator Chuck Schumer of New York, who was the direct recipient of Harris's largesse as the overseer of the Democrats' national Senate campaign effort. It was widely expected that Schumer would breeze to reelection and then replace retiring minority leader Harry Reid of Nevada as the Senate's top Democrat.

Deciding who gets assigned to what Senate committee is a complicated and murky process. There is no clearly articulated protocol. Even if there were, tradition decreed that virtually all the decisions would be made by Schumer. And that gave Harris good reason for optimism.

Committees weren't the only minefield Harris would have to traverse. In a legislative body that runs on seniority and alliances, there were other important relationships Harris would have to cultivate and manage. One of the most important ones would be with the senior senator from California, Dianne Feinstein. Given her seniority, Feinstein had amassed significant power in the upper house. She could help Harris, or not. Developing an alliance with Feinstein would be tricky. Friction dated to Officer Isaac Espinoza's funeral in 2004, when Feinstein publicly rebuked Harris for not seeking the death penalty against Espinoza's killer. Harris would have to walk a tightrope between being too deferential to Feinstein and being too brash or independent. The patchy relationship between Harris and Feinstein had improved. But there was a need for sensitivity and caution. Harris was entering Feinstein's world. Mostly, Harris, like the rest of the nation, would need to recalibrate and reassess, as Donald Trump, the great unknown, prepared to take office.

As is the tradition of the Senate, incoming freshmen were required to be in Washington early, on Monday, November 14, the start of a weeklong onboarding event known informally as the Senate Boot Camp.

Harris told staff she wanted two things. One was a holdover from the initial plan: they would hire as diverse a staff as possible. They'd been told, for instance, that there were few if any Black chiefs of staff at the time and only one who was a legislative director, another key position.

Her second decision was new: they would make sure anyone who had planned on joining a Hillary Clinton administration and was now out of work would be respected and listened to or met with, as possible.

That would mean hundreds of phone calls and emails to answer and dozens of meetings to schedule with Harris or with senior staff. Two of her closest aides, Debbie Mesloh, who had been with her since before she was ever elected, and Michael Troncoso, who had been an integral part of her staff at the Office of Attorney General of California, had moved to Washington to spearhead the effort and to make sure that everyone got a proper response. Both would stay for several months.

One silver lining of the 2016 election had been that three women of color would join the mostly White and male Senate. When Harris reported for duty in the basement of the Hart Senate Office Building, she found herself just down the hall from the other two. Catherine Cortez Masto of Nevada, an ally from their fight against banks in the wake of the foreclosure crisis, would be the nation's first Latina senator. Tammy Duckworth, the disabled war hero from Illinois, was the first Thai American woman elected to the Senate. They all bonded immediately.

To Harris's welcome surprise, Feinstein stepped up as a key partner and ally from the start. The display of generosity surprised — and even shocked — some of her staff, who had hoped for the best but prepared for the worst. Feinstein and outgoing senator Barbara Boxer helped Harris with the many unexpected logistical issues, like office space politics. Feinstein also helped Harris with staffing and offered up her own staff to help with anything Harris needed. And Feinstein gave Harris some advice that would not only help shape her time in the Senate but propel her into the political stratosphere: Harris should think about joining the Senate Select Committee on Intelligence, more commonly known as Senate Intel.

As one of the longest-serving committee members, Feinstein cautioned that it was a beast of a job, with grueling hours, long committee hearings, and numerous closed sessions at which some of the nation's most sensitive and urgent matters are discussed in secret. Because senators cannot hire their own staffers to help them with the daily deluge of top-secret information, a lot of the work falls on senators themselves, and the workload is huge. Feinstein warned Harris that if she landed on the committee, she could expect to receive a bulging packet of classified intelligence reports and memos to pore over late into the night in order to be ready for the morning barrage of decisions and meetings.

Feinstein also warned Harris that there was another drawback to being on the committee. Because all of its work, by nature, is classified, it's largely a thankless and anonymous task. And there was almost nothing Harris could do while on the committee to make a name for herself in the Senate or to establish a national profile and further her political career. As such, many senators, especially freshmen and those with aspirations to higher office, historically looked elsewhere when submitting their committee assignment requests. Harris put in for the job anyway.

It was a busy time. Harris was entertaining offers from several ranking Democrats on key committees, including Wyden of Oregon, who was infuriating Republicans with his deft poking as ranking member of the Finance Committee. One of the first questions Wyden asked Harris after the election was: "Hey, Kamala, you got any interest in being on the Finance Committee?" Wyden also wanted to see Harris on the Environment and Public Works Committee, given their mutual interest in protecting western states from enormous wildfires. And Wyden knew her reputation as a tough inquisitor would come in handy.

Everyone wanted Harris "because she's that talented and valuable as a senator," Wyden recalls telling her. "She knows there are queues and all the rest, but I think it'd be fair to say that there are a lot of ranking members that were hoping she'd be on their committees." Harris responded by telling Wyden about her own agenda and what she wanted to accomplish.

"I kind of got the feeling that if she had her way," Wyden said, "she'd be on a whole bunch of committees."

When Schumer announced the committee assignments on December 20, 2016, Harris hit the equivalent of a political jackpot. She didn't get a seat on the Judiciary Committee, given the queue of senators many years her senior, but she did get a seat on four committees, all of them high profile. One was Senate Intel. Another was Environment and Public Works. Harris was also assigned to the Senate Budget Committee, one of the key committees with jurisdiction over the Affordable Care Act. And she was given another slot that guaranteed a national spotlight: a seat on the Homeland Security and Governmental Affairs Committee. Harris wasted no time in announcing her new posts, saying they had put her in the perfect position to take on the Trump administration and the president-elect himself.

"These four committees will be key battlegrounds in the fight for the future of our country," Harris said. "At a time when so many Californians and Americans are uncertain about our future, I will aggressively fight for our families and the ideals of our nation."

That Harris was well on her way to making a name for herself on the national stage wasn't a shock to any Californian who had gotten to know her. But she was shifting her ways. Perhaps it was that she no longer had to be mindful that she was representing the State of California in litigation and could be freer to express her opinions. Clearly, Trump's election — and hers — was having an impact. Given her status, Harris prepared to lead the resistance to this most unlikely, unorthodox, divisive, and, as she came to view him, racist president.

27
The Resistance

On January 3, 2017, Vice President Joe Biden administered the oath of office to Kamala Harris as California's forty-fifth senator. The daughter of Shyamala Gopalan and Donald Harris, immigrants from India and Jamaica who came to America in search of higher education and better lives, was the second Black woman to serve in this most exclusive club and the first woman of Indian descent.

Harris arrived having been briefed by the best political minds in Washington and California on how to succeed in the Senate. Above all, hire a good staff and come prepared. She did that and more. But nothing could have prepared Harris — or the rest of the Senate — for the maelstrom that began with the start of the 115th session of Congress.

Instead of what all of Washington had expected — a friendly handoff of the levers of power from President Obama to Hillary Clinton, former rivals who had become aligned — Donald J. Trump was crashing the party. Trump's intention was to undo as many achievements by Obama and congressional Democrats as possible.

Trump's nominees for positions overseeing that dismantling would undergo confirmation hearings immediately, in a Senate that was more bitterly divided along party lines than any person could remember.

Republicans, who controlled the Senate and House of Representatives, would ram through everything the incoming administration wanted on critical issues, including immigration, the environment, health insurance, taxes, and Supreme Court nominees. Democrats could do little more than protest.

In the days leading up to Trump's inauguration, outgoing Obama administration officials were gravely concerned about intelligence suggesting that Trump's campaign, and perhaps the president-elect himself, might have colluded with Russia in ways that helped him defeat Hillary Clinton. Working in secret, Obama's national security team raced to investigate any potential ties before Trump took the reins of power on January 20. The Obama administration's goal was to document and safeguard incriminating information lest Trump try to whitewash the matter. All of that made for a tense time between the start of Congress and Trump's inauguration.

Democrats saw Harris, who had spent twenty-six years in law enforcement, much of it as a line prosecutor, as someone whose skills would come in handy. Although she hadn't tried a case in more than a decade, she could use her courtroom experience to cross-examine uncooperative Trump administration officials in ways few other senators could.

That, no doubt, was one of the reasons Senate Democratic leader Chuck Schumer put her on so many important committees, including one that is usually out of reach for freshmen: the Senate Intelligence Committee.

One of its longest-ever serving members, Ron Wyden, couldn't remember the last time a first-year senator was given a seat on Intel. But it was becoming increasingly clear in the days after Harris's swearing-in that her election to the Senate could not have been better timed, for herself and her political aspirations and for a Democratic Party on the ropes.

Between Intel, Homeland Security, Environment and Public Works, and Budget,

Harris became a front-line responder trying to hold the Democratic line against many, if not most, of the issues at the heart of Trump's agenda. Her role in that effort, or counter-effort, would only grow and help inform and define Harris's tenure in the Senate and, in time, her run for the White House.

Senator Kamala Harris's sixth day in office, January 10, 2017, was a harbinger of the contentious and exhaustively busy times to come. In the morning, the Homeland Security Committee held a confirmation hearing for retired Marine Corps general John F. Kelly. As head of the U.S. Southern Command, Kelly oversaw all American military operations in Central America, South America, and the Caribbean from November 2012 to January 2016. As Trump's nominee for the powerful post of Homeland Security secretary, Kelly would run point on many issues of critical importance to the border state of California, and the nation. The four-star general came so well regarded that the bipartisan outpouring of support for him, and the fawning lawmaker compliments, was noteworthy even for Congress.

"This is a remarkable public servant," North Dakota Democrat Heidi Heitkamp gushed in Kelly's confirmation hearing. "But one of the reasons why I believe that DHS won the Cabinet lottery — and you can tell from perhaps this love fest that we are having with you today — is that you have such a breadth of experience in an area that is very challenging to our Southern Border and really our entire border security."

Harris wasn't nearly so celebratory when it was her turn to ask questions.

After thanking Kelly for his service, she began questioning whether he would carry out Trump's stated plans to build a border wall, deport thousands of people, expand the administration's enforcement authority, and increase the number of detention cells nationwide. Such issues might not matter much in the Dakotas. But they were of paramount importance and interest in California, where 40 percent of the population is Latino, most of them with roots in Central America, and 27 percent of the population is foreign born.

Harris homed in immediately on DACA, short for the Deferred Action for Childhood Arrivals program. One of Obama's signature programs, DACA gave protections to many young people, popularly known as Dreamers, whose parents sought better lives for themselves and their children and crossed the border into the United States with their children in tow. Although Dreamers were not U.S. citizens, most of them had no connection to their parents' home country. California has more Dreamers than any other state by far, 183,000, many of them in college and many others working. Deporting them was said to be one of Trump's first initiatives. Harris rightly wanted to know where Kelly stood.

"Are you familiar that under your predecessors, the director of Homeland Security made the decision and issued the information to the troops?" Harris asked. "It was not the President. Are you familiar with that?"

"Yes, ma'am," Kelly responded.

"OK. And do you agree that many of these young people were brought here as children and only know America as their home?" Harris asked.

"Many of them are in that category" was Kelly's reply.

"And do you agree," Harris continued, "that they are now studying at colleges and universities and graduate schools across our country, some are working in Fortune 100 companies, major institutions, and businesses, both small and large?"

"I am aware that some are, yes," Kelly said.

"And do you intend then to use the limited law enforcement resources of DHS to remove them from the country?"

"I will follow the law," Kelly said.

In her questioning, Harris had been polite but direct: throughout the hearing, she came across as much more of a polished lawmaker than the fearsome bulldog of a prosecutor that some of her colleagues expected. But in this case, she got an answer to her question. Kelly was suggesting, without stating it directly, that he would oversee a policy that would lead to the deportation of Dreamers. It was a direct threat to more than 150,000 people in Harris's home state.

Harris would save her verdict for Kelly until nine days later, when she issued a statement saying she would vote against him.

"Unfortunately, I can't look Dreamers in the face and offer them any guarantee that General John Kelly won't deport them," she said. "And, without that guarantee, I can't support his nomination for the Department of Homeland Security. For ethical and moral reasons, we have to honor the promise made by the United States government to these kids."

Kelly was confirmed on an 88–11 Senate vote the next day, January 20, and sworn in hours later — on the same day as Trump's inauguration. Harris was one of the eleven; Feinstein voted aye.

An hour or so after Kelly's confirmation hearing concluded, Harris attended her first public hearing of the Senate Intel Committee.

On the witness list were four of the government's top national security officials, who were there to brief senators on a just-released intelligence report about Russia's multipronged effort to sway the presidential election in Trump's favor.

At the time, public speculation — and alarm — about the Trump campaign's possible assistance from Russia had reached a fever pitch, and the president-elect was doing little to refute it except to denounce it as "fake news."

While still in office, in December 2016, President Obama had tasked the Office of the Director of National Intelligence, FBI, CIA, and National Security Agency with compiling the top-secret report titled *Assessing Russian Activities and Intentions in Recent US Elections.* A much-redacted, declassified version of it had been released a few days in advance of the hearing, and its conclusions were chilling.

The report said Russia had indeed carried out a comprehensive cyber campaign to sabotage the presidential election and help Trump and that it was personally ordered by Russian president Vladimir Putin.

"Russian efforts to influence the 2016 US presidential election represent the most recent expression of Moscow's longstanding desire to undermine the US-led liberal democratic order," the report said, "but these activities demonstrated a significant escalation in directness, level of activity, and scope of effort compared to previous operations."

Trump and Obama were both briefed on the report and given a copy of it.

Afterward, Trump issued a statement trying to spread the blame, asserting that not only Russia but China and other countries and groups too may have sought to breach Democratic and Republican computer systems. And, he added, "there was absolutely no effect on the outcome of the election."

The public report, however, hadn't addressed the issue of the outcome of the election. And while the highly classified version of the report contained the same findings, it was far more detailed regarding what it said were "key elements of the influence campaign." Those details were explosive enough to rock the Senate and the rest of Washington.

Among its findings, according to the *Washington Post,* was that U.S. spy agencies had unverified but credible intelligence that Moscow had kompromat, or embarrassing and compromising information, on Trump's personal life and finances. That meant the soon-to-be occupant of the White House and world's most powerful man was potentially subject to blackmail and coercion by one of America's most aggressive enemies after it had helped him get elected.

Those findings were reportedly contained in a two-page summary attached to the full report. That addendum, the *Washington Post* reported, also included allegations of ongoing contact between members of Trump's inner circle and Kremlin representatives.

As California attorney general, Harris had been privy to sensitive law enforcement information about transnational gangs, terrorist threats, and more. The Senate Intelligence Committee operates on a different and far deeper level of secrecy. Its entire staff works out of a bunkerlike SCIF, or sensitive compartmented information facility, within a windowless vault in the bowels of the Senate office complex. For Harris, who had walked into the Senate a few days earlier, being "read in" on matters so vital to national security was eye-opening.

The Intel hearing itself was a spectacle. It was carried live by major cable news networks, and with more than 150 cameras trained on the senators, it had all the trappings of the Watergate impeachment hearings. By the time it was her turn, many of the critical questions had already been asked.

So Harris instead put a series of well-informed questions to Director of National Intelligence James Clapper about whether U.S. intelligence agencies were making sure that the computer networks and personal devices of the president-elect and his transition team were protected from Russia's ongoing cyber-penetration efforts.

"We've done what we can to educate the transition team about the pitfalls of mobile devices in secure areas and the like," Clapper said.

"Do you believe your education efforts have been successful?" Harris asked.

"You'd have to ask them, I think," Clapper said cryptically.

In the coming months, one media report after another documented exactly the kind of careless security breaches that Harris had inquired about, including top Trump officials using private cell phones and computers to conduct White House business. Harris asked a few more questions of FBI director James Comey before everyone headed into a closed session, but nothing contentious.

Two days later, though, Harris began to go on the offensive, in the confirmation hearing for Trump's nominee for CIA director, Congressman Mike Pompeo, a Republican from Kansas.

Harris bore in, starting with the findings of the just-released intelligence report.

"Do you fully accept its findings, yes or no?" Harris asked Pompeo about the intel report.

"I've seen nothing to cast any doubt on the findings in the report," Pompeo responded.

Harris also took a detour into some mostly uncharted waters for the committee, giving her Senate colleagues evidence both of her preparedness for hearings and her willingness to inject progressive politics into intelligence matters.

She questioned Pompeo at length about his known skepticism about climate change despite a near unanimous consensus from U.S. government scientists, wanting to determine exactly how skeptical he really was. And more important, Harris asked Pompeo if his personal beliefs would negatively influence the CIA's ongoing efforts to gather intelligence about how global warming was already triggering rising instability and conflict around the world.

When Pompeo dodged, Harris came back a second time, late in the hearing, to pin him down.

"Mr. Pompeo, on the issue of climate change, I understand you're not a scientist. What I'd like to know and what I want to hear from you is I want a CIA Director who is willing to accept the overwhelming weight of evidence when presented, even if it turns out to be politically inconvenient or requires you to change a previously held position."

Harris got Pompeo on the record as saying that he would.

She then told the nominee for CIA director she was concerned that the Trump administration would adopt discriminatory practices that undermined the CIA's efforts to recruit and retain LGBTQ and Muslim American employees, "who serve often with great distinction at the agency" and at great risk to themselves.

During a series of questions about the specific laws that apply, Harris elicited from Pompeo an assurance that all employees would be protected equally. Those early hearings, and others, showed that Harris was not the overnight sensation the media would later make her out to be. Nor was she a spotlight-hogging self-promoter. She was getting the work done.

Kamala Harris showed up well prepared. During hearings, she would spread out and open up her thick binders of documents and notes and write her questions on the fly on little white Post-its. Harris was also a quick study of the Senate's arcane rules of procedure and protocol. And she appeared to be respectful of her colleagues and cognizant of her place in the Senate hierarchy.

As she set out to do, Harris hired a smart and diverse staff, bringing east her top Sacramento deputy, Nathan Barankin, as her Senate chief of staff, Capitol Hill veterans Rohini Kosoglu as deputy chief of staff, and Clint Odom, who would be the Senate's only Black legislative director, and Tyrone Gayle, a twenty-nine-year-old African American press secretary who had worked on Hillary Clinton's campaign. To oversee her national media strategy, Harris hired Lily Adams. The granddaughter of the late Texas governor Ann Richards, Adams had served in a similar role for Hillary Clinton. She quickly became well regarded among Senate staffers and known for playing an integral role in preparing Harris for high-impact moments, like her questioning of top Trump officials. Harris's go-to political consultants in San Francisco, Ace Smith, Sean Clegg and Dan Newman, continued to advise her as well.

Harris reached out to other Democrats and Republicans alike to work on issues of mutual interest. One was Kentucky Republican senator Rand Paul. They shared an interest in reforming the cash bail system. They also agreed to cosponsor legislation to protect undocumented youth under DACA. And she asked Arizona Republican senator John McCain out for coffee. He shared with her the wisdom of his time in Congress and on the campaign trail.

All the while, Harris's publicity machine was busy broadcasting her positions across Twitter and other social media on signature issues and trumpeting news of her strident concerns about Trump, his administration's policies, and their alleged wrongdoing and cover-ups.

Harris built a loyal and national Twitter following, often focusing on Trump's actions against immigrants, working families, and people of color. As winter turned to spring, Harris became more aggressive in her questioning of witnesses in a never-ending gauntlet of Intel, Homeland Security, Environment, and Budget hearings. She began appearing with increasing frequency on the nation's most-watched news shows and in the pages of its most prominent newspapers. Her global profile grew, thanks to the huge cadre of foreign correspondents in Washington to chronicle the Trump administration for their audiences back home.

By early summer, Harris had emerged as one of the Trump administration's most aggressive and high-profile critics. Keeping true to her 2016 election-night speech, Kamala Harris was fast becoming a leader in the Democratic resistance to Trump in the Senate. More broadly, she was seen as a symbol of a new generation in Washington.

With Harris's arrival, change had come to the Senate. More was yet to come.

28
"I'M ASKING THE QUESTIONS"

On January 29, 2017, Senator Kamala Harris, following in the footsteps of parents who marched for civil rights in the 1960s, joined protesters outside the White House who were denouncing President Trump's declaration that he was banning travel from seven majority-Muslim nations, an order that proved to be illegal.

In Washington, Republican senators John McCain and Lindsey Graham condemned the ban, warning it "will become a self-inflicted wound in the fight against terrorism." Back in California, the Muslim travel ban confirmed some of the worst fears of the anti-Trump resistance. Lieutenant Governor Gavin Newsom, already running for governor, joined a thousand people at an impromptu protest at San Francisco International Airport. They sang the Woody Guthrie protest ode "This Land Is Your Land."

That night, Harris called Secretary of Homeland Security John Kelly at his home to voice her concerns and those of her constituents and to elicit details about the administration's plans.

"Why are you calling me at home with this?" Kelly gruffly replied to the U.S. senator. Harris, stunned at the response, tried to explain. The call ended quickly with Kelly saying he'd get back to the senator. He never did, she writes in her autobiography.

In the months ahead, Harris gradually amped up the intensity of her cross-examinations of Trump administration officials. She took that to a fierce new level on June 6, 2017, when Kelly came before the Homeland Security Committee. Harris was itching for this day.

Harris grilled Kelly on Trump administration threats to cut off federal anti-terrorism funds to cities that didn't enforce harsh new immigration detention orders, a direct threat to California's major cities, even when those cities' lawyers concluded it would expose them to civil liability.

Harris's questions came in rapid-fire succession, and she frequently cut off Kelly in an effort to get him to provide responsive answers. Visibly frustrated, the normally unflappable former general began protesting that he couldn't get a word in edgewise.

Finally, an exasperated Kelly said, "Would you let me finish once?"

"Excuse me?" Harris replied. "I'm asking the questions."

So it went. Republicans on the committee weren't happy. Harris didn't seem to care that she had ruffled their feelings.

On June 7, 2017, Deputy Attorney General Rod Rosenstein appeared before Senate Intel. Senators wanted to know about his role in Trump's decision a month earlier to fire FBI director James Comey. They also intended to question Rosenstein about his decision to appoint Robert Mueller as a special counsel to oversee the Justice Department probe into possible ties between Russia and Trump's presidential campaign.

When Harris's turn came, she peppered Rosenstein with yes-or-no questions and, as with Kelly, interrupted when he started to dodge. Harris's focus was on getting Rosenstein to commit to writing a letter granting Mueller complete independence as a bulwark against White House interference or retaliation.

As she spoke, she pointed at Rosenstein, pen in hand. Flustered, he explained that the issue was complicated and that his response would require "a very lengthy conversation" with Harris.

"Can you give me a yes-or-no answer?" Harris replied.

"It's not a short answer, Senator," Rosenstein said.

"It is," Harris shot back. "Either you are willing to do that, or you are not."

As Harris's questioning got increasingly testy, committee chairman Richard Burr, a Republican from North Carolina, cut her off. Looking in her direction, Burr said, "Would the senator suspend? The chair is going to exercise its right to allow the witnesses to answer the question. . . ."

Harris, incredulous, was not accustomed to being told to, in essence, stifle herself. She whipped her head around to glare at Burr. Squinting her eyes in disapproval, she listened as his rebuke of her continued before a live TV audience estimated to be in the millions. Burr told Harris he was exercising his right as chairman by giving Rosenstein "the courtesy, which has not been extended all the way across," of responding how he saw fit. When Harris tried to explain her line of questioning, Burr cut her off again. Democrats stayed silent, some looking at their notes. Kamala Harris was definitely leaving an impression.

The exchange went viral immediately: old White male senators had "shushed" Harris, the only Black woman on the committee. As it exploded on Twitter, the rancorous partisan bickering worsened between Democratic and Republican senators and between Democrats and the Trump administration.

Within hours, Harris and her staff had shrewdly exploited the incident by coming up with a meme:

"Courage, Not Courtesy."

That went viral as well, and so did related merchandise. "RT this if you've ordered your 'Courage, Not Courtesy' sticker and want your friends and family to get one too," Harris tweeted. Some of it, unaffiliated with Harris, added the words HARRIS 2020. Six days after that, Harris herself would engineer her most viral moment of all.

The Intel Committee's witness that day on June 13, 2017, was Jeff Sessions, though some of Harris's staffers made a point of saying aloud his full name, Jefferson Beauregard Sessions III, in recognition that, like his father and grandfather, he was named for the Confederate president and a Confederate general. As a U.S. senator from Alabama, Sessions was the first major Republican to endorse Trump's presidential run in February 2016. But as attorney general, he followed Justice Department guidelines and recused himself from the Trump-Russia probe, citing a conflict of interest stemming from his appointed role as the head of the Trump campaign's national security advisory council. That infuriated Trump, because it put a civil servant, Rosenstein, in charge of the investigation. For those and other reasons, Sessions's testimony was must-see TV, and some were tuning in to see Harris cross-examine him. They were curious what she could draw out about what he knew about possible Trump connections to Russia during and after the campaign, about why Trump fired Comey, and about Trump's efforts to derail the probe.

"Smoke the hell out of Jeff Sessions Tuesday," Jim Spears, a Louisiana voter, a college teacher, and an occasional tweeter, said in a tweet to Harris. "I'm eager for the grill." Spears was one Democratic voter who thought Harris was the Democrats' best weapon against Sessions, that she would "just cut through Jeff Sessions' bullshit and racism to get whatever answers she needed."

Harris's rapid questioning looked especially jarring in contrast with Sessions, a seemingly mild-mannered, elfin five-foot-five septuagenarian with a southern drawl. His genteel disposition aside, he had taken the hardest line possible against immigration when he was in the Senate. Sessions spent much of the hearing dodging questions.

"I don't recall," he restated.

Harris interrogated Sessions about whether he had met Russian business leaders or intelligence operatives at the 2016 Republican National Convention in Cleveland, Ohio, which, as it turned out, was a focus of Kremlin operations. He said he had not. Then, he said, he wanted to clarify his answer given how many people he'd met in Cleveland. Harris continued to press him, and a visibly rattled Sessions pleaded with her to slow down.

"I'm not able to be rushed this fast," Sessions stammered. "It makes me nervous."

As many of her current and former staffers can attest, Harris can have that effect on people. She kept at it, demanding more specificity from Sessions about what law or policy he was invoking in saying he couldn't discuss key issues or share documents with the committee. Sessions replied, "I'm not able to answer the question." Harris wasn't buying it.

"You rely on that policy. Did you not ask your staff to show you the policy that would be the basis for refusing to answer the majority of the questions that have been asked of you?"

As she continued, once again, Harris was shut down.

"Senator Harris, let him answer," one of the senior Republicans on the committee told her.

Afterward, Republican senators and conservative commentators accused Harris of being disrespectful and failing to follow Senate rules of order. Old-time Washington hands, especially old men, were having difficulty with Harris's audacity and her tenacity. But no one who knew her back in California had any doubt that this was Kamala Harris's way.

29
"Yes or No"

Kamala Harris's star was rising after the June 2017 hearings where she grilled top Trump administration officials John Kelly, Jeff Sessions, and Rod Rosenstein.

Not surprisingly, Republicans were critical of Harris's style. She also was irritating some of her fellow Democrats and career Homeland Security officials who had no political ax to grind but felt insulted by her.

In private, some Democrats believed her pugilistic tone was mostly for show. Others suspected her thirst for the spotlight was part of a long-range plan to "pull an Obama" by staying just long enough in the Senate to get the credentials needed to run for president. Fueling that view, Harris announced in mid-April that she had just returned from a weeklong trip to the Middle East, an important way for a senator seeking a place on the national stage to burnish her foreign policy credentials. In Iraq, she met with California service members supporting local forces in fighting ISIS, inquiring whether they had the support they needed there and also when they returned home during and after deployment. She traveled to Jordan to witness firsthand the devastating impact of the Syrian refugee crisis caused by President Bashar al-Assad's regime.

"It is critical we have a sound, detailed, and long-term national security strategy to combat terrorism in the Middle East, and an immigration policy that provides a safe haven to those fleeing violence and oppression," Harris said in a press release on her return.

The trip wasn't part of any formal congressional delegation. Rather, she went because of her positions on the Senate Intel and Homeland Security Committees, she explained. However, Harris wasn't on committees with direct oversight of the military, such as Armed Services or Foreign Relations. That didn't escape notice on Capitol Hill, where some veterans recalled that Senator Barack Obama won a prized seat on the Foreign Relations Committee to beef up his foreign policy credentials ahead of his presidential run.

On the Homeland Security Committee,

the resentment ran deep, said a former senior Homeland Security official, who left the department in the summer of 2020 and spoke on condition of anonymity. Some senators and committee staff believed Harris was shirking her share of the tedious work that made up the vast majority of committee business, a galling transgression for a first-year senator. Worse, some officials came to believe that her brusque and antagonistic style was jeopardizing bipartisan efforts on critical security matters that had been years in the making.

"The impression that I am left with is that she's not well liked by the majority of people that had to interact with her on the Homeland Security Committee," said the former senior Department of Homeland Security official, who dealt with senators and committee staff.

Harris could be disrespectful to top-level Department of Homeland Security officials undergoing Senate confirmation, no matter what issues they would be overseeing. That might have been understandable if they would be enforcing Trump's immigration policies, which affected Californians directly. But Homeland Security has 240,000 employees who deal with many apolitical issues and are devoted to trying to keep

Americans safe.

The resentment about that ran so deep at the Department of Homeland Security that when current and former senior officials were coming out publicly in support of Joe Biden, at least four of them decided not to after he named Harris as his running mate, said the former Homeland Security official, who had worked in Republican and Democratic administrations and left in order to come out publicly against Trump. "They were like, 'Sorry, I can't do it.' "The former official added, "Something about the way that she operated really bothered these individuals. For them, it seemed like she was always about the politics and not about the mission."

An issue that rubbed some officials wrong was that Harris declined to meet with many people Trump nominated for the highest positions in Homeland Security. Instead, she chose to grill them in public confirmation hearings with yes-or-no questions about complex topics that could not be answered in simple ways. The Trump nominees' inability or refusal to answer questions might make for good sound bites, but it did little to provide the public with answers to some of the most important policy issues of the day. It also didn't help promote the kind of good governance that's needed for the Senate to succeed at its oversight role. Perhaps most important, it didn't help foster productive relationships between top department officials and one of the senators, Harris, who oversaw them.

Traditionally, the kinds of fraught issues that Harris liked to ask about in public hearings are discussed initially in private meetings. Those meetings, known as courtesy calls, come at the end of an exhaustive process for the select few political appointees deemed so critical to the department's mission that they require confirmation by the full Senate.

These appointees are required to send enormous amounts of personal and professional background information to the oversight committee. After digesting that information, the committee sends the nominee a lengthy series of policy questions. Once the nominees reply, they meet with the committee staff, potentially for hours. The last stop is the courtesy call with senators. It's the most important: it's how senators and senior staff get a feel for the nominees and their management style. The calls are akin to an interview for a big job. In less partisan times, the meetings could make the difference between confirmation and rejection. Even if they agree to disagree, the senator and nominee can establish some rapport and trust.

In the spring of 2017, Elaine Duke, nominated by Trump to the second-highest-ranking position in the Department of Homeland Security, sought a meeting with all the Homeland Security Committee members. She especially wanted to meet with Democrats so she could provide them with detailed answers to issues that were in the headlines and that seemed too complicated for the structure of a public hearing. Duke, a career civil servant, had spent twenty-eight years in public service, working in the administrations of Obama and George W. Bush. Almost all the Senate Democrats met with her privately, but not Harris. Harris asked her questions in public.

"I know I'm not the only one she didn't want to meet with," said Duke, who is widely seen as an apolitical moderate. "My understanding is that in general she did not meet with any of the Republican nominees."

Duke said Harris's prosecutor-like questions seemed more geared to making headlines than collectively figuring out the best way forward, leaving her wondering: "Are you trying to glean information for oversight or are you trying to indict?"

Duke was confirmed on an 85–14 vote in 2017, with Harris voting against her confirmation and Feinstein for it. She served until April 2018, including five months as acting Homeland Security secretary. She had no comment when asked whether Biden's choice of Harris as his running mate influenced her decision to not publicly support the Democratic nominee.

"When you look at her public record, the hearings and the campaign, is there an underlying anger there?" Duke asked. "And will that help, or further divide the country in terms of moving away from compassion and more toward anger?"

Donald Trump's leadership style as president was the same as it was during his campaign. He was playing a part in a reality show, with enough interesting characters and plotlines to keep audiences riveted and glued to their screens. Whether she did so intentionally or not, Harris was one of a few Democrats to play Trump's own game. She was becoming an easy-to-identify character herself. She did so in Trump's way, too, by grabbing the spotlight to get her message out and change the narrative.

Under normal circumstances, lawmakers

are criticized for acting like politicians and seeking the limelight. Perhaps because of jealousy or competition, blatant self-promotion is seen as a vice, not a virtue. But as Trump took over Washington, Harris rose above the din. Her ability to come up with pithy sound bites, viral videos, and eye-catching headlines elevated her from being a bit player in the show to becoming a star. The more Republicans made her the public face of the Democratic resistance, the more the Republicans made Harris's star rise even higher. Reporters helped, too, seizing on the narrative that Harris was helping create that she was engaged in a David and Goliath battle with Trump and his administration.

That story line was especially popular with reporters who had flocked to Washington to cover the Trump drama for the folks back home. What perpetrators of that narrative often overlooked was that Harris was by no means the only Democrat battling Trump and scoring victories. Many other Democratic lawmakers were also expertly pinning down administration officials on a variety of issues and provoking Trump enough for him to single them out.

One was Congressman Adam Schiff, the Democrat from the Los Angeles suburb of

Burbank who considered running for the Senate seat Harris won and now was leading the House version of the Trump-Russia investigation. Another was a first-term congresswoman from New York, Alexandria Ocasio-Cortez.

The Senate was full of Trump resisters, too, including at least two former prosecutors who hadn't called nearly as much attention to their backgrounds as Harris did. Senator Sheldon Whitehouse oversaw scores of prosecutors as the U.S. attorney for Rhode Island. Richard Blumenthal of Connecticut had been the state's attorney general for more years than Harris served as California's attorney general. All six of the other Democrats on the Intel Committee were skilled at getting answers from even the most hostile of witnesses. The committee's ranking Democrat, Senator Mark Warner, was particularly good at it.

Some of the old guard, like Feinstein, were renowned for being thoroughly prepared, asking informed questions, and getting the answers they needed. But where Harris would rely on direct confrontation, Feinstein acted more on instinct.

Feinstein elicited perhaps the biggest money quote of the Trump-Russia hearings during her questioning of former FBI director James Comey. Comey's appearance, a day after Rosenstein's, came amid media reports that Trump had invited him to the White House for a private dinner for two, demanded loyalty from him, and then, when Comey refused, fired him without cause. The fact that Comey had taken detailed contemporaneous — and court-admissible — notes of everything made his appearance especially significant.

So did the fact that Trump, in response to those reports, hinted in a tweet that maybe there were secret White House tapes that would prove Comey wrong.

Comey spent hours testifying, often giving long and sometimes rambling answers to friendly questions from committee Democrats, including Harris. In the middle of his response to a question from Feinstein, he said, "Look, I've seen the tweet about tapes. Lordy, I hope there are tapes," before returning to the subject at hand. A video clip of that exchange was posted to the internet and viewed by millions before the day was out.

In normal times, Harris's brash confidence and unapologetic ambition would have generated more friction within the ultra-competitive Senate. But the timing of her arrival proved fortuitous. From the start of the 115th Congress, Senate Democrats quickly realized that they faced a far greater threat from the Trump administration than they did from one another. Most pulled together in response.

Many of the staffers who make the Senate run found Harris to be far more approachable than most of her colleagues. That, in turn, paid off handsomely for her.

"In my interactions with her, I've found her to be extremely personable and funny when it comes to dealing with staff," said one senior staffer to a Democratic senator on the Intel Committee. "Many senators have somewhat of an imperious attitude when it comes to staffers, but that definitely isn't the case with Senator Harris."

Wyden and Harris formed a special bond. The two were often seen walking and talking in the Senate hallways together, the six-foot-four Wyden towering over Harris, who is five foot two. Wyden, who went to college on a basketball scholarship, and Harris spent a lot of their work downtime talking about her Golden State Warriors and his Portland Trailblazers.

"Kamala Harris comes to play every day. I mean, every single day. She's prepared, she's focused, she's smart, she's effective.

She does her homework," Wyden said. "And that's really the coin of the realm of the Senate: who's doing their homework and who's just throwing press releases out for a ten-second sizzle and is not really serious about that."

For years, Wyden doggedly pursued lines of questioning that raised awareness about a raft of significant issues and concerns. He had, for example, railed for more than sixteen years about government overreach on surveillance, torture, drone strikes, and other U.S. intelligence and judicial matters in prosecuting the war on terrorism. But he often found himself voted down by a 13–2 or even a 14–1 margin. With Harris on the committee, he found an ally. She voted with him on many of the most significant issues before the committee, after doing her own research.

Although Harris's vote was not enough usually to tip the balance in most cases, her support made a big difference in helping Wyden promote an amendment that would have prohibited the use of Section 215 of the Patriot Act to collect Americans' internet search history and web browsing records. They lost by one vote. In January 2017, after Wyden was reelected to his fourth term, he took his daughter Scarlett to his ceremonial swearing-in in the Old Senate Chamber. The redheaded four-year-old drew laughs by giving Biden, who was swearing in senators, an unusual but skeptical look.

"I actually showed it to a few people on the floor because they had asked me about it," Wyden said. "And so there was a group of us and everybody said, 'What's she doing in it?' And Kamala piped up and said, 'Scarlett's giving the vice president of the United States side-eye, everybody! That's what's going on!' "

Thinking about the episode later, Wyden concluded that Harris truly did bring to the Senate something new. She shares recipes. She wears Chuck Taylors. She invites senators over for small dinners. She has an interesting family. She loves basketball.

"She is somebody who is just a very interesting person to be around."

30
Harris v. Kavanaugh

On October 9, 2017, Senator Dianne Feinstein announced via Twitter that she would run in 2018 for another term, although she hadn't exactly figured out the newfangled world of Twitter. She had, at last count, 7,557 Twitter followers. Kamala Harris, adept at the no-longer-new modes of communication, had 6.9 million. This would come in handy.

In California and Washington, many Democrats had hoped that Feinstein would step aside after a storied Senate career that began in 1992. At the end of another six-year term, she would be ninety-one. But Feinstein believed she had plenty left to give. As the ranking Democrat on the Senate Judiciary Committee, she was deeply involved in the confirmation and, occasionally, rejection of President Trump's nominees to lifetime appointments to the federal bench. Within minutes of Feinstein's announcement, Harris sent a fund-raising letter to her own supporters asking for contributions to Feinstein's reelection campaign.

"Since joining the Senate in January, I have found few better allies in our fight to stop the radical agenda of Donald Trump than Dianne," Harris wrote. "She's joined with us in every major fight."

But that alliance was about to be tested.

Kamala Harris could not block the confirmation of Brett Kavanaugh to the Supreme Court in September 2018, though it wasn't for lack of trying. Through that hearing, Harris showed a wider public that she was unafraid to confront powerful men, that she was a warrior, and that she understood the need to comfort women who had been harmed.

Democrats knew the math. With Republicans holding fifty-one of the one hundred seats, Senate leader Mitch McConnell had the votes to confirm Kavanaugh. Democrats could, however, mess with the process. Harris helped with that.

As the confirmation hearings opened on Tuesday, September 4, 2018, Iowa senator Chuck Grassley, chairman of the Judiciary Committee, was eighty-four, the second-oldest member of the Senate, a year younger than Feinstein, the ranking Democrat on the committee. When Grassley gaveled the hearings open, Democrats, starting with Harris, interrupted him. It was, of course, orchestrated.

"We cannot possibly move forward, Mr. Chairman, with this hearing," Harris said, seconds into Grassley's opening. Harris, like the other Democrats, pointed out that Democrats were given forty-two thousand pages pertaining to Kavanaugh's background just fifteen hours before and had not had an opportunity to review them.

While protesters demonstrated outside, some of them wearing the crimson *Handmaid's Tale* costumes, Democrat Cory Booker of New Jersey boomed, "Mr. Chairman, what is the rush? What are we trying to hide by not having the documents out front?"

Grassley, in his folksy tone, repeatedly declared the postponement requests as being out of order, and the hearing proceeded. Senators, legal experts, and character witnesses spent nearly seven hours giving interminable opening statements and offering their opinions, good and bad, of Kavanaugh.

In the coming days, Democrats sought to elicit information from Kavanaugh, and he avoided giving them answers. Harris was in the thick of it, though in proceedings marked by outbursts and acrimony, she was actually one of the tamer combatants, most likely because she was still very much the junior member of the committee, which included Cory Booker and Amy Klobuchar of Minnesota, each of them planning presidential campaigns. Pundits couldn't resist making cracks about how the trio was regarding the hearing as a launchpad for higher office. Republican senators seemed less amused by that prospect, accusing Democrats of unfairly piling on Kavanaugh to score points with their party and voters, as if Republicans wouldn't do the same if circumstances were reversed.

Harris's turn to face Kavanaugh came late on the first full day when senators had an opportunity to question the nominee. Her questioning proved confusing. "Judge, have you ever discussed Special Counsel Mueller or his [Trump-Russia] investigation with anyone?"

Sure, he answered. He had discussed the Mueller investigation with other judges. Harris then asked if he'd ever discussed it with anyone from the law firm of Trump's personal lawyer, Marc Kasowitz. Either Kavanaugh didn't remember or he did a good job of pretending that was the case. As he fumbled with vague and noncommittal responses, Harris kept at it. In a moment of drama, she added, "Be sure about your answer, sir."

Republican senators cut in. Senator Mike Lee of Utah interrupted Harris's questioning to say law firms have so many lawyers, and change them so frequently, that Kavanaugh shouldn't be expected to remember.

"They're constantly metastasizing," Lee said. "They break off; they form new firms. They're like rabbits. They spawn new firms. There is no possible way we can expect this witness to know who populates an entire firm."

After a brief skirmish by other senators over who can interrupt the proceedings and when, Harris returned to the same point: Had Kavanaugh talked to anyone at Trump's personal attorney's law firm?

"I think you can answer the question without me giving you a list of all employees of that law firm," she told him.

Ultimately, Harris concluded that Kavanaugh hadn't denied speaking to anyone at the firm and moved on. The exchange became one of the most talked about of the entire hearing. But it was, at best, inconclusive. Kasowitz and others claimed such a conversation had never happened. Harris was lampooned in the media and by conservatives about trying to be too dramatic, only to have her attempt fall flat. While her aides said she had specific information, that information never became public. She seemed to have asked a question not knowing the answer, something a practiced prosecutor would not do. But if that line of questioning flopped, she found a way to recover.

Harris had found a 1999 op-ed that Kavanaugh wrote for the *Wall Street Journal* about an obscure court case in which he twice used the term "racial spoils system." What did that term mean? she asked Kavanaugh. He dodged, and she repeated the question, and he dodged again. That happened four more times, and Harris finally gave up, but not before lecturing the federal judge.

"You should know that the same year you wrote your op-ed, a magazine published a cover story — a magazine that is described as being a white supremacist magazine — published a cover story about what are called, quote, the racial spoils system, of, quote, affirmative action, the double standard in crime, sensitivity toward Black deficiencies, and everything else." Harris also cited the writings of a "self-proclaimed Euro-centrist" who referred to "racial spoils."

She pointed out that a Supreme Court justice ought to be aware that certain terms "are loaded and associated with a certain perspective and, sometimes, a certain political agenda."

"Well, I take your point," Kavanaugh replied. "And I appreciate it."

Harris then turned to cases with outsized implications in which the Supreme Court held that states could not prohibit married or unmarried people from using contraceptives. She asked Kavanaugh six different ways if he believed they were correctly decided. He dodged those questions, too, until Harris cornered him by saying Chief Justice John Roberts and Justice Samuel Alito both believed the matter was correctly decided.

"That's what they said," Kavanaugh responded, though he was still being vague on the issue of whether the right to privacy was applied correctly to the use of contraceptives.

"Do you believe the right to privacy protects a woman's choice to terminate a pregnancy?" she asked.

Kavanaugh obfuscated. Harris quoted Ruth Bader Ginsburg from her confirmation hearing in 1993: "This is something central to a woman's life, to her dignity. It's a decision she must make for herself. And when government controls that decision for her, she's being treated as less than a fully adult human responsible for her own choices."

Kavanaugh continued dodging, most likely because he thought he knew where Harris was headed. In reality, Harris was headed down a path that caught Kavanaugh unaware:

"Respectfully, Judge, as it relates to this hearing, you're not answering that question, and we can move on," Harris said.

In a way that seemed like almost an afterthought, she asked, "Can you think of any laws that give government the power to make decisions about the male body?"

Kavanaugh played dumb, asking if she had a more specific question.

"I'll repeat the question," Harris said. "Can you think of any laws that give the government the power to make decisions about the male body?"

Cornered, with a hushed audience and the cameras close up on his face, he replied, "I'm not — I'm not — I'm not thinking of any right now, Senator."

Of course he wasn't. There are no such laws.

The exchange was picked up in news stories that day. Cable pundits discussed it. It became a classic viral moment. Planned Parenthood and other advocates of women's right to control their own bodies pinned it to their pages.

Unlike Kavanaugh, the Yale-Yale man who had graduated at the top of his classes, Harris went to a public law school in San Francisco's Tenderloin district and definitely was not at the top of her class. But she knew the law well enough, and she displayed the trial lawyer's skill of asking a question that cut to the core of what was at stake.

It was, however, a small victory, certainly not sufficient to derail Kavanaugh's confirmation. Another development, unknown to all the senators except for Dianne Feinstein, would have an impact on the process.

On July 5, 2018, Christine Blasey Ford, a psychology professor from Palo Alto, California, called the receptionist for her congresswoman, Anna Eshoo, wanting to pass along information about what Kavanaugh did to her when he was seventeen and she was fifteen, some forty years earlier. She also wanted to somehow stop what she worried would happen: that Kavanaugh would be nominated to the U.S. Supreme Court. She also wanted to remain anonymous. Four days later, President Trump did what Blasey Ford feared by nominating Kavanaugh.

Ford told Eshoo her story on July 20. Eshoo called Feinstein to inform her about it, without revealing Blasey Ford's name. Feinstein asked Eshoo to have her constituent write her story in a letter. She did. Feinstein, honoring Blasey Ford's confidentiality request, held the letter close, failing to tell even Democratic leaders about it. Time was ticking away. In her book about Kavanaugh's confirmation, *Supreme Ambition,* Ruth Marcus of the *Washington Post* writes that, on September 9, with Kavanaugh's confirmation seemingly assured, Eshoo spoke to Harris, telling her about the letter and saying "that nothing seemed to have been done about the allegation."

Harris, Marcus writes, was furious and called Feinstein, "demanding answers about this secret letter." Democratic senators convened in a private caucus and confronted Feinstein. Marcus quotes Harris as telling Feinstein that there would be repercussions: "You've got to figure this out."

In the days ahead, pieces of the story

began leaking in the *Intercept* and the *New Yorker.* Then on September 16, Blasey Ford went public with her allegations in an explosive story in the *Washington Post.* Blasey Ford didn't remember all the details of what happened forty years earlier or even the year. But she alleged that Kavanaugh and his prep school friend Mark Judge maneuvered her into an upstairs bedroom at a party in a wealthy suburb of Washington, D.C., and that Kavanaugh pinned her down and groped her while also trying to take her clothes off. When she tried to scream, she said, a drunken Kavanaugh put his hand over her mouth to mute her screams.

"I thought he might inadvertently kill me," the *Washington Post* story quoted her as saying. Ford said she escaped when someone jumped on top of them, sending them all to the floor.

The allegations set off a remarkable series of accusations between supporters of Blasey Ford and Kavanaugh. Democrats and Republicans on the Judiciary Committee bickered and sniped, and people in and out of the Senate questioned why Feinstein failed to let the rest of the world in on the allegations contained in Blasey Ford's letter.

Feinstein responded with a statement: "That individual strongly requested confidentiality, declined to come forward or press the matter further, and I have honored that decision. I have, however, referred the matter to federal investigative authorities."

When Kavanaugh was forced to return before the committee on September 27 to respond to Blasey Ford's allegations, the two sat side by side at witness tables. Each offered far different but equally riveting testimony.

Harris, drawing on her experience as a prosecutor who had held the hands of victims of sex crimes, began by apologizing to Blasey Ford for her treatment by Republicans trying to neutralize her as a threat to Kavanaugh's confirmation:

"Dr. Ford, first of all, just so we can level set, you know you are not on trial. . . . You are sitting here before members of the United States Senate Judiciary Committee because you had the courage to come forward, because as you have said, you believe it was your civic duty." Harris then guided Blasey Ford through a series of questions as she would any victim of a sexual assault.

Turning to Kavanaugh, Harris tried to extract a commitment from him that he would ask the White House to order the FBI to do a supplemental background investigation in order to, once and for all, get to the bottom of the allegations. She was not successful. The next day, the Republican-controlled Judiciary Committee voted to send his confirmation to the full Senate, and on October 6, 2018, Kavanaugh was confirmed by the slimmest margin in the court's history, 50–48.

In the Kavanaugh hearing, there was the unmistakable echo of the confirmation of Clarence Thomas in 1991, when Kamala Harris was a deputy district attorney in Oakland. Then, a law professor, Anita Hill, was the reluctant witness. In 2018, Blasey Ford, the psychology professor, didn't want to testify. In 1991, Dianne Feinstein watched Hill testify on a television while waiting for a flight at Heathrow Airport. Voters' reaction against the treatment of Hill by men in the Senate helped Feinstein win election to the Senate in 1992, the "Year of the Woman." As a senator twenty-six years later, Feinstein took it upon herself to withhold Blasey Ford's letter, out of concern for the impact on Blasey Ford's life and because she sought to protect her request for confidentiality. Harris worried, too, about the impact on Blasey Ford, but she also believed the central allegation needed to be investigated.

In 2019, *Time* magazine listed Kavanaugh and Blasey Ford as being among its top one hundred most influential people from the year before. Mitch McConnell wrote the blurb that accompanied Kavanaugh's photo. He referred to "unhinged partisanship and special interests" that sought to "distract" the Senate from considering his sterling credentials. Harris wrote the blurb that appeared next to Blasey Ford's photo:

> Her story, spoken while holding back tears, shook Washington and the country. Her courage, in the face of those who wished to silence her, galvanized Americans. And her unfathomable sacrifice, out of a sense of civic duty, shined a spotlight on the way we treat survivors of sexual violence. Christine Blasey Ford's ambition wasn't to become a household name or make it onto this list. She had a good life and a successful career — and risked everything to send a warning in a moment of grave consequence. At her core, she is a teacher. And through her courage, she forced the country to reckon with an issue

that has too often been ignored and kept in the dark.

Their friction over Feinstein's handling of Blasey Ford's letter aside, Harris stuck by her endorsement of Feinstein's reelection. Feinstein won another six-year term in November 2018.

31
A Death in the Family

Ever since she flummoxed Attorney General Jeff Sessions, Kamala Harris had become a favorite of Samantha Bee, Stephen Colbert, and other late-night comics. Increasingly, she had also become a target for Fox News commentators, Donald Trump, and the people in his orbit. Jason Miller, a President Trump loyalist and a talking head on CNN, accused Harris of being "hysterical" during her questioning of Sessions, a classically sexist characterization.

"Really? Really, if anyone was hysterical maybe it was the old man saying that her questions were scaring him," Colbert said, defending Harris in one episode.

Harris's questioning of Sessions elevated her above the crowd of Democratic senators. Her star rose even higher after her performance in the Kavanaugh confirmation hearings. In the closing weeks of the 2018 midterm campaign, she was in high demand. She filled every request possible, even though, unnoticed by her public, she was again confronting the fragility of life. One of her close staffers was sick with cancer, and Harris was quietly aware that he was not likely to make it.

On the surface, Harris kept moving. Clearly contemplating a presidential run, Harris made stops in all the most important states: Iowa, New Hampshire, South Carolina, Nevada. As Election Day neared, she spent at least $709,500 of her campaign funds to help Democratic Senate and House candidates and made donations to state parties and candidates in Florida, Wisconsin, Pennsylvania, Michigan, Iowa, New Hampshire, and South Carolina and back home in Orange County, California.

Reporters were there in South Carolina on October 19, 2018, as Harris denounced Republican efforts to dismantle the Affordable Care Act and unnamed forces sowing "hatred and division." The crowd sang "Happy Birthday" to her, a day before she turned fifty-four. A week earlier, Joe Biden visited South Carolina, the state that would propel him to the Democratic presidential nomination, as it did Hillary Clinton and Barack Obama before him.

Along the way, Harris proposed a middle-class tax cut intended to help people earning $100,000 or less and to raise taxes on big banks. Her proposal was intended to counteract the tax cut President Trump and congressional Republicans had pushed through in 2017. Trump's tax cut greatly benefited corporations and wealthy individuals, but by limiting federal deductions for state and local taxes, the measure cost people in California, New York, and other states that have high property values and that levy high state income taxes.

From South Carolina, she jetted to Iowa. CNN's Maeve Reston was in Cedar Rapids on October 23, reporting that a young English teacher told Harris that the senator "had spoken for all the women who have experienced sexual assault when she questioned the then–Supreme Court nominee Brett Kavanaugh and Christine Blasey Ford."

Harris invited the woman to come close and folded her in a hug as the woman wept.

Reston offered her analysis: "It is far too early to assess Harris' viability within an enormous field of likely 2020 candidates. But with her prosecutorial style and unflappable demeanor during the Kavanaugh hearings, she clearly forged a unique connection with women, one that could serve as a powerful driver in her campaign if she decides to run."

With a headline saying Kamala Harris "May Be the Antidote to Trump," *Des Moines Register* columnist Rekha Basu wrote about the enthusiastic reception Harris was receiving in Iowa, following her performance in the Senate Judiciary Committee confirmation hearings for Kavanaugh. Basu wrote, "And when, at one point, she walked out of the hearing room in frustration, she gave voice to women everywhere who were feeling the same way. 'I can't sit here anymore and be a part of this,' she could be heard saying in a hallway. 'It was so disgusting that they were pushing this through.' "

The column continued: "She comes across as whip smart, warm, impassioned and, maybe most importantly, someone who embodies the aspirations and struggles of every American." And this: "Hearing Harris address the Iowa Asian-Latino Coalition earlier brought reminders of the transcendent power of America's first mixed-race president, and his contention that there was only one America. Lately, that has not rung true. But imagine adding a female perspective to Barack Obama's diverse background."

Edward-Isaac Dovere, among the reporters following Harris in Iowa, wrote in the *Atlantic* on October 26, 2018, that "everywhere she's been, and in the airports in between, from women across ages and races. Crying. Saying thank you. Telling her their own stories."

And he quoted her: "It's about diagnosis and then there needs to be treatment, right? That's also speaking truth — the diagnosis: You have cancer. So that is the truth, now let's deal with it: What's the treatment required? To deny it and not speak the truth means to let it fester."

The statement was at once a metaphor and literal. The beast that is cancer was on her mind that week.

Like many young men drawn to working in politics, Tyrone Gayle was smart, hardworking, savvy, and idealistic. He had a winning smile, could be funny, and could be sharp-tongued with a reporter who annoyed him. In 2012, he worked to elect Tim Kaine of Virginia to the U.S. Senate. In 2014, he was press secretary for the Democratic Congressional Campaign Committee. In the 2016 presidential campaign, he was one of Hillary Clinton's top press officers.

During the 2016 campaign, Gayle was

diagnosed with colon cancer but, after treatment, appeared to have beaten it. In 2017, newly elected senator Kamala Harris hired him as her first press secretary. He quickly became integral to Harris's operation and to her life in D.C. He helped shape her media strategy and keep up on the news she needed to know. They also shared a common heritage. His parents were Jamaican immigrants, as was her father. He helped her build her Spotify playlist. Where her tastes went to Bob Marley and hip-hop, he persuaded her Boyz II Men was worth a listen.

Then his colon cancer reappeared, no doubt reminding Harris of her mother's battles with cancer in 2009. Although Tyrone often had no choice but to be absent from the office, Harris made a point of keeping him in her loop, texting him, calling him, soliciting his advice, telling him he looked handsome as his hair fell out and he lost weight. On May 5, 2018, she wished him all the best when he married the love of his life, Beth Foster. Harris and her husband had thrown a wedding shower for the couple in April and gave them a crystal vase. Beth and Tyrone had met in 2012 when she worked on President Obama's reelection campaign and Gayle was working for Senator Kaine.

A little less than six months later, on October 25, 2018, Lily Adams, Gayle's friend and Harris's communications director, got a call from Beth Foster Gayle. The situation was dire. Adams got in her car and drove to New York. She also relayed the information to Harris. The senator canceled whatever obligations she had that day, thirteen days before the midterm elections, and headed to Reagan Washington National Airport, got a shuttle to New York, and made her way to Memorial Sloan Kettering Cancer Center on the Upper East Side of Manhattan.

Beth Foster Gayle told the story to Anderson Cooper of CNN:

"And she unobtrusively came into the hospital room. She held Tyrone's hand. She told funny stories about him. And she said, 'Goodbye.'

"And she hugged me just as everything in my entire world was falling apart. And she looked deep in my eyes and told me that she would have my back forever. And it is a moment I will never forget for as long as I live."

As the election neared, Trump returned to his old playbook by attacking immigrants and trying to stoke voters' fears. He warned that a supposed caravan of immigrants was making its way north from Central America. As if an invasion were coming, the commander in chief dispatched soldiers, supposedly to defend the southern border against unarmed, destitute, and desperate immigrants.

On October 26, the day after Gayle died, evidence surfaced that Trump's bellicosity played havoc with the minds of people already on the edge. On that day in Plantation, Florida, federal authorities arrested Cesar Sayoc Jr., a onetime wrestler and stripper, who had been living in a van plastered with pro-Trump signs and messages condemning the media and Democrats. He was charged with sending bombs to several prominent Democratic critics of President Trump, including Harris. Each package had a photo of the intended recipient with red Xs over her or his face. None went off, and Sayoc was sentenced to twenty years in prison in 2019.

Harris went about her political business, appearing in Atlanta and speaking at Spelman College, America's oldest private historically Black liberal arts college for women:

"We can honor the ancestors by voting

early. And certainly in the next 10 days, we can send a message that if someone is trying to suppress our vote, then we will vote them out of office. Because that is a fight worth having."

In the days ahead, she would visit Florida, where she stumped for Democrats Senator Bill Nelson and Tallahassee mayor Andrew Gillum, who was running for governor (both lost); Wisconsin, where she campaigned for the defeat of Republican governor Scott Walker (he lost, too); Iowa again; Arizona; and several other states. Democrats reclaimed control of the House of Representatives in 2018, though not the Senate. She would remain in the minority.

But her star was ascending, and she was setting out to win the biggest race of all. First, though, she had an important stop to make.

On the weekend after Election Day, Tyrone Gayle's family and friends gathered for a memorial at the Howard Theatre, not far from where Harris got her undergraduate degree. In her eulogy to Gayle, Harris called him "a warrior, a gentle friendly warrior." She said, "He understood that those of us sitting in these powerful offices have a sacred responsibility to do everything we can for those people who aren't sitting in those offices." She added, "He made me a better public servant. And a better person."

32
"For the People"

Kamala Harris, her closest advisers, and her family converged on the Park Hyatt Residence, Maya Harris's Manhattan apartment overlooking Central Park on July 28 and 29, 2018. They were there to discuss what Harris's consultants — Ace Smith, Sean Clegg, Juan Rodriguez, and Dan Newman — had been calling the "Thing." Should she do the Thing? What if she did the Thing? How would the Thing play out? What effect would the Thing have on their work and their lives?

The Thing was the most consequential decision of Harris's career and probably theirs: whether she should run for president of the United States. Maya Harris, Tony West, Doug Emhoff, Smith, Clegg, Rodriguez, and Harris's Senate chief of staff, Nathan Barankin; his successor, Rohini Kosoglu; Harris's communications director, Lily Adams; and a few others gathered in the building's conference room and gave their best analyses. Pollster David Binder, who had been Obama's pollster, had done a deep inquiry. Participants in focus groups said she came off as strong and having moral authority, as opposed to President Trump, who could not be trusted.

The competition among Democrats would be tough, but her life experience, her career as a prosecutor, and her positions on the side of immigrants could set her apart. Her fund-raising team believed that with her connections to the Bay Area and Los Angeles — the ATM for Democratic presidential candidates — Harris would have a leg up raising money.

Harris mostly listened, though more than once she told the group that if she decided to run, she would run to win. She was not interested in running for second place. Most important, she did not want to lose to Donald Trump. Beating Trump was the existential issue. She understood that a small fraction of presidential candidates ever win their party's nomination, and that at best, her chance of getting into the general election would be 10 percent. She had to want to run, and know why she was running. If she made it to the general election, she wanted to be as certain as possible that she would be a strong general election candidate.

In 2017, the California State Legislature voted to move the state's primary up to the first Tuesday after the first Monday in March, a step that her campaign team helped choreograph. If Harris decided to do the Thing, she thought she'd have a home state advantage over the competitors. She needed to do well enough in Iowa and New Hampshire, better in Nevada, and win in South Carolina. That would give her momentum for the March 3 primary in delegate-rich California. With a win in California, she'd be hard to stop.

No one was a cheerleader. They all tried to remain sober about the path forward. On the final day, it fell to Tony West to argue the cons. There'd be a toll emotionally and physically. Harris needed to know that a full campaign would lay her and her family bare, that every word she uttered would be scrutinized as never before. It was a huge risk, not just for her but for the people she loved, including Doug's children, Harris's stepchildren. They'd all be subject to opposition research. Harris had been in the Senate less than two years. Shouldn't she build more of a record? What if they threw a party and no one came? That would damage her standing and perhaps derail her career.

At the end of it, the politician who had been criticized on occasion as being overly cautious decided to jump in. All the way in.

Harris dashed through the next months, though the dash was controlled and calculated. As her campaign team staffed up and quietly rented space for a headquarters in Baltimore, Harris barnstormed from the confirmation hearings for Supreme Court justice Brett Kavanaugh in September to the campaign trail, stumping for candidates running in the 2018 midterms, many of them in states relevant to the Democratic presidential primary.

In committee hearings that fall and early winter, she questioned Trump administration officials about the treatment of pregnant refugees in custody at the border, and she demanded that the Department of Homeland Security reunite children who had been separated from their parents. She introduced legislation to require that Border Patrol and Immigration and Customs Enforcement agents wear body cameras, and she was one of the authors of antilynching legislation. She toured the destruction caused by the Camp Fire, which killed eighty-six people that fall and destroyed the Northern California town of Paradise. An inconvenient piece of unfinished California business surfaced. In early December 2018, the *Sacramento Bee* reported that in 2017, after Harris had been sworn in as senator, California attorney general Xavier Becerra settled a harassment claim against Harris's director of the Division of Law Enforcement for $400,000. He had come with her to her Senate staff. The settlement was an embarrassment for the senator on multiple levels, at least in part because it reflected on her role as a manager. Her aides said she didn't know that the complaint was filed, let alone that it was being settled. But the Division of Law Enforcement is a major part of the California Department of Justice and its director reports to the attorney general. Harris forced the aide to resign from her Senate staff after the *Bee* story appeared. He had been with her since she was San Francisco district attorney in the mid-2000s. Time to move on. She visited Afghanistan later in December.

In March 2017, two months after she was sworn into the U.S. Senate, Harris had transferred $1 million-plus left over in her attorney general campaign bank account to another campaign account called "Harris for Governor 2026," just in case. The money was sitting there in 2018, after she made the decision to run for president. So she contributed it to favored charities: $100,000 to the Los Angeles Brotherhood Crusade, which helps low-income residents; $71,000 to the Coalition for Humane Immigrant Rights of Los Angeles; $100,000 to a firefighters fund; $50,000 to the Anti-Recidivism Coalition; $41,000 to the California Peace Officers' Memorial, which tends to a monument across from the capitol that includes the names of all California peace officers who have been killed in the line of duty, Isaac Espinoza among them; and $37,500 to the United Farm Workers. She gave money to organizations that promote science education for girls, shelter domestic violence victims, and provide services to domestic workers. The giving was generous and knowing. Each recipient could help a candidate running in a California primary in March 2020.

Although Harris had not formally announced her candidacy, the *New York Times, Washington Post,* and others reported in year-end stories that Harris was getting ready to run, as were Senators Cory Booker, Kirsten Gillibrand, and Elizabeth Warren. Bernie Sanders also was running, and Joe Biden was likely to enter the race. CNN identified twenty-nine potential Democratic presidential candidates, including four from California.

The release of her autobiography, *The Truths We Hold,* at the start of 2019 generated some buzz, and many questions. The title was intentional. The campaign was going to be about truth and justice, although when she talked about the book in interviews, she told interviewers she was not prepared to make any announcement about her plans at that moment.

On January 9, 2019, during a morning appearance on the ABC talk show *The View,* one of the cohosts, Whoopi Goldberg, opened with "So, I'm supposed to ask you, are you running?"

"I'm pleased to announce on *The View* that I'm not ready to make my announcement," Harris replied, smiling. They laughed uproariously.

"I'm very tempted," Harris said, once the laughter quieted. "But I'm not yet ready."

She waited to make her announcement on ABC's *Good Morning America,* on January 21, the day of service named in honor of Martin Luther King Jr. "The American people deserve to have somebody who is going to fight for them, who is going to see them, who will hear them, who will care about them, who will be concerned about their experience and will put them in front of self-interest," Harris said.

Her kickoff rally was on the next Sunday, January 27, in Oakland. Her consultants knew how to put on a show in Oakland, having done it in October 2007 when they managed Hillary Clinton's California presidential campaign and drew fourteen thousand people to downtown Oakland. They worked assiduously to make certain Harris's crowd would be even more impressive, and it was. American flags and red, white, and blue bunting draped Oakland City Hall; the sun was shining, and twenty thousand people showed up. Harris talked about Martin Luther King Jr. and recalled that Shirley Chisholm had made her historic announcement as the first Black woman running for president more than forty years earlier.

Harris's speech was full of populist themes and mentions of African American heroes. She told the crowd that she was born at the Kaiser Permanente hospital not far away and had worked in the Oakland courts as an Alameda County deputy district attorney, saying how proud she was when she stood in a courtroom and said, "Kamala Harris, for the people."

"For the people" was her theme that day.

It was meant to reflect the rationale for her run.

"I'm running to be president, of the people, by the people, and for all people," she said.

One of the faces in the crowd was Jackie Phillips, the principal at Cole School in Oakland who had known Harris as the teenager who was always ready to have fun but who also was determined to make something of herself. She was "proud beyond words."

The event got rave reviews. Even President Trump, aficionado of big crowds, acknowledged in a *New York Times* interview that Harris's Oakland event was "the best opening so far."

It was Harris's way: enter the race early, show strength, and, perhaps, thin the field. There was plenty of promise. She got off to a great start. But a statewide race in California was one thing. A national campaign was quite another.

33
Timing Is Everything

Fox News proclaimed that Kamala Harris was the front-runner less than two weeks after she announced her candidacy. That was not true then or ever. Joe Biden was the front-runner from start to finish. But Harris was in the top tier, and that meant she was being scrutinized as never before.

Journalists and commentators questioned whether she'd been as good a prosecutor as she had claimed to be. Some wondered if she'd been too good and had become so steely and tough that she would lack the common touch that Obama had on the trail and not connect with her next jury, the American people. The *Los Angeles Times* asked Feinstein whether she would support Harris. The senior senator damned Harris with faint praise: "I'm a big fan of Sen. Harris, and I work with her. But she's brand-new here, so it takes a little bit of time to get to know somebody." Biden was her man.

Harris based her campaign in Baltimore, though she had no connection to Baltimore. She did know that in the United States, news travels east to west, and that to be taken seriously, she needed to be in the East. Maya Harris was campaign chairwoman in the East, while much of Harris's brain trust remained in San Francisco. Juan Rodriguez, who managed her Senate campaign, was campaign manager. He was not yet thirty-five. Born in Burbank, Rodriguez is the son of immigrants from El Salvador who came to the United States at age nineteen to escape the violence in their homeland and seek a better life. His mom worked cleaning houses. His dad was a carpenter. He went to UCLA, then got a master's degree in business administration from Pepperdine University in Malibu, and worked as an intern for Los Angeles mayor Antonio Villaraigosa before rising in Harris's organization.

In the campaign, competing factions soon developed. Setbacks, including some self-inflicted ones, caused rifts. Harris had a habit of ducking reporters and showing up late for events, and she had shifting stands on single-payer health care, and small messages on legalizing the commercial sale of marijuana and decriminalizing prostitution between consenting adults — an idea that appalled some of the people who applauded her when in 2016 she brought the first criminal case against the owners of Backpage.

In February, she told an interviewer on *The Breakfast Club* podcast that she had smoked marijuana in college, offering: "Half my family's from Jamaica. Are you kidding me?"

Donald Harris, her father, was not amused, and he blogged that his deceased grandmothers and parents "must be turning in their graves right now to see their family's name, reputation and proud Jamaican identity being connected, in any way, jokingly or not with the fraudulent stereotype of a pot-smoking joy seeker and in the pursuit of identity politics." He removed the post, but not until it was widely reported. For Harris, the episode was an unforced error, a lesson that in a presidential campaign, every word uttered by the candidate matters.

Coming from California and having run three statewide races, Harris should have had a fund-raising edge. She didn't. Despite her impressive kickoff in Oakland, Harris raised $12 million in the first quarter of

2019, a mediocre showing. By comparison, Senator Barack Obama raised more than $25 million in the first quarter after he announced his candidacy, and that was twelve years earlier in 2007.

In a large field that included strong women, such as Elizabeth Warren, Amy Klobuchar and Kirsten Gillibrand, Harris was not standing out. She wasn't as far to the left as Warren or Bernie Sanders. Nor did she capture the imagination of voters who flocked to former South Bend mayor Pete Buttigieg. Buttigieg stood out as the only candidate who, as he put it, was "the only left-handed, Maltese-American, Episcopalian, gay millennial war veteran in the race." He was Harvard educated and a Rhodes Scholar, and he seemed to answer the yearning of voters, including many in California that Harris might have been counting on, who wanted a generational change. Worse for Harris, she could not define her reason for running beyond being someone who would prosecute the case against Trump, and she could not pull voters away from Joe Biden.

Harris's first big chance to turn the race came in the first debate, on June 27, 2019. An hour into it, she paused, inhaled, turned to Biden, and attacked him over his work decades earlier in the Senate with segregationist senators to restrict busing to achieve school desegregation.

"It was hurtful to hear you talk about the reputations of two United States senators who built their reputations and career on the segregation of race in this country. And it was not only that, but you also worked with them to oppose busing. And, you know, there was a little girl in California who was part of the second class to integrate her public schools, and she was bused to school every day. And that little girl was me."

Her willingness to attack the front-runner on the defining issue of race in the United States made clear that she was running to win. Her fund-raising spiked upward. She got a jolt in polling. Journalists concluded that she was the clear winner in the first debate. But the win and the polling spike were fleeting. A *New York Times* story the following day reflected a recurrent problem for Harris. Her spokesman said she supported busing as a method for school integration but "declined to provide additional information." After raising the issue, she was dodging the issue. From the *New York Times:*

The question for Ms. Harris is whether she can sustain her momentum from Thursday. Since the start of her campaign, she has performed well when working from a well-crafted plan but has sometimes suffered from self-inflicted wounds when forced to speak extemporaneously. And, as is often the case when one candidate attacks another in a multicandidate field, it remains to be seen if she helped herself or merely wounded Mr. Biden.

The attack surprised Biden and seemed to hurt him on a personal level. He later said on *The Tom Joyner Morning Show,* "I thought we were friends, and I hope we still will be." Biden in that interview recalled that in 2016, she asked him to come to the California Democratic Convention in San Jose and endorse her candidacy for U.S. Senate. He did. His appearance and heartfelt speech cemented the California Democratic Party's endorsement of Harris over Loretta Sanchez.

That was then. In 2019, Harris was doing what she thought she needed to do to win.

In a general election, Harris's background as a prosecutor, someone who had put people in prison for their bad acts, would play well. But in the primary, she was challenged by social justice activists who questioned whether she was, in fact, a "progressive" prosecutor.

"Time after time, when progressives urged her to embrace criminal justice reforms as a district attorney and then the state's attorney general, Ms. Harris opposed them or stayed silent. Most troubling, Ms. Harris fought tooth and nail to uphold wrongful convictions that had been secured through official misconduct that included evidence tampering, false testimony and the suppression of crucial information by prosecutors," Lara Bazelon, an associate professor at the University of San Francisco School of Law, wrote in an opinion piece in the *New York Times.* Bazelon's piercing analysis appeared on January 17, 2019. It resonated throughout the campaign.

In the second Democratic presidential primary debate held at the end of July in Detroit, Congresswoman Tulsi Gabbard of Hawaii picked up on that theme and was brutal. As a prosecutor, Gabbard said, Harris "put over 1,500 people in jail for marijuana violations" and failed to investigate evidence that might have exonerated a death row inmate, a reference to the Kevin Cooper case. It was out of context. But on a stage crowded with ten candidates, Harris was not able to aptly respond. She made it worse when she appeared on CNN with Anderson Cooper. Rather than taking an affirmative position or setting the record straight, she came off as imperious: "This is going to sound immodest, but obviously I'm a top-tier candidate and so I did expect that I'd be on the stage and take some hits tonight. When people are at zero or one percent or whatever she might be at, so I did expect to take some hits tonight."

Harris backtracked on some of her positions she had taken as a district attorney and attorney general, notably saying she regretted that in some counties, parents of habitually truant children were jailed as a result of the law she advocated. Their incarceration was an "unintended consequence," she said in 2019. But just a few years earlier, January 2015, when she was sworn in for her second term as attorney general, she said in her inauguration speech, "It's time to say that in the State of California it is a crime for a child to go without an education." The episode raised the basic question: Kamala Harris took positions, but what were her principles?

By early November, the campaign was running out of money, and it fell to campaign manager Juan Rodriguez to impose layoffs and face the vitriol from people who were let go.

Rodriguez had been the starting quarterback of his high school football team as a junior and senior. Quarterbacks learned how to take a sack. In the crumbling Harris campaign, the blitz was on. The *New York Times* deconstructed Harris's faltering campaign on November 29, in a piece that ran nearly three thousand words under a headline that read: "How Kamala Harris's Campaign Unraveled."

"The 2020 Democratic field has been defined by its turbulence, with some contenders rising, others dropping out and two more jumping in just this month. Yet there is only one candidate who rocketed to the top tier and then plummeted in early state polls to the low single digits: Ms. Harris."

Rodriguez was taking the sack. But quarterbacks don't get sacked unless there is a breakdown around them. So it was in Harris's campaign. The tone of any campaign is set from the top. Maya Harris second-guessed strategists, who knew it was folly to get between the Harris sisters. Messaging was flat. There was way too much internal drama. Campaign aides who lost their jobs because money was running out were sniping as they left.

Democrats don't win their party's presidential nomination without winning primaries in southern states, and Harris needed to do well in South Carolina where Black voters were key. Harris's campaign, like the campaigns of the other Democrats, did not anticipate the unshakable strength of Joe Biden's support among Black voters. Harris's failure to move up in the polls affected her fund-raising, and without money, she couldn't buy airtime in the early states for ads that might have helped her in the polls. It was a vicious circle. By the end of 2019, Harris had raised $40.3 million, slightly more than half of the $76 million raised in 2019 by Pete Buttigieg. Harris failed to catch on with small-dollar donors, who provide much of the Democratic presidential candidates' money. Federal Election Commission statistics show 54 percent of her donations came in increments of $200 or less, way below Massachusetts senator Elizabeth Warren, who received 74 percent of her $127 million in increments of $200 or less. On one day in the summer, Harris raised a mere $4,000 in online donations.

There was, however, one hope.

Presidential candidates are restricted to

raising $2,800 per donor for the primary and another $2,800 for the general. Given the cost of campaigning, candidates end up relying on super PACs, especially during the primary. Super PACs, which must operate independently from candidates, can accept donations of unlimited size. Seeing that the campaign was failing, one of Harris's wealthy supporters and two former campaign aides banded together to create a super PAC called People Standing Strong. The committee raised $1.2 million. Of that, $1 million came from M. Quinn Delaney, a wealthy liberal from Oakland who funds candidates and campaigns she believes advance the cause of racial justice. Delaney and her husband, real estate developer Wayne Jordan, are among Harris's most loyal supporters.

Timing in politics matters. At 11:42 a.m. EST on December 3, 2019, *Politico*'s Christopher Cadelago broke the news that a super PAC supporting Harris had started reserving airtime in Iowa — this after Harris's campaign, running on fumes, had not aired a single ad in Iowa since September. Dan Newman and Brian Brokaw, the consultants working on People Standing Strong, had wired $501,000 to television stations in Iowa to start airing a pro-Harris ad and were preparing to send another $500,000. It was to be the largest purchase of airtime on behalf of any candidate who was not a self-funding billionaire.

"We were her only shot. We needed to be on the air," said Brokaw, who had managed Harris's 2010 run for attorney general.

The ad almost certainly would have grabbed voters' attention and perhaps set Harris apart from the pack. The spot featured Harris's greatest hits, clips of her grilling Justice Brett Kavanaugh, Attorney General William Barr, and former attorney general Jeff Sessions, with her signature: "I'm asking you a very direct question. Yes or no?"

"I'm not able to be rushed this fast. It makes me nervous," Sessions fumbles in the ad.

The narrator's voice: "Kamala Harris exposes Republicans. She makes them nervous. And leaves them unable to defend their lies and corruption. She'll do the same to Donald Trump. . . . Kamala Harris, the Democrat for president that Donald Trump fears most."

On December 3, three hours and six minutes after his first scoop, Cadelago reported another big story: "Kamala Harris is ending her presidential campaign after months of failing to lift her candidacy from the bottom of the field — a premature departure for a California senator once heralded as a top-tier contender for the nomination."

Brokaw and Newman were stunned. They couldn't believe what they were hearing. She could not be dropping out, not yet anyway. But she was. Brokaw called Delaney to relay the news and promised to try to get her money back. He did retrieve most of it.

Harris pulled out of the race after conferring with her team and realizing she had no money. By dropping out early, she could save herself the embarrassment of losing big in the Iowa caucuses and, worse, in her home state. Her name would not appear on California's March 3 primary ballot. That was for the best. Polls showed she was going to lose California. An embarrassing loss would have raised questions about her viability as a candidate in years to come.

But soon another opportunity would present itself.

34
DANCING IN THE RAIN

With her presidential aspirations put aside, Kamala Harris returned to the work for which she was elected: representing California in the U.S. Senate. After a bare-knuckled and exhausting run, her work in the Senate was intended to rehabilitate her with voters back home and, maybe, with Joe Biden.

The House of Representatives had presented the articles of impeachment of President Donald Trump to the Senate on January 16, 2020. With Senate leader Mitch McConnell in charge of the proceeding, the outcome of the Senate trial was never in doubt. When he rejected Democrats' requests to call witnesses, Harris had no opportunity to claim the national spotlight, as she had when she questioned Attorney General Sessions and Supreme Court candidate Brett Kavanaugh.

Between the end of the impeachment trial in February and August, when she stepped back onto the national stage, Harris introduced thirty-three bills and resolutions. Some were partisan, like the resolution that condemned Trump adviser Stephen Miller "for his trafficking in bigotry, hatred, and divisive political rhetoric." The resolution urged that Miller resign. He didn't.

The bills got little or no press attention. Some sought to address issues unique to California: restoring and enhancing access to public lands, including the South Fork Trinity River–Mad River in Northern California, and cleaning up pollution in the Tijuana River to the far south at the California-Mexico border.

Other measures reflected issues she had raised on the campaign trail. There were environmental justice bills to protect people living in poor communities from the impact of pollution from industrial developments and to fund research into safe alternatives to chemicals in consumer products including cosmetics. The latter was intended to protect women working in salons, not the sort of issue old men in the Senate would see a need to address in their legislative packages.

One of her bills sought to fund research into uterine fibroids. Another, the Black Maternal Health Momnibus Act of 2020, urged the Department of Health and Human Services to address high maternal and infant mortality rates among Black women and to require that the Federal Bureau of Prisons award grants to prisons and jails to improve maternal health among pregnant women behind bars.

Harris was quick to address the COVID-19 pandemic, introducing legislation in March to increase financial aid to individuals thrown out of work as states were issuing lockdown orders. As the pandemic spread, she introduced legislation to protect renters against eviction, provide funding for small businesses, require that the president appoint a special envoy focused on pandemic preparedness, increase funding to states for voting by mail, and study racial and ethnic disparities among minorities who contracted COVID-19. Another bill sought to provide aid so that small- and mid-sized restaurants could partner with governments including Indian tribes to provide food to people in need.

Harris was a Democrat in a Republican-controlled Senate in an election year in which she had sought to be a presidential nominee. All that meant that she had zero chance of winning passage of any of her bills. But each bill was a statement about the sort of issue she would address, once she got the opportunity.

During the Democratic presidential candidate debate on March 15, 2020, Joe Biden, heading toward the Democratic nomination, announced that he would pick a woman to be his running mate. Harris's friends wanted to help.

One was Michael Tubbs. Tubbs was elected mayor of Stockton, the city where he grew up, in 2016 at age twenty-six, after serving a four-year term on the city council. He had won that seat while finishing up at Stanford University, sixty-one miles and another world away. Tubbs, the son of a single mom who was a teenager when she had him and a father who was in prison, had been an intern in the Obama administration White House. As mayor, Tubbs had his work cut out for him. The city of three hundred thousand was emerging from bankruptcy, and his predecessor had pleaded guilty to misappropriating public funds and, separately, to furnishing alcohol to a minor, after initially being accused of secretly recording teen camp counselors in a game of strip poker.

"I decided it would be cowardly for me to continue to do research and write essays about all of Stockton's problems and not try to do something about them," Tubbs told *Sacramento Bee* reporter Cynthia Hubert in 2017, explaining why he came home.

As Mayor Tubbs worked to revive his city, Senator Harris would call to check in, dispensing advice and seeing if there was anything she could do from Washington. On her birthday in 2019, as she was running for president, Harris called Tubbs to congratulate him on the birth the day before of Michael Malakai Tubbs Jr., his and his wife's firstborn.

"Tell him Auntie Kamala can't wait to meet him," she told the mayor.

Tubbs phoned California Lieutenant Governor Eleni Kounalakis, asking about mounting a lobbying campaign for Harris. Kounalakis told Harris that she would be willing to start one on Harris's behalf. But Harris declined. She wanted to be Biden's running mate, but figured Biden knew where she was and how to find her. In the end, events would compel Biden to think harder about choosing Harris.

On May 25, George Floyd died, pinned under the knee of a Minneapolis cop for eight minutes and forty-six seconds, after police were called about him buying a pack of cigarettes with a counterfeit twenty-dollar bill. Two months earlier, police in Louisville, Kentucky, thinking they were searching the home of drug dealers, shot and killed Breonna Taylor, an unarmed twenty-six-year-old emergency room technician who was in her bed. Harris put on a mask to protect against COVID-19 and walked to the White House to join a protest on May 30.

Some vice presidential candidates aggressively campaigned for the job. Harris wanted it, but her campaign was more subtle. She knew she was on the short list of potential appointees. Rohini Kosoglu, who had been Harris's chief of staff in the Senate and later on the presidential campaign, made sure Biden aides vetting Harris had everything they needed. Kosoglu also made sure Biden knew that Harris's messaging on her long-held views on race and criminal justice issues would not conflict with his stands. If there were conflicts, Biden's views would control. Of the Black women under consideration, Harris was the only one who had won major statewide contests and had run in a national campaign.

There was damage control to be done. It was well known that Joe Biden's wife, Dr. Jill Biden, had called Harris's attack over race on her husband during the June 27 debate "a punch to the gut." Appearing on *The Late Show with Stephen Colbert* in June, Harris attempted an explanation about why she had challenged Biden over race: "It was a debate. The whole reason — literally, it was a debate. It was called a debate." On the prospect of being picked as Biden's running mate, she said, "I'd be honored, if asked, and I'm honored to be a part of the conversation. Honestly, let me just tell you something. I will do everything in my power, wherever I am, to help Joe Biden win."

In July and August, other candidates emerged and gained traction, notably Congresswoman Karen Bass, a Los Angeles Democrat and chair of the Congressional Black Caucus. Her allies included some politicians who had national aspirations and realized that Harris would be the immediate front-runner for the Democratic presidential nomination after Biden served four or eight years. Bass seemed like a less likely presidential contender. Most concerning, Harris's supporters in California believed the men advising Biden, including former senator Christopher Dodd and former Pennsylvania governor Ed Rendell, were buying into a narrative that Harris was disliked and losing support among Democrats in California and that Bass would be a solid alternative. Certainly, Harris had made her share of enemies among Democrats. But she also had a core of support. Bass had never been fully vetted on a national stage, and negative stories appeared, including that she had heaped words of praise on Fidel Castro, not something that would play well in Florida, and that she had offered kind words about Scientology in a speech that was easily found online.

Lt. Gov. Kounalakis became engaged.

"I didn't ask for permission," Kounalakis said.

In the small world of San Francisco politics, Mark Buell, Harris's first campaign finance chair, introduced then district attorney Harris and Kounalakis. Kounalakis's father is Angelo Tsakopoulos, who arrived in the United States at age fifteen, penniless from Greece, in 1958, worked his way through Sacramento State College, and became the Sacramento region's largest developer. He also held the fund-raiser where Buell's future wife, Susie Tompkins, met Bill Clinton and became involved in politics. Harris and Kounalakis started having lunch together and bonded. (Harris calls her on her birthday and sings her "Happy Birthday.") Before running for lieutenant governor in 2018, Kounalakis had been a major campaign donor who had supported Hillary Clinton in 2008 and 2016 and became the Obama administration's first ambassador to Hungary. Kounalakis lives in the same San Francisco apartment building as Buell, with the same 360-degree view of the Bay Area. She and Mark and Susie Buell often coordinate their fund-raising efforts, with donors stopping at her apartment for wine or cocktails and then riding the elevator up a few floors for dinner at the Buells. When Kounalakis decided to run for lieutenant governor, Harris called to say, "I am going to endorse you and you are going to win."

On July 31, 2020, Kounalakis called the Biden campaign requesting a Zoom meeting. That call happened three days later. Kounalakis lined up an impressive list of Harris's backers: San Francisco mayor London Breed, Oakland mayor Libby Schaaf, Long Beach mayor Robert Garcia, California treasurer Fiona Ma, California secretary of state Alex Padilla, Mayor Tubbs, and former governor Gray Davis. Each person was allotted two minutes to tell why Harris was the right choice. Some of the people had professional stories. Others were personal. Garcia of Long Beach said Harris was the first person who called offering condolences after his mother died of COVID-19 on July 26.

Tubbs pointed out that Harris had run three times statewide, had run for president, and was "battle-tested and vetted." "Kamala Harris is singular," Tubbs said.

Kounalakis argued she was a "transformational woman" in American politics. "There is no stereotype for Kamala Harris."

On August 11, a Tuesday, Biden called Harris via Zoom.

"You ready to go to work?"

Biden had kept his final decision a closely held secret. On the Saturday before the Tuesday when he made his choice public, Harris and her closest advisers had no clue that she would be his pick.

"Oh my God. I'm so ready to go to work," Harris answered.

The opinion of Biden's son Beau about Harris, forged when the state attorneys general challenged the banks in 2011 and 2012, weighed heavily on his decision.

"There is no one's opinion I valued more than Beau's and I'm proud to have Kamala standing with me on this campaign," Biden said after the selection.

Being vice president was not the outcome

Harris envisioned when she launched her presidential campaign in 2019. She had entered the presidential race to win, and she did not intend to be anyone's vice president. From Biden's perspective, the choice made sense. She rose in the rough-and-tough politics of San Francisco and had been vetted by investigative journalists and some of the best opposition researchers from both parties. She had run hard races and won and lost. Her good and not-so-good traits were known to Biden's team. She would match well in a debate with Vice President Mike Pence and didn't have a habit of making mistakes on the trail. She also would bring excitement and maybe even some dance moves to a ticket led by a man who would be the oldest person ever elected president. As politicians say, she was operational.

She also had a story to tell, a story that is unique and also very American.

After Biden selected Harris, she reached out to Wanda Kagan, her high school friend in Montreal, wondering if she would allow Harris to share her story. Kagan did not hesitate. In a video tweeted on September 23, 2020, Harris told the story without mentioning Kagan's name, recalling that a best friend in high school "would come to school and just be sad and there were times when she just didn't seem to want to go home." When the friend confided that she was being abused, Harris told her, "You have to come stay with us." Her friend's pain was one reason Harris wanted to become a prosecutor, she said on the video.

Two days before the election on November 3, 2020, Kagan thought back to her days in high school and what had become of the girl who helped her through the toughest of times.

"The U.S. is getting the best of the person, like that's who she is. That's who she always was," Kagan said.

On October 19, 2020, Democratic vice presidential nominee Kamala Harris was at a campaign rally in Jacksonville, Florida. It was raining. Harris was wearing her Chuck Taylors, and the speakers were blasting her walk-off music, Mary J. Blige's "Work That."

Just because the length of your hair ain't long And they often criticize you for your skin tone Wanna hold your head high . . . .

Girl be yourself.

Harris tipped her umbrella back and moved with the beat, smiling wide, laughing, reveling in where she found herself, and maybe where she had come from.

Ronald Reagan's presidential speechwriter Peggy Noonan tsked in a *Wall Street Journal* column four days later that "it was embarrassing" to see the vice presidential candidate dancing and that Harris was coming off as frivolous.

The Recount posted a fifteen-second clip of Harris dancing in Jacksonville. It got 2.3 million views and counting.

Beth Foster Gayle had just gotten up and was making coffee at her D.C. home on the morning of October 25, bracing herself for the day ahead. It was the second anniversary of the death of her husband, Tyrone Gayle, Harris's first Senate press secretary.

Such days bring with them hard, happy, sad memories. Her phone buzzed with a text. It was from the Democratic vice presidential nominee, from somewhere on the campaign trail. Kamala Harris wanted to pass along what she had seen at the rally in Jacksonville, Tyrone's hometown. Someone held a sign that read: DO IT FOR TYRONE. In other words, the person holding the sign wanted Harris to win the election for the young man who died too soon. Harris wanted Beth to know that someone else was remembering Tyrone.

The gesture brightened the start of the rough anniversary, and it reflected a facet of Kamala Harris that few people would ever see. She could be tough, often too tough, with those around her. In her climb, she had left people behind feeling used, and she left work undone as she moved fast from one important job to the next. But she also took time to show she cared and to display that all-too-rare quality, empathy. On this day, she knew one person would be feeling pain, and she wanted to let that person know someone was thinking of her.

It was Kamala Harris's way.

ACKNOWLEDGMENTS

For understandable reasons, Kamala Harris and her family did not grant interviews or provide help in the reporting of *Kamala's Way.* Harris was focused on running a national campaign during September and October when I was writing this book.

I relied on dozens of sources who had firsthand knowledge of the events to which they spoke. Many of them are identified in these pages; others had good reasons to remain anonymous. My sincere thanks to each of them for helping inform me and readers of *Kamala's Way.*

Josh Meyer, my friend from our days at the *Los Angeles Times,* deserves a special acknowledgment. This book could not have been written without his reporting and insights about Washington. Josh's hard-edged reporting is second to none. In this project, he used his decades of experience in the ways of Washington to provide invaluable help in reporting and writing chapters on Harris's very busy time in the Senate and on her efforts to win Biden's selection as his running mate. Josh turned all of this around on a tight deadline, which makes me even more appreciative.

Andy Furillo, my dear friend and the best courthouse reporter I know, helped immensely with reporting, insights, and descriptions of Harris's time at the San Francisco Hall of Justice.

Sasha Hupka provided invaluable help reaching important people in this book and researching Harris's time in Berkeley and Oakland. Sasha is a meticulous reporter and fine writer and has a great future in journalism. Thanks also to Yumi Wilson, who teaches the next generation of journalists at UC Berkeley, for recommending Sasha.

Kristina Rebelo was a most amazing fact-checker and line editor. Karina Robinson is an incredible historical researcher, genealogist, and fact-checker who helped with my understanding of Harris's roots. Thanks to California State Librarian Greg Lucas and his great staff. The California State Library is one of California's true gems.

Kamala's Way would not have happened without Michael Duffy, *Washington Post* opinion editor at large. He suggested that I undertake this project and suggested it again when I hesitated, and he called the most amazing editor, Priscilla Painton of Simon & Schuster, on my behalf. Thank you, Priscilla, for your steady hand, insights, and thoughtful editing and for taking a chance on a first-time author.

Thanks as well to my friend Scott Lebar, a great journalist and *Sacramento Bee* managing editor who, when contacted by an agent looking for someone to write about Kamala Harris, gave her my name. Thank you, Karen Brailsford of Aevitas Creative Management, for helping me navigate the world of publishing and for taking a chance on me.

I got to know Kamala Harris when I was a columnist and later editorial page editor at the *Sacramento Bee.* Thank you, Stuart Leavenworth, for hiring me. My deepest gratitude goes to Cheryl Dell, who as publisher of the *Bee* entrusted me with the high honor of being editorial page editor.

My sincere thanks to Shawn Hubler, Joyce Terhaar, Foon Rhee, Erika D. Smith, Gary Reed, Ginger Rutland, Mariel Garza, Jack Ohman, Pia Lopez, and the late Rex Babin, my colleagues at the *Bee*'s editorial board.

The fact-based reporting of Christopher Cadelago, John Diaz, Michael Finnegan,

Leah Garchik, Joe Garofoli, John Howard, Carla Marinucci, Melanie Mason, Phil Matier, Maeve Reston, Jerry Roberts, Andy Ross, Phil Trounstine, Karen Tumulty, Lance Williams, Phil Willon, and others helped inform this book. Thanks to Dave Lesher at CalMatters.org for hiring me to a position where I could watch as Kamala Harris ascended.

And thank you to Tony and Tess, Clara and Ken, and Libby and Grayson for your love and support. Above all, thank you to my wife, Claudia. Your love, support, and understanding makes everything possible.

NOTES

1: Shyamala's Daughter

"My mother, Shyamala Gopalan Harris": Kamala Harris (kamala-harris), "My Mother, Shyamala Gopalan Harris, Was a Force of Nature . . . ," Instagram, March 1, 2020, https://www.instagram.com/p/B9MndAdnoHs/?utm_source=ig_web_copy_link.

"My mother had been raised": Kamala Harris, *The Truths We Hold* (New York: Penguin, 2019), 7.

"a standout in appearance": Ellen Barry, "How Kamala Harris's Immigrant Parents Found a Home, and Each Other, in a Black Study Group," *New York Times,* September 13, 2020.

"A culture that worships": Scott Duke Harris, "In Search of Elusive Justice," *Los Angeles Times,* October 24, 2004.

"no great anxiety or desire": Stephen Carter, "Harris Departure Stirs Turmoil: Econ

Dept. Loses Radical Prof," *Stanford Daily,* January 25, 1974.

"had they been a little older": K. Harris, *Truths We Hold,* 6.

In a 2018 essay: Donald J. Harris, "Reflections of a Jamaican Father," Jamaica Global, August 18, 2020.

"My father is a good guy": Peter Byrne, "Kamala's Karma," *SF Weekly,* September 24, 2003.

In her official biography: "Kamala D. Harris, 32nd Attorney General," State of California Department of Justice, https://oag.ca.gov/history/32harris#:~:text=Born%20and%20raised%20in%20the,graduate%20studies%20at%20UC%20Berkeley.

"My roots go back": D. Harris, "Reflections of a Jamaican Father."

"Managing slaves was a means": Christer Petley, *Slaveholders in Jamaica: Colonial Society and Culture during the Era of Abolition* (London: Pickering & Chatto, 2009), 1.

"more than a third": Ibid., 2.

"In Jamaica, sexual relations": Ibid., 7.

"the sexual opportunism of white men": Ibid.

"Brown worked hard to repress": Ibid., 117.

"the great deterioration": Ibid., 159.

"They fell in love": Maura Hohman, "Kamala Harris Details Being Raised by a Single

Mom, Importance of Family in DNC Speech," *Today,* August 19, 2020, https://www.today.com/news/dnc-speech-kamala-harris-details-being-raised-single-mom-t189876.

Police shot to death: "Flashback: Ronald Reagan and the Berkeley People's Park Riots," *Rolling Stone,* May 15, 2017.

"There's no reason why": Chuck McFadden, "Armed Black Panthers in the Capitol, 50 Years On," *Capitol Weekly,* April 26, 2017.

Newton had been a charismatic leader: Henry Weinstein, " 'Free Huey': A White Man's View: Nowhere to Run, Nowhere to Hide," *Daily Californian,* May 20, 1968.

"The Huey Newton I saw": Thomas Orloff (retired district attorney for Alameda County, California), in discussion with the author, October 2020.

he was gunned down: Mark A. Stein and Valarie Basheda, "Black Panther Founder Huey Newton Is Killed," *Los Angeles Times,* August 23, 1989.

"she was raising two black daughters": K. Harris, *Truths We Hold,* 10.

"This #BlackHistoryMonth": Kamala Harris (kamalaharris), "My Mother Was Very Intentional . . . ," Instagram, February 9, 2020, https://www.instagram.com/p/B8W

nPWzn-EN/?utm_source=ig_web_copy_link.

"the thought of moving away": K. Harris, *Truths We Hold,* 19.

At Westmount, Kamala Harris: Dan Bilefsky, "In Canada, Kamala Harris, a Disco-Dancing Teenager, Yearned for Home," *New York Times,* October 5, 2020.

"what she went through with me": Wanda Kagan (lifelong friend) in discussion with the author's researcher, Sasha Hupka, November 1, 2020.

2: That Little Girl

That would change in the ensuing decades: Dan Morain and Paul Jacobs, "Worlds of Politics, Law Often Mix for Speaker," *Los Angeles Times,* April 1, 1991.

"what is to prevent the Legislature": California Secretary of State, "Proposed Amendments to the Constitution: Propositions and Proposed Laws Together With Arguments," Sacramento: California Office of State Printing, 1964.

"It would legalize and incite bigotry": Proposed Amendments to the Constitution: Propositions and Proposed Laws Together with Arguments to Be Submitted to the Electors of the State of California at the General

Election, Tuesday, Nov. 3, 1964, California State Archives, Secretary of State, September 1, 1964.

first Black legislator: Conor Dougherty, "Overlooked No More: William Byron Rumford, a Civil Rights Champion in California," *New York Times,* August 7, 2019.

"felt that if in so-called 'liberal' California": William Byron Rumford, "The Fair Housing Bill and Proposition 14, 1963–1964," interview by Edward France and Joyce Henderson, *Legislator for Fair Employment, Fair Housing, and Public Health,* Earl Warren Oral History Project, Online Archives of California, 1973, https://oac.cdlib.org/view?docId=hb8n39p2g3;NAAN=13030&doc.view=-frames&chunk.id=div00040&toc.depth=1&toc.id=&brand=oac4.

On May 29, 1967: Reitman v. Mulkey, 387 U.S. 369 (1967).

"The children fell in love": Neil V. Sullivan and Evelyn S. Stewart, *Now Is the Time: Integration in the Berkeley Schools* (Bloomington: Indiana University Press, 1970), 203.

"I believe that our schools": Ibid., x.

"Is it possible for one": Ibid., 7.

But in the fall of 1970: Natalie Orenstein,

"Did Kamala Harris' Berkeley Childhood Shape the Presidential Hopeful?," Berkeley-side, January 24, 2019, https://www.berkeleyside.com/2019/01/24/did-kamala-harris-berkeley-childhood-shape-the-presidential-hopeful.

"The children of Berkeley": Sullivan and Stewart, *Now Is the Time,* 171.

"I would like to speak": NBC News, "Democratic Presidential Debate — June 27," YouTube video, June 27, 2020, https://www.youtube.com/watch?v=cX7hni-zGD8.

Harris's campaign seized: Kamala Harris (@KamalaHarris), "There Was a Little Girl in California Who Was Bussed to School . . . ," Twitter, June 27, 2019, https://twitter.com/KamalaHarris/status/1144427976609734658?s=20.

3: An Education, Apartheid, and a Slaughter

"We would dance": Kamala Harris (@KamalaHarris), "Being a Graduated of @HowardU . . . ," Twitter, June 19, 2019, https://twitter.com/KamalaHarris/status/1141375083807748096?s=20.

"On any given day": K. Harris, *Truths We Hold,* 22.

"She used to laugh at my cooking": Karen Gibbs (lifelong friend of Harris) in discussion with the author, October 2020.

Bishop Desmond M. Tutu accused: Gene Kramer, Associated Press, November 7, 1984.

"We talked of many things": Willie L. Brown, *Basic Brown: My Life and Our Times* (New York: Simon & Schuster, 2019), 207.

In a letter to President Reagan: Dan Morain, "How the 'Duke' Helped Mandela," *Sacramento Bee,* July 21, 2013.

"We must not turn our backs": Ibid.

"How would we feel": Ibid.

"Mandela praised the California political leaders": Dan Morain, "Mandela Ends Tour by Promising to Return," *Los Angeles Times,* July 1, 1990.

"I don't think there was anything": Author interview with Willie Brown, 2013.

"There was nothing about her": Matthew D. Davis (San Francisco attorney) in discussion with the author, October 2020.

"We were able to hit": Jane Gross, "California Becomes the First State to Vote Curbs on Assault Rifles," *New York Times,* March 13, 1989.

former Los Angeles mayor Tom Bradley: Joe Mathews, "It Was Guns, Not Race, That

Affected Bradley," *Politico,* November 4, 2008.

"You do not grieve alone": Doug Willis, "Five Children Killed in Schoolyard Shooting Remembered at Memorial Service," Associated Press, January 23, 1989.

"These bills are not going": Carl Ingram, "Governor Signs Assault Weapon Legislation," *Los Angeles Times,* May 25, 1989.

4: A Taste of Politics

the number of murders: Crime Trends in the City of Oakland: A 25-Year Look (1987–2012), Chief Justice Earl Warren Institute on Law and Social Policy, University of California, Berkeley School of Law, February 2014, https://www.law.berkeley.edu/files/Crime_Trends_in_the_City_of_Oakland_-_A_25-Year_Look.pdf.

a horse-drawn funeral procession: Dan Morain, "Garish Oakland Funeral: 1,000 Witness Last Ride of Slain Drug Ring Kingpin," *Los Angeles Times,* August 30, 1986.

"I knew that the people": "Kamala Harris Officially Launches 2020 Presidential Campaign," CNN, January 28, 2019, https://lite.cnn.com/en/article/h_812f00af9ad82880d57b91b881207ccb.

"She did stand out a bit": Nancy O'Malley

(Alameda County districct attorney) in discussion with the author, September 2020.

Law professor Anita Hill: Elise Viebeck, "Joe Biden Was in Charge of the Anita Hill Hearing. Even He Says It Wasn't Fair," *Washington Post,* April 26, 2019.

Oakland schools were so troubled: Dan Morain, "In His Own Image: Elihu Harris Vows to Improve Perceptions — and Reality — of Life in Oakland," *Los Angeles Times,* January 6, 1991.

The California State Legislature had installed: Dan Morain, "State Audit Blasts Oakland School District," *Los Angeles Times,* January 25, 1990.

Barbara Boxer and Dianne Feinstein: Dean E. Murphy, "Boxer, Feinstein Rivalry Is Softened by Historic Election," *Los Angeles Times,* November 8, 1992.

one of seven Democratic congresswomen: Maureen Dowd, "The Thomas Nomination: The Senate and Sexism," *New York Times,* October 8, 1991.

"Can you think of any laws": "Supreme Court Nominee Brett Kavanaugh Confirmation Hearing, Day 2, Part 5," C-SPAN, September 4, 2018, https://www.c-span.org/video/?449705-15/supreme-court-nominee-brett-kavanaugh-confirmation-

hearing-day-2-part-5.

They had Friday lunch dates: Leah Garchik, "Friday Lunches at Le Central Were Legendary," *San Francisco Chronicle,* April 2, 2002.

Ever clever with a quip: Thomas B. Rosenstiel and Dan Morain, "Herb Caen's 50 Years: Prophet of 'The City' Sees Decline," *Los Angeles Times,* April 16, 1987.

The scandal became public: Daniel M. Weintraub and Dan Morain, "Keene's Records Subpoenaed; Aide Investigated," *Los Angeles Times,* September 10, 1988.

California's three strikes law: Dan Morain, "Column One: California's Profusion of Prisons," *Los Angeles Times,* October 16, 1994.

So, in late November: Dan Morain, "2 More Brown Associates Get Well-Paid Posts," *Los Angeles Times,* November 29, 1994.

"It's safe to say": Ibid.

When the clerk got to: Dan Morain and Carl Ingram, "Brown Blocks GOP Assembly Takeover as 1 Republican Bolts," *Los Angeles Times,* December 6, 1994.

"new first-lady-in-waiting": Herb Caen, "Cut Along Dotted Lines," *San Francisco Chronicle,* December 14, 1995.

" 'It's all over' ": Herb Caen, " 'Twas the Day After," *San Francisco Chronicle,* December

26, 1995.

In 2019, Brown, the octogenarian: Willie Brown, interview by Susan Leigh Taylor, Stan Bunger, and Phil Matier, KCBS Radio Morning News, KCBS, February 1, 2019.

On January 8, 1996: "San Francisco Mayoral Inauguration," C-SPAN, January 8, 1996, https://www.c-span.org/video/?69289-1/san-francisco-mayoral-inauguration.

"She was very bright": Tom Orloff (retired district attorney for Alameda County, California) in discussion with author, October 2020.

"It's appropriate for what he did": Peter Fimrite, "Life Term for Fremont Man Who Scalped Girlfriend," *San Francisco Chronicle,* September 28, 1996.

5: Setting Her Sights

"political hack": "Why Bill Fazio Is the Choice for D.A.," editorial, *San Francisco Chronicle,* November 26, 1995.

a late revelation that a paternity suit: Carla Marinucci, "Hallinan Tells of Fling, Son, Paternity Suit," *San Francisco Examiner,* February 3, 2012.

The California Supreme Court overruled: Hallinan v. Committee of Bar Examiners, 65

Cal. 2d 447, December 15, 1966.

"vehemently denies almost dying": William Claiborne, "San Francisco Prosecutor Tries Something Different," *Washington Post,* February 20, 1996.

But the turmoil he caused: Maura Dolan, "A Liberal Lays Down the Law in S.F.," *Los Angeles Times,* April 5, 1997.

"I didn't choose it": Phillip Matier and Andrew Ross, "Blow-by-Blow Description of DA's Tussle," *San Francisco Chronicle,* May 3, 1996.

"She's a terrific prosecutor": Phillip Matier and Andrew Ross, "Matier & Ross — Brown's Creative Financing Underwrites Far-Flung Trade Jaunts," *San Francisco Chronicle,* February 2, 1998.

"This friend of mine": Andy Furillo (Kamala Harris researcher) in discussion with the author, October 2020.

"an intelligent lawyer who had a heart": Louise Renne (former San Francisco city attorney) in discussion with the author, September 2020.

"Suddenly, she had become this": Matthew D. Davis (San Francisco attorney) in discussion with the author, October 2020.

6: Becoming a Boldface

"Being able to cross over": Brown, *Basic Brown,* 54.

"She was very determined": Libby Schaaf (Oakland Mayor) in discussion with the author, October 2020.

"And they were treated": Jackie Phillips (former Cole School principal) in discussion with the author's researcher, Sasha Hupka, October 2020.

She was photographed: Pat Steger, "Fairy-Tale Wedding for Getty-Jarman in Napa Valley," *San Francisco Chronicle,* June 21, 1999.

A piece in Harper's Bazaar: Stacy Finz, The Daily, *San Francisco Chronicle,* March 15, 2001.

A society columnist noted: Carolyne Zinko, "Moreno Lets It All Hang Out/All-Star 'Monologues' Draw High-Powered V-Day Supporters," *San Francisco Chronicle,* February 17, 2002.

She attended an October 2002 gala: Catherine Bigelow, "Elton John's 'Your Song' Is Their Song at Star-Studded Fund-Raiser," *San Francisco Chronicle,* October 18, 2002.

though Jet *magazine ran a photo:* "Kamala Harris with Montel Williams and His

Daughter, Ashley at the Eighth Annual Race to Erase MS in Los Angeles," YouTube video, May 18, 2001, https://www.youtube.com/watch?v=e8iZw2yWb7M.

"I was at that event": Phil Matier and Andy Ross, "Costs of BART Talks Picking Up Speed of Runaway Train," *San Francisco Chronicle,* July 16, 2001.

"hardly a figure of respect": "Bumbling into a Second Term," editorial, *San Francisco Chronicle,* August 23, 2000.

As retold by the Los Angeles Times: Evan Halper, "Meet One of Hillary Clinton's Biggest Donors in California. They Hardly Ever Talk Politics," *Los Angeles Times,* July 3, 2016.

"socialite with a law degree": Michael Kruse, "How San Francisco's Wealthiest Families Launched Kamala Harris," *Politico,* August 10, 2019.

"Once I was convinced": Mark Buell (friend of Harris and philanthropist) in discussion with the author, October 2020.

7: Severing Heads. Figuratively.

Schwarzenegger, the one to beat: Gary Cohn, Carla Hall, and Robert W. Welkos, "Women Say Schwarzenegger Groped, Humiliated Them," *Los Angeles Times,*

October 2, 2003.

"I'm thinking about running": Louise Renne (former San Francisco city attorney) in discussion with the author, October 2020.

"She'd do the speech": Mark Buell (Harris friend and philanthropist) in discussion with the author, October 2020.

"I was tired of the old": John Keker (top criminal defense attorney) in discussion with the author, October 2020.

In 1989, Keker had led: Dan Morain, "Ready for Combat: The Man Who Would Prosecute Oliver North Is a Marine Veteran Known for His Tough Courtroom Stance," *Los Angeles Times,* January 12, 1989.

"We were trying to reimagine": Debbie Mesloh (Harris friend and first campaign worker; campaign spokeswoman) in discussion with the author, October 2020.

"She just beamed": Laura Talmus (Harris friend and fund-raiser) in discussion with the author, September 2020.

The training was for candidates: Jane Ganahl, "Finding Their Voices: Training Program Helps Women Shape Political Dreams," *San Francisco Chronicle,* February 23, 2003.

made a point of distancing herself: Byrne, "Kamala's Karma."

"The bottom line is": Phillip Matier and

Andrew Ross, "Brains, Brio, Beauty — and Wounded Feelings," *San Francisco Chronicle,* November 10, 2003.

Guilfoyle gained notoriety: Phillip Matier and Andrew Ross, "Contract Reportedly Out on Life of Dog Case Prosecutor," *San Francisco Chronicle,* November 21, 2001.

"It is obviously a gender victory": Demian Bulwa, "Harris Defeats Hallinan after Bitter Campaign," *San Francisco Chronicle,* December 10, 2003.

8: Officer Down

At about 9:30 p.m.: People v. Hill, A117787, January 13, 2011.

Police, having been tipped: Demian Bulwa and Jaxon Van Derbeken, "Suspect in Slaying of SFPD Officer in Custody," *San Francisco Chronicle,* April 12, 2004.

"To hesitate is to die": People v. Hill, A117787, January 13, 2011.

Neighborhood kids drew a picture: Demian Bulwa and Jaxon Van Derbeken, "Suspect in Slaying of SFPD Officer in Custody/ Bayview 'War Zone' Site of Fatal Shooting Late Saturday Night," *San Francisco Chronicle,* April 12, 2004.

"It's so utterly unnecessary": Ibid.

she would not seek death for Hill: Jaxon Van

Derbeken, "Not Guilty Plea in Killing of Officer," *San Francisco Chronicle,* April 15, 2004.

"We, the command staff": Jaxon Van Derbeken, "S.F. Police Push Hard for Death Penalty," *San Francisco Chronicle,* April 21, 2004.

no other similar instance in which prosecutors: Matthew B. Stannard, "San Francisco D.A. Won't Pursue Death in Cop Slaying," *San Francisco Chronicle,* April 14, 2004.

forty-three of eighty members: Assembly Joint Resolution No. 82, California Legislature, 2003–2004 Regular Session (2004).

"Isaac paid the ultimate price": Matthew B. Stannard, "Police Mourn Hero Who Refused to Give Up," *San Francisco Chronicle,* April 17, 2004.

"This is not only the definition": Ibid.

"You could feel the shock": Bill Lockyer (former California attorney general) in discussion with the author, September 2020.

Feinstein had her own history: John Balzar, "Feinstein Support of Death Penalty Draws Party Boos," *Los Angeles Times,* April 8, 1990.

"For those who want this defendant": Kamala

Harris, "Justice for Officer Espinoza, Peace for the City," *San Francisco Chronicle,* April 23, 2004.

9: Getting "Smart" on Crime

"Sunnydale, also called 'The Dale'": Leslie Fulbright, "Life at the Bottom: S.F.'s Sunnydale Project," *San Francisco Chronicle,* February 3, 2008.

The Los Angeles Times *detailed the 2008 case:* Michael Finnegan, "San Francisco's D.A.'s Program Trained Illegal Immigrants for Jobs They Couldn't Legally Hold," *Los Angeles Times,* June 22, 2009.

"There were no crowds": Matthew D. Davis (classmate of Harris's from Hastings and a friend) in discussion with the author, October 2020.

redefined prostitution: Assembly Bill No. 3042 Sentencing, California State Legislature (2004).

"It's finally in black and white": Lee Romney, "Bill Would Fight Child Prostitution," *Los Angeles Times,* September 5, 2004.

"There is a very direct connection": Don Thompson, "Calif. Bill Could Jail Parents if Kids Miss School," Associated Press, May 13, 2020.

"I just want these kids": Ibid.

10: Harris and Obama

"That was probably not": Dan Morain, "Republicans Dismiss Harris at Their Peril," *Los Angeles Times,* February 8, 2019; Buffy Wicks (Obama's chief California organizer in 2007 who later joined his White House staff) in discussion with the author, February 2019.

"I am so psyched": Carla Marinucci, "Excitement Surrounds Obama's Visit to Oakland," *San Francisco Chronicle,* March 18, 2007.

Obama was on a fund-raising blitz: Dan Morain and Doug Smith, "Clinton and Obama in a Dead Heat," *Los Angeles Times,* April 16, 2007.

"one of the most extraordinary": SanBenito.com, December 11, 2007, https://sanbenito.com/softball-pitch-for-2008/.

"I have my own legacy": Catherine Kim and Zack Stanton, "55 Things You Need to Know About Kamala Harris," *Politico,* August 11, 2020.

11: The Mad Dash

"long had focused on running": Dan Morain, "Kamala Harris, an Early Barack Obama Backer, Begins Her Ascent," *Los Angeles*

Times, November 12, 2008.

They lingered a little too long: Ace Smith (Harris's chief strategist, political consultant) in discussion with the author, October 2020.

"In movie terms, we are dying": Scott Martelle, "Top of the Ticket," *Los Angeles Times,* September 7, 2007.

"For as long as I could remember": Kamala Harris, "Everyone Gets Sick. And We Deserve Better," *New York Times,* December 29, 2018.

"Kamala has spent": "LA Mayor Antonio Villaraigosa Endorses Kamala Harris for Attorney General," Facebook, April 16, 2010, https://www.facebook.com/notes/kamala-harris/la-mayor-antonio-villaraigosa-endorses-kamala-harris-for-attorney-general/417633530662/.

found that Harris based her statement: Peter Jamison, "A Lack of Conviction," *SF Weekly,* May 5, 2010.

"They should only bring cases": Kate Chatfield (policy director of the Justice Collaborative; also affiliated with University of San Francisco law school) in discussion with the author, October 2020.

On that same day, a separate jury: Bob Egelko, "SF Man Awarded $10 Million after Jury Finds Police Framed Him for

Murder," *San Francisco Chronicle,* April 6, 2018.

Trulove was an aspiring rapper: Jaxon Van Derbeken, "Reality TV Figure's Courtroom Drama," *San Francisco Chronicle,* February 3, 2010.

"brave eyewitness who stepped": Jaxon Van Derbeken, *San Francisco Chronicle,* February 10, 2010.

a state court of appeal reversed Trulove's conviction: People v. Trulove, CA1/2, A130481A (Cal. Ct. App. 2014).

a new jury in San Francisco acquitted Trulove: Jaxon Van Derbeken, "Ex-Reality TV Show Contestant Acquitted of Murder in S.F. Retrial," *San Francisco Chronicle,* March 11, 2015.

a federal jury awarded him $14.5 million: Paul Elias, "San Francisco Pays $13.1 Million to Man Framed for Murder," Associated Press, March 19, 2019.

the San Francisco Board of Supervisors settled: Ibid.

"Kamala Harris tried to be progressive": Marc J. Zilversmit (San Francisco criminal defense attorney and appellate attorney) in discussion with the author, September 2020.

"People saw the prison system": Ace Smith (Harris's chief strategist) in discussion

with the author, October 2020.

Authorities were investigating Bell: Jeff Gottlieb and Ruben Vives, "Is a City Manager Worth $800,000?" *Los Angeles Times,* July 15, 2010.

12: Change Comes to California

"Against almost any other opponent": "Cooley Has Edge in Experience for Attorney General," editorial, *Sacramento Bee,* October 8, 2010.

predicted Harris would lose: Bridget Bowman, "When Kamala Harris Lost on Election Night, but Won Three Weeks Later," *RollCall,* July 16, 2019.

"This, needless to say, is corruption": Jeff Gottlieb, Ruben Vives, and Jack Leonard, "Bell Leaders Hauled Off in Cuffs," *Los Angeles Times,* September 22, 2010.

"This is not about Kamala Harris": Steve Cooley (Los Angeles County district attorney) in discussion with the author, October 2020.

"dear, dear friend": Alexander Burns, "California's High-Stakes AG Race," *Politico,* November 18, 2010.

Under the headline: Marisa Lagos, "Corruption Fighter Accepted Many Gifts," *San Francisco Chronicle,* August 9, 2010.

"cannot withstand any level": Hollingsworth v Perry, 704 F. Supp. 2d 921 (2010) 123.

"Now that Proposition 8 has been found": "State Attorney General Debate," Kamala Harris, Ken Cooley," October 5, 2010, ATS Video from webcast.ucdavis.edu on July 24, 2015, https://video.ucdavis.edu/media/State+Attorney+General+Debate+-+Kamala+Harris%2C+Ken+Cooley+10-05-2010/0_s5l4d8po.

13: Attorney General Harris

More than one million Californians: Edmund G. Brown Jr., *Governor's Budget Summary, 2011–12,* State of California, January 10, 2011, 1.

"She understood the issues": Dane Gillette (former chief of Criminal Division, California Attorney General's Office) in discussion with the author, October 2020.

the U.S. Supreme Court in a 5–4 decision: Brown v. Plata, 563 U.S. 493 (2011).

"Shane Taylor was a mistake": Howard Broadman (former Superior Court judge) in discussion with the author, October 2020.

14: The Relic

In 2006, Michael Morales: Morales v. Hickman, 415 F. Supp. 2d 1037 (N.D. Cal. 2006).

Robert Lee Massie, the last San Franciscan: Jim Herron Zamora et al., "Massie Executed for 1979 S.F. Murder," *San Francisco Chronicle,* March 27, 2001.

the case of Ernest Dewayne Jones: Jones v. Chappell, 31 F. Supp. 3d 1050 (C.D. Cal. 2014).

"not supported by the law": "Attorney General Kamala D. Harris Issues Statement on Appeal of Court Ruling on California's Death Penalty," press release, State of California Department of Justice, August 21, 2014, https://oag.ca.gov/news/press-releases/attorney-general-kamala-d-harris-issues-statement-appeal-court-ruling-california.

The state appealed Carney's ruling: Jones v. Davis, 806 F. 3d 538 (9th Cir., 2015).

"immoral, discriminatory": "Senator Kamala Harris on California Death Penalty Moratorium," press release, Kamala D. Harris, March 13, 2019, https://www.harris.senate.gov/news/press-releases/senator-kamala-harris-on-california-death-penalty-moratorium.

The following day, she told reporters: "Kamala Harris Calls for Federal Moratorium on Executions," Associated Press, March 14, 2019.

California has 691 condemned men: "Condemned Inmate List (Secure)," California Department of Corrections and Rehabilitation, updated October 7, 2020, https://www.cdcr.ca.gov/capital-punishment/condemned-inmate-list-secure-request/.

Between June 24 and July 29: "Coronavirus Prison Fatalities Surpass Two Decades of Executions," Death Penalty Information Center, August 31, 2020, https://deathpenaltyinfo.org/news/coronavirus-prison-fatalities-surpass-two-decades-of-executions-covid-19-has-killed-more-california-death-row-prisoners-than-the-state-has-executed-in-27-years.

"They'd rather execute": Aldrin Brown and David E. Hendrix, "Evidence on Trial: Kevin Cooper Is on Death Row for the 1983 Massacre of Four People in Chino Hills," *Press-Enterprise,* August 20, 2000.

On May 17, 2018: Nicholas Kristof, "Was Kevin Cooper Framed for Murder?" *New York Times,* May 17, 2018.

15: Wedding Bells

"We stood together performing": K. Harris, *Truths We Hold,* 111.

"Too much. Too fast. Too soon": Dean Murphy, "Some Democrats Blame One of Their Own, *New York Times,* November 5, 2004.

"San Francisco's gay-marriage mayor": "Court Challenges in Pipeline for San Francisco Gay Marriages," *The Big Story with John Gibson,* television newscast, John Gibson, Fox News Network, February 17, 2004.

"If every public official": Lockyer v. City and County of San Francisco, 17 Cal. Rptr. 3d 225 (2004).

"In view of the substance": Adam Liptak, "California Supreme Court Overturns Gay Marriage Ban," *New York Times,* May 16, 2008.

More than 75 percent: "Supplement to the Statement of Vote: Statewide Summary by County for State Ballot Measures," General Election — Statement of Vote, November 4, 2008, California Secretary of State, https://elections.cdn.sos.ca.gov/sov/2008-general/ssov/10-ballot-measures-statewide-summary-by-county.pdf (accessed September 2020).

"We canvassed the entire state": Jessica Garrison, Cara Mia Dimassa, and Richard C. Paddock, "Nation Watches as State Weighs Ban," *Los Angeles Times,* November 5, 2008.

George left little doubt: "Brief for the State of California as Amicus Curiae in Support of Respondents," *Hollingsworth v. Perry,* 12-144, U.S. (2013).

"Chickens gained valuable rights": Ronald George, Induction Ceremony American Academy of Arts and Sciences, "The Perils of Direct Democracy: The California Experience," Remarks by Chief Justice Ronald M. George, Cambridge, Massachusetts, October 10, 2009.

filing a brief on February 27, 2013: "Brief for the State of California as Amicus Curiae in Support of Respondents," *Hollingsworth v. Perry,* 12-144, U.S. (2013).

Two days after the Supreme Court ruled: Maura Dolan, "Prop 8: Gay Marriages Can Resume in California, Court Rules," *Los Angeles Times,* June 28, 2013.

"On my way to S.F.": Kamala Harris (@KamalaHarris), "On My Way to S.F. City Hall . . . ," Twitter, June 28, 2013, https://twitter.com/KamalaHarris/status/350744403272413185?s=20.

"By virtue of the power": KRON 4, "Raw

Video Wedding of Kris Perry and Sandy Stier," YouTube, https://www.youtube.com/watch?v=_RcpgACc6JY.

16: The Damned Photos

161 laws in total: John Myers, "Even Rivals Say Mark Leno Is One of Sacramento's Most Accomplished Lawmakers. Now, His Time Is Up," *Los Angeles Times,* August 29, 2016.

"protect innocent Californians": Attorney General Harris testimony, California Senate Public Safety Committee, California State Senate Session 2011–2012 (2011). Audio recording. California State Senate Media Archive.

I spent a cold January night: Dan Morain, "When Confiscating Guns in California Make Sense," *Sacramento Bee,* January 22, 2013.

"Babies. Babies. Babies": Erin Lehane (Harris friend) in discussion with the author, October 2020.

17: Mortgage Meltdown

"As Attorney General of California": Kamala Harris (@Kamala-Harris), "As Attorney

General of California . . . ," Twitter, February 23, 2019, https://twitter.com/KamalaHarris/status/1099498399454384128?s=20; Facebook, February 23, 2019, https://www.facebook.com/KamalaHarris/posts/10157501079732923?comment_id=10157501137007923.

"They seemed to be under the misimpression": K. Harris, *Truths We Hold,* 97.

Miller, meanwhile, concluded: Brady Dennis, "N.Y. Bumped from 50-State Foreclosure Committee," *Washington Post,* August 23, 2011.

The Los Angeles Times *quoted:* Alejandro Lazo, "Kamala Harris Pressured to Reject Bank Foreclosure Settlement," *Los Angeles Times,* September 30, 2011.

Harris announced that she was: California attorney general Kamala Harris, letter to U.S. associate attorney general Thomas Perrelli and Iowa attorney general Tom Miller, September 30, 2011.

"The banks were furious": K. Harris, *Truths We Hold,* 94.

"There were periods": Ibid., 100.

On January 23, 2012: Nelson D. Schwartz and Shaila Dewan, "Political Push Moves a Deal on Mortgages Inches Closer," *New York Times,* January 23, 2012.

"The reality," Rodriguez told me: Dan Morain, "A Shallow Promise of Justice in Housing Scandal," *Sacramento Bee,* January 26, 2012.

Schneiderman sat by Michelle Obama: Edward-Isaac Dovere, "The Battle That Changed Kamala Harris," *Atlantic,* August 20, 2020.

"Hundreds of thousands of homeowners": "Attorney General Kamala D. Harris Secures $18 Billion California Commitment for Struggling Homeowners," press release, State of California Department of Justice, February 9, 2012, https://oag.ca.gov/news/press-releases/attorney-general-kamala-d-harris-secures-18-billion-california-commitment.

"This issue has never been": "Kamala Harris Among the Rising Dem Stars at DNC," *All Things Considered,* radio newscast, Richard Gonzales, NPR, September 3, 2012.

However, many Californians: Phil Willon, "$25-Billion Foreclosure Settlement Was a Victory for Kamala Harris in California, but It Wasn't Perfect," *Los Angeles Times,* October 16, 2016.

"protecting legally exposed mortgage fraudsters": David Dayen, "Kamala Harris Celebrates Her Role in the Mortgage

Crisis Settlement. The Reality Is Quite Different," *Intercept,* March 13, 2019, https://theintercept.com/2019/03/13/kamala-harris-mortage-crisis/.

"For the banks, the settlement": Dayen, "Kamala Harris Celebrates Her Role."

Matt Levin, the housing reporter: Matt Levin, "Big Investment Firms Have Stopped Gobbling Up California Homes," CalMatters, *Los Angeles Daily News,* April 5, 2018.

"She made it happen": Author interview with Mark Leno, October 2020.

18: Phenomenal Women

"It was incredible": Joe Garofoli, "Kamala Harris Gets Key Convention Slot," *San Francisco Chronicle,* September 4, 2012.

"If you really want to know": Kamala Harris, draft of a speech provided to author, September 2012.

Kamala Harris provided Politico: Burgess Everett and Elana Schor, "Kamala Harris Keeps 'Em Guessing," *Politico,* March 8, 2018.

19: "Just a Dude"

Emhoff represented a Los Angeles company: Jukin Media, Inc. v. QWorldstar, Inc., 2:16-

cv-06800 (C.D. Calif. 2017).

Emhoff tells his recollection: Chasten Buttigieg, "Chasten Chats with Douglas Emhoff and Sen. Kamala Harris (w/Special Appearance from Pete Buttigieg!)," YouTube, April 21, 2020, https://www.youtube.com/watch?v=D7xyMtJSi0U.

"He's cute": K. Harris, *Truths We Hold,* 126.

"I was like just a dude": C. Buttigieg, "Chasten Chats with Douglas Emhoff."

"Like a lot of career": Ronald Wood (Los Angeles attorney) in discussion with the author, October 2020.

"He was the sweetest guy": Mark Buell (friend of Harris and philanthropist) in discussion with the author, October 2020.

"She looked truly very happy": Erin Lehane (Harris friend) in discussion with the author, October 2020.

"these dad moves": Doug Emhoff (@DouglasEmhoff), "If I Can Do These Dad Moves . . . ," Twitter, June 30, 2019, https://twitter.com/DouglasEmhoff/status/1145458269298630661?s=20.

"the evolved hubby": Manuel Roig-Franzia, "Doug Emhoff Paused His Career for His Wife Kamala Harris's Aspirations — and Became the Campaign's 'Secret Weapon,' " *Washington Post,* October 28, 2020.

20: Woman in a Hurry

"I hope so": Dan Morain, "Kamala Harris Stays on Message, Which Means She Bobs and Weaves," *Sacramento Bee,* August 9, 2014.

"Acapulco Gold": Debra J. Saunders, "Will California's Next Top Cop Support Legal Pot?" *San Francisco Chronicle,* October 10, 2014.

"Substantial evidence presented": Jennifer Medina, "Judge Rejects Teacher Tenure for California," *TEACHERWISE* (blog), June 10, 2014, https://teacherwise.wordpress.com/2014/06/10/judge-rejects-teacher-tenure-for-california/.

Harris won only twenty-six: "Statement of Vote: November 4, 2014, General Election," California Secretary of State, https://elections.cdn.sos.ca.gov/sov/2014-general/pdf/ 2014-complete-sov.pdf, 34–36.

She was a Republican: Dan Morain, "Chief Justice of the California Supreme Court Leaves the Republican Party, Citing Kavanaugh," CalMatters, December 13, 2018, https://calmatters.org/politics/2018/12/chief-justice-of-the-california-supreme-court-leaves-the-republican-party-citing-kavanaugh/.

Harris spoke in ambitious terms: "Attorney

General Kamala D. Harris Sworn In, Delivers Inaugural Address," press release, State of California Department of Justice, January 5, 2015.

21: Joe Biden Gives Harris a Hand

"She has been dubbed": Rory Carroll, "Kamala Harris: The 'Female Obama' Plots Her Course on the Road to Washington," *Guardian* (UK edition), January 14, 2015.

"smart, tough, and experienced": Elizabeth Warren, "I'm Supporting Kamala," Elizabeth Warren for Senate, January 14, 2015, https://elizabethforma.com/im-supporting-kamala/.

"exactly the kind of leader": Dan Morain, "Harris' Senate Ambitions Now Are More Sizzle than Substance," *Sacramento Bee,* January 17, 2015.

"His loyalty and his relationship": Christopher Cadelago, "Willie Brown: Villaraigosa Should Sit Out U.S. Senate Race," *Sacramento Bee,* January 23, 2015.

It was a fundamentally offensive: "Willie Brown's Guide to Losing Friends and Alienating Voters," editorial, *Sacramento Bee,* January 27, 2015.

She is one of seven kids: Michael Finnegan, "Loretta Sanchez's Public Image a Factor in Senate Race," *Los Angeles Times,* May 14, 2015.

she was prone to gaffes: Dan Morain, "Dan Morain: Loretta Sanchez Runs Against Kamala Harris and Herself," *Sacramento Bee,* January 22, 2016.

broke into an odd dance move: Kenny Ducey, "A History of Cam Newton and the 'Dab,' " *Sports Illustrated,* February 7, 2016, https://www.si.com/extra-mustard/2016/02/07/nfl-super-bowl-cam-newton-dab-dance-celebration#:~:text=Back%20in%20October%2C%20Cam%20Newton,for%20making%20the%20dance%20popular.

press was denied access: Carla Marinucci, "Kamala Harris' 'Bizarre' Move: No Press at Kickoff Event," *San Francisco Chronicle,* April 3, 2015.

"spending hundreds of thousands": Christopher Cadelago, "Kamala Harris Spending Big Chunk of Money Raised for Senate Race," *Sacramento Bee,* October 29, 2015.

a campaign shake-up: Phil Willon, "Kamala Harris Shakes Up Senate Campaign Staff," *Los Angeles Times,* November 17, 2015.

Then an anvil fell: Alex Roarty, "Posh Hotels and Pricey Airfare: Meet the Senate Candidate Driving Democrats Crazy," *Atlantic,* December 6, 2015.

To have even an outside chance: Dan Morain, "Harris' Senate Ambitions Now Are More Sizzle Than Substance," *Sacramento Bee,* January 17, 2015.

"Our people are not the problem": Dan Morain, "Joe Biden Calls for Some Political Civility in Uncivil Times," *Sacramento Bee,* March 5, 2016.

Sanchez blundered: Phil Willon and Jazmine Ulloa, "Rep. Loretta Sanchez Implies Obama Endorsed Senate Rival because They Are Both Black," *Los Angeles Times,* July 22, 2016.

22: Picking Her Shots

"When you have a candidate": Christopher Cadelago, "Loretta Sanchez, Kamala Harris Wrangle Over Trump University," *Sacramento Bee,* September 14, 2016.

"isolated" and "impatient": Floyd Norris, "Corinthian Colleges Faltering as Flow of Federal Money Slows, *New York Times,* June 26, 2014.

The company nearly doubled: Chris Kirkham, "Corinthian Closing Its Last Schools; 10,000 California Students Displaced," *Los Angeles Times,* April 26, 2015.

Warren also was one of a dozen: "Twelve Senators Urge Education Department to Protect Students while Continuing Oversight of Other For-Profit Colleges," U.S. Senate Committee on Heath, Education, Labor & Pensions, June 26, 2014, https://www.help.senate.gov/ranking/newsroom/press/twelve-senators-urge-education-department-to-protect-students-while-continuing-oversight-of-other-for-profit-colleges.

23: Fighting the Forever War

On its website, Planned Parenthood's: "9 Reasons to Love Kamala Harris," Planned Parenthood, https://www.plannedparenthoodaction.org/elections/kamala-harris (accessed October 27, 2020).

In July 2015, he and an entity: Paige St. John, "Kamala Harris' Support for Planned Parenthood Draws Fire after Raid on Anti-Abortion Activist," *Los Angeles Times,* April 7, 2016.

a gunman raving about body parts: Julie Turkewitz and Jack Healy, "3 Are Dead in Colorado Springs Shootout at Planned Parenthood Center," *New York Times,*

November 27, 2015.

"Planned Parenthood is a well-respected": Christopher Cadelago, "Kamala Harris to Review Group behind Planned Parenthood Abortion Videos," *Sacramento Bee,* July 24, 2015.

"They worked at their normal": Kathy Kneer (president and CEO of Planned Parenthood Affiliates of California) in discussion with the author, October 2020.

"ongoing security requests/needs": Jill E. Habig, email message provided to the author by source, April 5, 2016.

they seized Daleiden's computers: St. John, "Kamala Harris' Support for Planned Parenthood."

"We had no advance word": Kathy Kneer (president and CEO of Planned Parenthood Affiliates of California) in discussion with the author, October 2020.

"California has public programs": Reproductive FACT Act, AB-775, California State Assembly (2015).

"exists to protect": "About NIFLA," NIFLA, https://nifla.org/about-nifla/ (accessed October 27, 2020).

"Forcing speech is not": National Institute of Family and Life Advocates, letter to California Assembly Committee, Bill

Analysis of Assembly Bill 775, April 14, 2015.

"Now, we're finding out": Dan Morain, "Howan Abortion Rights Law Ended Up Bankrolling Anti-Abortion Forces in CA," CalMatters, November 4, 2019, https://calmatters.org/politics/2019/11/abortion-law-california-settlement-nifla-becerra-daleiden-sekulow/.

"I am proud to have": "Attorney General Kamala D. Harris Issues Statement on Governor Brown Signing Reproductive FACT Act into Law," press release, State of California Department of Justice, October 9, 2015, https://oag.ca.gov/news/press-releases/attorney-general-kamala-d-harris-issues-statement-governor-brown-signing.

"Licensed clinics must provide": Adam Liptak, "Supreme Court Backs Anti-Abortion Pregnancy Centers in Free Speech Case," *New York Times,* June 26, 2018.

His legal team consisted of: Morain, "How an Abortion Rights Law Ended Up Bankrolling Anti-Abortion Forces."

Attorney General Becerra filed: The People of the State of California v. David Robert Daleiden and Sandra Susan Merritt, San Francisco Superior Court (2017).

"It's pretty obvious": "NEW VIDEO: Planned

Parenthood and Kamala Harris Colluded to Weaponize CA Video Recording Law against Disfavored Speech," Center for Medical Progress, October 6, 2020, https://www.centerformedicalprogress.org/2020/10/new-video-planned-parenthood-and-kamala-harris-colluded-to-weaponize-ca-video-recording-law-against-disfavored-speech/.

24: "Go Get 'Em"

"Human trafficking is a modern": The State of Human Trafficking in California, Human Trafficking Work Group, California Department of Justice, 2012.

Craigslist, under pressure: Claire Cain Miller, "Craigslist Says It Has Shut Its Section for Sex Ads," *New York Times,* September 15, 2010.

"increasingly concerned about human trafficking": National Association of Attorneys General letter to Samuel Fifer, August 31, 2011.

"to investigate and prosecute": National Association of Attorneys General letter to Senators John Rockefeller IV and John Thune and Representatives Frederick Upton and Henry Waxman, July 23, 2013.

"made me sick to my stomach": Maggy Krell

(former California Department of Justice; special counsel to Planned Parenthood Affiliates of California) in discussion with the author, October 2020.

California unsealed the complaint: "Attorney General Kamala D. Harris Announces Criminal Charges against Senior Corporate Officers of Backpage.com for Profiting from Prostitution and Arrest of Carl Ferrer, CEO," press release, State of California Department of Justice, October 6, 2016, https://oag.ca.gov/news/press-releases/attorney-general-kamala-d-harris-announces-criminal-charges-against-senior.

"Somebody needed to start it": Carissa Phelps (advocate for children; author and attorney) in discussion with the author, October 2020.

"This is a frightening abuse": Mike Masnick, "Merry Christmas: Kamala Harris Files Brand New Criminal Charges against Backpage Execs after Last Ones Were Tossed Out," *Techdirt* (blog), December 23, 2016, https://www.techdirt.com/articles/20161223/15495736339/ merry-christmas-kamala-harris-files-brand-new-criminal-charges-against-backpage-execs-after-last-ones-were-tossed-out.shtml.

California could pursue money laundering:

Don Thompson, "Judge Allows Money Laundering Charges against Backpage Execs," Associated Press, August 23, 2017.

On April 9, 2018: Tom Jackman and Mark Berman, "Top Officials at Backpage.com Indicted after Classifieds Site Taken Offline," *Washington Post,* April 9, 2018.

The federal case resulted: United States of America v. Michael Lacey, CR-18-00422-PHX-SPL (BSB) (D. Ariz. 2018).

25: "I Intend to Fight"

"drawing all the interest": George Skelton, "Capitol Journal: Few Are Paying Attention to California's Senate Contest — because It May Be Putting Them to Sleep," *Los Angeles Times,* October 10, 2016.

a failed businessman armed: Julie Tamaki and Dan Morain, "Baffling Portrait of S.F. Gunman Emerges," *Los Angeles Times,* July 3, 1993.

"She tried to be reassuring": Erin Lehane (Harris friend) in discussion with the author, October 2020.

"Those in the know point": Phillip Matier and Andrew Ross, "How Kamala Harris Turned U.S. Senate Contest into a Cakewalk," *San Francisco Chronicle,* November

6, 2016.

"Auntie Kamala, that man": K. Harris, *Truths We Hold,* ii.

"Do we retreat or do we fight?": KCRA-Sacramento, "Kamala Harris Election Night Speech, 2016," YouTube video, May 1, 2016, http://bit.ly/1kjRAAn.

"You are not alone": Phil Willon, "Newly Elected Kamala Harris Vows to Defy Trump on Immigration," *Los Angeles Times,* November 10, 2016.

26: Stepping onto the National Stage

roughly the same amount that Warren: Katharine Q. Seelye, "A New Senator, Known Nationally and Sometimes Feared," *New York Times,* November 10, 2012.

One silver lining: Amber Phillips, "One Election Bright Spot for Democrats: Women of Color," *Washington Post,* November 10, 2016.

"Hey, Kamala, you got any interest": Ron Wyden (senior U.S. Senator for Oregon) in discussion with the author's researcher, Josh Meyer, October 2020.

When Schumer announced: "Schumer Announces Senate Democratic Committee Memberships for the 115th Congress," press release, December 20, 2016, http://

static.politico.com/be/b6/1ba2e7f1465fadebe406e448aaad/ senate-democratic-committee-assignments.pdf.

"These four committees will be": "Harris Appoints Community Leader, Veteran Organizer and Champion of Immigrant Communities to Lead State Operation," press release, Kamala D. Harris, December 18, 2016, https://www.harris.senate.gov/news/press-releases/harris-appoints-community-leader-veteran-organizer-and-champion-of-immigrant-communities-to-lead-state-operation.

27: The Resistance

"This is a remarkable public servant": Nomination of John F. Kelly, Hearing before the Committee on Homeland Security and Governmental Affairs, U.S. Senate, 115th Cong., 1st Sess., January 10, 2017.

40 percent of the population: Hans Johnson and Sergio Sanchez, "Just the Facts: Immigrants in California," Public Policy Institute of California, May 2019, https://www.ppic.org/publication/immigrants-in-california/.

"Unfortunately, I can't look Dreamers": Ron Wyden (senior U.S. Senator for Oregon) in discussion with the author's researcher,

Josh Meyer, October 2020.

"Russian efforts to influence": Background to "Assessing Russian Activities and Intentions in Recent US Elections": The Analytic Process and Cyber Incident Attribution, Office of the Director of National Intelligence, January 6, 2017, https://www.dni.gov/files/documents/ICA_2017_01.pdf.

"there was absolutely no effect": Greg Miller and Adam Entous, "Declassified Report Says Putin 'Ordered' Effort to Undermine Faith in U.S. Election and Help Trump," *Washington Post,* January 6, 2017.

U.S. spy agencies had unverified: Ibid.

"We've done what we can": Open Hearing on the Intelligence Community's Assessment on Russian Activities and Intentions in the 2016 U.S. Elections, Hearing before the Select Committee on Intelligence of the United States Senate, 115th Cong., 1st Sess., January 10, 2017.

"Do you fully accept its findings": Open Hearing to Consider the Nomination of Hon. Mike Pompeo to Be Director of the Central Intelligence Agency, Hearing before the Select Committee on Intelligence of the United States Senate, 115th Cong., 1st Sess., January 12, 2017.

"who serve often": "Senator Kamala D. Harris Presses Pompeo on Russian Inter-

ference in the Election & National Security Impact of Global Climate Change," press release, Kamala D. Harris, January 12, 2017, https://www.harris.senate.gov/news/ press-releases/senator-kamala-d-harris-presses-pompeo-on-russian-interference-in-the-election-and-national-security-impact-of-global-climate-change.

28: "I'm Asking the Questions"

"will become a self-inflicted wound": Nicholas Fandos, "Growing Number of G.O.P. Lawmakers Criticize Trump's Refugee Policy," *New York Times,* January 29, 2017.

"Why are you calling": K. Harris, *Truths We Hold,* 157.

"Would you let me finish once?": Ian Schwartz, "Let Me at Least Finish Once Before You Interrupt Me," *RealClear Politics,* June 6, 2017.

"Can you give me": Jeremy Herb, "Senators Try to Quiet Harris, but She Doesn't Back Down," CNN, June 7, 2017.

"RT this if you've ordered": Kamala Harris (@KamalaHarris), "RT This If You've Ordered . . . ," Twitter, June 10, 2017, https://twitter.com/KamalaHarris/status/873678921841201152?s=20.

"Smoke the hell": Jim Spears a.k.a. QuaranTweeting (@QuaereNon), "Smoke the Hell Out of Jeff Sessions Tuesday . . . ," Twitter, June 10, 2017, https://twitter.com/QuaereNon/status/873679800552103936?s=20.

"just cut through Jeff Sessions' bullshit": Jim Spears (Louisiana college professor) in interview with the author's researcher, Josh Meyer, October 2020.

"I'm not able to be rushed": "Attorney General Testimony on Russian Investigation," C-SPAN, June 13, 2017, https://www.c-span.org/video/?429875-1/attorney-general-calls-collusion-accusations-detestable-lie.

"I'm not able to answer the question": Ibid.

29: "Yes or No"

"It is critical we have": "Senator Harris Returns from Trip to the Middle East," press release, Kamala D. Harris, April 17, 2017, https://www.harris.senate.gov/news/press-releases/senator-harris-returns-from-trip-to-the-middle-east.

"I know I'm not the only one": Elaine Duke (American civil servant and former U.S. Deputy Secretary of Homeland Security) in discussion with the author's researcher,

Josh Meyer, October 2020.

"Look, I've seen the tweet": "James Comey: Lordy, I Hope There Are Tapes," C-SPAN, June 8, 2017, https://www.c-span.org/video/?c4672714/james-comey-lordy-hope-tapes.

"In my interactions with her": Ron Wyden (senior U.S. Senator for Oregon) in discussion with the author's researcher, Josh Meyer, October 2020.

"Kamala Harris comes to play": Ibid.

30: Harris v. Kavanaugh

"We cannot possibly move forward": "Supreme Court Nominee Brett Kavanaugh Confirmation Hearing, Day 1, Part 1," C-SPAN, September 4, 2018, https://www.c-span.org/video/?449704-1/brett-kavanaugh-confirmation-hearing-begins-amid-democratic-objections-public-protests.

"Judge, have you ever discussed": "Supreme Court Nominee Brett Kavanaugh Confirmation Hearing, Day 2, Part 5," C-SPAN, September 4, 2018, https://www.c-span.org/video/?449705-15/supreme-court-nominee-brett-kavanaugh-confirmation-hearing-day-2-part-5.

"You should know that": Ibid.

"that nothing seemed to": Ruth Marcus, *Supreme Ambition: Brett Kavanaugh and the Conservative Takeover* (New York: Simon & Schuster, 2019), 240.

"demanding answers": Ibid., 241.

"You've got to figure": Ibid., 246.

Ford went public: Emma Brown, "California Professor, Writer of Confidential Brett Kavanaugh Letter, Speaks Out about Her Allegation of Sexual Assault," *Washington Post,* September 16, 2018.

"That individual strongly requested": Ibid.

"Dr. Ford, first of all": "Supreme Court Nominee Brett Kavanaugh Sexual Assault Hearing, Professor Blasey Ford Testimony," C-SPAN, September 27, 2018, https://www.c-span.org/video/?451895-1/professor-blasey-ford-testifies-sexual-assault-allegations-part-1.

In 2019, Time *magazine:* "*Time* 100 Most Influential People, 2019," *Time,* https://time.com/collection/100-most-influential-people-2019/.

31: A Death in the Family

"Really? Really": Lorena O'Neil, "Samantha Bee, Stephen Colbert Criticize Jason Miller Calling Kamala Harris 'Hysterical,' " *Hollywood Reporter,* June 15, 2017.

"hatred and division": Bill Barrow and Meg Kinnard, "Kamala Harris: Midterms a Fight for 'the Best of Who We Are,' " Associated Press, October 19, 2018.

"had spoken for all": Maeve Reston, "Kamala Harris Receives a Hero's Welcome from Women in Iowa," CNN, October 25, 2018, https://www.cnn.com/2018/10/25/politics/kamala-harris-iowa-women/index.html.

"May Be the Antidote": Rekha Basu, "Kamala Harris' Passion, Optimism, Warmth May Be the Antidote to Trump's Snide Divisiveness," *Des Moines Register,* October 23, 2018.

"everywhere she's been": Edward-Isaac Dovere, "Kamala Harris's Anti-Trump Tour," *Atlantic,* October 26, 2018.

"And she unobtrusively": Beth Foster Gayle, interview by Anderson Cooper, *Anderson Cooper 360,* CNN, August 12, 2020.

"We can honor the ancestors": "Harris at Spelman College: 'Go Forward Unburdened, Unwavering, and Undaunted by the Fight,' " press release, Kamala D. Harris, October 26, 2018, https://www.harris.senate.gov/news/press-releases/harris-at-spelman-college-go-forward-unburdened-unwavering-and-undaunted-by-the-fight.

"a warrior, a gentle friendly warrior": KCRA-Sacramento, "Tyrone Gayle Memorial Service," YouTube video, November 10, 2018, https://www.youtube.com/watch?v=DId5FtJ_N48.

32: "For the People"

"So, I'm supposed to ask": "Sen. Kamala Harris Says She's 'Not Yet Ready' to Announce if She'll Run for President," *The View,* season 22, episode 77, ABC, January 8, 2019, https://abcnews.go.com/theview/video/sen-kamala-harris-shes-ready-announce-shell-run-60236162.

"The American people deserve": "Sen. Kamala Harris Announces 2020 Presidential Run," *Good Morning America,* ABC, January 21, 2019, https://www.goodmorningamerica.com/news/video/sen-kamala-harris-announces-2020-presidential-run-60518540.

"I'm running to be president": Kamala Harris, "I'm Running to Be President of the People . . . ," Facebook, January 28, 2019, https://www.facebook.com/KamalaHarris/posts/im-running-to-be-president-of-the-people-by-the-people-and-for-all-people-im-run/10157431129232923/.

"the best opening so far": Peter Baker and

Maggie Haberman, "Trump, in Interview, Calls Wall Talks 'Waste of Time' and Dismisses Investigations," *New York Times,* January 31, 2019.

33: Timing is Everything

"I'm a big fan": Jennifer Haberkorn, "Feinstein Says She Supports Joe Biden for 2020, and Notes That Sen. Kamala Harris Is 'Brand-New Here,' " *Los Angeles Times,* January 3, 2019.

"Half my family's from Jamaica": Breakfast Club Power 105.1 FM, "Kamala Harris Talks Gender Pay Gap, Climate Control, Russian Interference + More," YouTube, July 12, 2019, https://youtu.be/QPwlZxBVoeA.

"must be turning": Sinéad Baker, "Kamala Harris' Father Said She Disgraced Her Jamaican Family by Using a 'Fraudulent Stereotype' to Joke About Smoking Weed," *Business Insider,* February 21, 2019.

"the only left-handed": Chelsea Janes and Amy B. Wang, "Pete Buttigieg Is Ending His Presidential Bid," *Washington Post,* March 1, 2020.

"The question for Ms. Harris": Julie Bosman and Katie Glueck, "Civil Rights Discussion 'Shouldn't Be about the Past,' Biden

Says," *New York Times,* June 28, 2019.

"I thought we were friends": Arlette Saenz, Jessica Dean, and Eric Bradner, "Joe Biden Previews More Aggressive Approach Ahead of Next Democratic Debate," CNNPolitics, July 28, 2019.

"Time after time": Lara Bazelon, "Kamala Harris Was Not a 'Progressive Prosecutor,' " *New York Times,* January 17, 2019. See also Phil Willon, "Kamala Harris Should Take Bolder Action on Police Shootings, Civil Rights Advocates Say," *Los Angeles Times,* January 18, 2016; and Kate Kelly, "How Does Harris View Big Business? Her Time as California's Top Lawyer Offers Clues," *New York Times,* October 30, 2020.

"put over 1,500 people": Chris Cillizza, "How You Know Tulsi Gabbard Really Got Under Kamala Harris' Skin," CNN, August 1, 2019.

"This is going to sound immodest": Ibid.

"unintended consequence": Melanie Mason and Michael Finnegan, "Kamala Harris Regrets California Truancy Law That Led to Arrest of Some Parents," *Los Angeles Times,* April 17, 2019.

The New York Times *deconstructed:* Jonathan Martin, Astead W. Herndon, and Alexander Burns, "How Kamala Harris's

Campaign Unraveled," *New York Times,* November 29, 2019.

"We were her only shot": Brian Brokaw (managed Harris's 2010 run for attorney general) in discussion with the author, October 2020.

"Kamala Harris is ending": Christopher Cadelago and Caitlin Oprysko, " 'One of the Hardest Decisions of My Life': Kamala Harris Ends Once-Promising Campaign," *Politico,* December 3, 2019.

34: Dancing in the Rain

"for his trafficking in bigotry": H. Res. 858, 116th Congress, 2nd Sess. (2019–2020).

"I decided it would be": Cynthia Hubert, "Michael Tubbs, One of America's Youngest Mayors, Aims to Lift His Hometown of Stockton," *Sacramento Bee,* April 12, 2017.

"Tell him Auntie Kamala": Michael Tubbs (Stockton, California, mayor) in discussion with the author, October 2020.

"a punch to the gut": Alexander Burns and Katie Glueck, "Kamala Harris Is Biden's Choice for Vice President," *New York Times,* August 11, 2020.

"It was a debate": The Late Show with Stephen Colbert, "Sen. Kamala Harris on

Joining the Biden Ticket: I'd be Honored," YouTube, June 18, 2020, https://youtu.be/jkTOpWzC9Rc.

"I didn't ask for permission": Eleni Kounalakis (lieutenant governor of California) in discussion with the author, October 2020.

"You ready to go to work?": Joey Garrison, et. al, "Inside a Grueling Search for VP; How Joe Biden Came to Choose Kamala Harris," *USA Today,* August 14, 2020.

"There is no one's opinion": Joe Biden (@JoeBiden), "I First Met @KamalaHarris . . . ," Twitter, August 13, 2020, https://twitter.com/JoeBiden/status/1293970573559599105?s=20.

"would come to school": Kamala Harris (@KamalaHarris), "In High School, I Found Out My Best Friend . . . ," Twitter, September 23, 2020, https://twitter.com/KamalaHarris/status/1308779071204192256?s=20.

"The U.S. is getting": Wanda Kagan (longtime friend from high school in Montreal) in discussion with the author's researcher, Sasha Hupka, November 2020.

"it was embarrassing": Peggy Noonan, "A Good Debate, and It's Not Quite Over," *Wall Street Journal,* October 23, 2020.

ABOUT THE AUTHOR

Dan Morain has covered California policy, politics, and justice-related issues for more than four decades, including twenty-seven years at the *Los Angeles Times* and eight at the *Sacramento Bee,* where he was editorial page editor.

The employees of Thorndike Press hope you have enjoyed this Large Print book. All our Thorndike, Wheeler, and Kennebec Large Print titles are designed for easy reading, and all our books are made to last. Other Thorndike Press Large Print books are available at your library, through selected bookstores, or directly from us.

For information about titles, please call:
(800) 223-1244

or visit our website at:
gale.com/thorndike

To share your comments, please write:
Publisher
Thorndike Press
10 Water St., Suite 310
Waterville, ME 04901